AF531391

Foundations of News and Journalism

FOUNDATIONS OF NEWS AND JOURNALISM

Swati Chauhan
Navin Chandra

KANISHKA PUBLISHERS, DISTRIBUTORS
NEW DELHI-110 002

KANISHKA PUBLISHERS, DISTRIBUTORS
4697/5-21A, Ansari Road, Daryaganj
New Delhi -110 002
Phones : 2327 0497, 2328 8285
Fax : 011-2328 8285
E-mail : kanishka_publishing@yahoo.co.in

First Published: 1997
Second Edition: 2005
Third Edition: 2011

ISBN : 978-81-7391-203-3

PRINTED IN INDIA

Published by Madan Sachdeva for Kanishka Publishers, Distributors, 4697/5-21A, Ansari Road, Daryaganj, New Delhi-110 002, Typeset by Sunshine Graphics, Delhi, and Printed at Rajdhani Printers, Delhi.

Preface

There are many professions even today which have grown and reached hitherto on certain traditions and conventions. Some aspects of journalism also fall in this category. Yet here is an attempt to compile scientific and systematic guides towards fine-turning the skills of working as well as aspiring journalists. The journey of a newspaper starts from the reporters' beat. A good reporter has to keep his eyes, ears and senses open for the happening things. It is a faculty that is developed more by training than by mere instinct. Then it will take some deskwork also to make even a good report newsworthy. Flashing the news from distant location using the latest and closest available facility shall make one beat the competitors and deadlines. For this purpose a brief yet pointed awareness of the technologies of present and future is a must for all reporters and journalists.

Even best of the reports and features can be got beaten by an ordinary expression, commonplace language and localised diction. The fluency and effectiveness of the expression and lucidity and flow of the report is learnt by a sustained activity. This work has detailed discussions, examples and explanations to master the language for becoming a successful reporter and an effective journalist.

The book has earmarked chapters for honing the skills and talents of media person towards establishing a greater communication with their readers. The most important factor in this exercise will be to steer clear of the extremes keeping in mind the common reader who loves objectivity the most, in any media presentation.

Information Technology has affected the journalism to its inner most reaches. The computer literacy and proficiency have become essential for all media persons in whatever capacity or department they may be working. The book tries to document some trends and techniques that have emerged prominently in the media rooms. Now the people donot have to grope in dark as to where from to start their familiarity with the changed systems. The machines, software, techniques and applications have been discussed here in sufficient depth.

A journalist has to sometimes do an act of rope working even while knowing hazards of such a course. The book has highlighted the pitfalls which the community should try to keep away from. The reliable sources have tended to leave reporters and commentators in lurch and often to face malignation and smut. The book discusses the legal safeguards and other mechanisms which one may fall back on in the unlikely event of an error of judgement. The work closes with a distinct value addition that comes in the form of terms and expressions of general usage, frequently used abbreviations and common symbols. A complete hand book for journalists of today and tomorrow.

EDITORS

Contents

1

Successful Correspondent: Assets and Attributes

PEOPLE make news. Where people go, there news develops. From north of Spitzbergen to south of Little America, from Irving, Kansas, to Irkutsk, Siberia, and back again, news is predictable in some of its movements, unreliable as quicksilver in others.

But whether it is news long foreseen and prepared for, or news that breaks unexpectedly, the world seldom needs to wait every long for full details. A widespread organization of correspondents, plus almost instantaneous communication, and very rapid transportation, bring the facts to all larger cities and most of the smaller ones within a few moments, and usually within a few hours even from the more remote places. Newspapers and press associations have charted the news areas of the world and have spread a net to ensnare virtually anything that may be classified as news.

This network is comprised of telephone and telegraph lines, railroads, radio channels and ship lanes. Where these converge most thickly it is safe to assume that social, artistic, commercial, financial and governmental activities are greatest. And in those very places in which populations center, news is certain to grow luxuriantly. There journalists foregather.

The leading news centers of the world are London, Washington, New York, Paris, Berlin, Geneva, Rome, Madrid, Vienna, Moscow, Shanghai, Tokyo and Buenos Aires. In these thirteen cities press associations and newspapers concentrate their efforts.

Other important centers are Brussels, Lisbon, Copenhagen, Amsterdam, Stockholm, Oslo, Riga, Sofia, Budapest, Athens, Belgrade, Milan, Prague, Warsaw, Bucharest, Istanbul, Ankara, Jerusalem, Cairo, Cape Town, Bombay, Calcutta, Delhi, Bangkok, Singapore, Manila, Nanking, Peiping, Hong Kong, Hsinking, Canton, Melbourne, Wellington, Honolulu, Montreal, Ottawa, Havana, Mexico City, Rio de Janeiro, Lima, Santiago. Still others become important from time to time.

Staff correspondents are stationed in some of these secondary cities, particularly in such as Warsaw, Cairo, Bombay, Peiping, Mexico City and Rio de Janeiro, but it is far commoner to depend upon native correspondents, often regularly employed by some local paper, or upon aliens resident there for business or personal reasons. They send to the nearest "control bureau" of the foreign newspaper or press association served, a report of any matter which their experience tells them may be desired by that paper or agency. Every such "part time" correspondent is instructed as to what constitutes news in the view of the foreign paper, and he even receives instructions as to how to cover that type of news, how to write it, and how to transmit it.

The basis for world news collection is the press association. There is one association, and often more than one, in almost every country. About thirty of these national associations maintain an exchange arrangement by which each has its own correspondents covering the news of a certain area. The news gathered more or less independently is made available to all of the other associations. A representative of each may select, from this mass of information, such matter as he believes will be of interest to his own people. He verifies it if necessary, edits it, and possibly rewrites it before sending it for use at home. Or he may merely use it as a springboard for an entirely new story which he himself writes on the basis of information obtained from primary sources.

If a report comes to a control point bureau from some locality within the sphere of its interest, and circumstances seem to warrant, a special correspondent for the foreign newspaper may leave his bureau and journey to the place where the event has occurred to report upon it at first hand. This was particularly common, as a method, in the nineteen-twenties, when some correspondents were so constantly on the move about the continent of Europe that they sometimes were referred to as "swing men." International conferences in the capitals and watering places of Europe since 1920 have sent small armies of correspondents stampeding back and forth across the map.

The Correspondent and His Work

There must be efficient men in all strategic news centers. This is axiomatic and expensive, but it is the only way in which prompt and intelligent news coverage is possible. Accordingly, correspondents are at work twenty-four hours a day, around the world, in order that the newspaper reader may be well informed.

Just as no man ignorant of football could understand the game or write about it intelligently, so no man ignorant of public affairs could understand them, write about them, or edit reports about them without making mistakes in facts or perspective that would mislead and confuse readers, while injuring the reputation of the newspaper itself with persons who recognize its shortcomings.[1]

Facts are what the good correspondent wants, and facts make news, although what looks like news when published is not always fact, unhappily for the reader.[2] Much depends upon the discernment of the correspondent, who needs to understand the country in which he is living; and fully as much depends upon the common sense and social responsibility of the employing newspaper.

How to keep the home office happy is one problem of the correspondent, for that office occasionally seems to ask the impossible! Correspondents have been ordered by their offices to interview Kings, Emperors, Premiers, Generals, Chief Justices and all manner of high officials. Such exalted personages hold no awe for the far-off newspaper editor, secure in his own little half-acre, but rarely are they themselves free to grant press interviews, even if willing to do so.[3]

Up to about 1895 a correspondent in London or Paris for an American newspaper often sent his own opinion, his own editorial interpretation of events, rather than the bare facts. But in writing to-day, bowing to a demand for objectivity, the correspondent either presents the fact as unadorned as possible, as for a press association, or he confines himself to factual interpretation, as distinguished from editorial interpretation, for a newspaper or syndicate.[4]

To report the news without bias, intentional or otherwise, requires that the correspondent retain enough detachment so that he may see things not only objectively, but in the light of his own national interests. That is assuming him to be a native and a citizen of the country to which his dispatches go. This is not always the case, but there is a tendency to make it so, increasingly, on the supposition that only under such circumstances can readers feel the greatest confidence in the impartiality of the facts they are receiving, and only thus can the correspondent himself make clear to his readers—his countrymen—the reasons and the meanings underlying the news as it appears on the surface. To do this successfully he needs, actually, to keep free of personal or national prejudices, pro or con, and of influences that might corrupt impartiality.[5]

Well-recognized sources to which correspondents turn for news at any post include the newspaper and periodical press of the city or country itself, representing various shades of opinion, where variety is politically possible; the service of a local press association; the government offices, especially the ministry of foreign affairs; parliament and its members, foreign embassies, legations, and consulates; commercial attaches, banks and business houses, hotels, clubs, bars, educational institutions, the offices and homes of persons active in the affairs of the country or acquainted with the local situation in its various aspects, and willing to talk about it.

The foreign correspondent must, to an extent, make his own assignments; he must make his own decisions. His output of copy may be great and sometimes his merit is in knowing when *not* to send a story. Quality is more important than quantity in his product. He may produce much in the way of private reports to editorial writers and other editors, reports which do not appear in print, but which guide the editors in what they themselves write. The system helps to explain the exceedingly well-informed editorials, or leaders, which appear, for example, in *The Times* of London.

Because of the important position that a correspondent occupies in interpreting one country to another, he has been correctly referred to as an "unofficial ambassador." As such, his position can be as powerful as his sense of responsibility, his ability, and the reputation of his paper. Sir Willmott Lewis, as Washington correspondent for *The Times* of London, offered ten suggestions to correspondents:[6]

Sir Willmott Lewis's Advice to Correspondents

1. Take your work, but never yourself, seriously.
2. Know that there is no simple or immediate solution for any national or international problem.
3. Never forget that 99 times out of 100 the issue is not between right and wrong, but between right and right; but also that those who explain too much prepare the way for those who excuse too much.
4. Remember always that prejudice is dishonesty—patriotic prejudice as much as any other kind.
5. Be chary of moral exaltation, and of moral indignation no less, for good and evil mingle in the best and worst of causes.
6. Remember that if you do not like a country, there are a thousand chances that the fault is not in the country, but in you.
7. Be prepared to find that the best and the worst give way under closer scrutiny.
8. Pray nightly that the generalizing and abstracting habit of mind may not prevail over the practical.
9. Be very sure that of all the influences which seek to destroy your independence of mind, the most respectable will be the most dangerous.
10. Know that the sort of patriot who maintains that the women of his country are more chaste and the statesmen

> of his country more stupid than those of any other country, is wrong on both these counts and may be wrong on every count.

The correspondent must be *persona grata* in the country to which he is assigned. If he is not well liked, he cannot hope for success. He needs to be a gentleman, in every sense of the word, and he needs to be well educated, whether through formal university instruction or otherwise. Modern languages are indispensable, although correspondents often learn a tongue only after having been assigned to a post requiring it. Some even have maintained that it is possible for a correspondent to act without a speaking and reading knowledge of the language of the country in which he is working. While correspondents may have succeeded thus handicapped, there can be no argument about the desirability of knowing languages. History, economics, logic, philosophy and finance are other subjects considered of the greatest value. In most instances, newspapers and press associations prefer to have the correspondent serve an apprenticeship in the home office because, it teaches him home office needs, conditions and attitudes.[7]

One notably successful correspondent and bureau chief has advocated this preparation as ideal for foreign work: A good liberal arts training, with history, economics and modern languages prominent in the curriculum. After leaving college, join a paper in as big a city as possible. Get on the city hall run, covering municipal affairs and politics, learning all about methods and operations. Then get to the state capital and ultimately to Washington as a correspondent. Then go abroad with any press association or newspaper bureau, and work up to the directorship of the bureau.

This correspondent believes that there will be increased opportunities for journalists with an interest in foreign work.

In general, a foreign correspondent is paid at a somewhat better rate than the reporter at home. That is necessary because living costs are greater, if requirements of comfort and convenience are equal, and it often is necessary to do considerable entertaining and to maintain a standard sufficiently high to command the respect of those persons with whom he must deal. It is almost essential for a foreign correspondent to follow such a policy because the name of his paper probably means nothing in the foreign land, and his prestige and reception will depend upon his own manner, personality, acquaintanceships, and style of living.[8]

The correspondent needs to be level-headed, not only to avoid being deceived by propagandists and by those trying to escape unwelcome publicity, but to avoid yielding to personal temptations and to keep from seeing stories where none exist and so becoming an unwitting sensationalist. If he knows the local situation thoroughly he is less likely to fall victim to rumors and statements deliberately intended to mislead him. This attitude of independent judgment is stressed by many good correspondents. It means independence of all groups and individuals interested in shaping his opinions and so influencing his writing. Sir Willmott Lewis has expressed it by saying that a correspondent must protect his "intellectual virginity" at any cost, adding that, in forming judgments, he must keep trying to discern the great tidal movements underlying the froth on the sea of public affairs. The ability of the correspondent to recognize the tidal movements and to differentiate those movements from the waves and the spray on the surface is the measure of his success. Also, he must report both the people and the government; almost any people is likable; but governments seldom are.

So far as concerns the Anglo-Saxon press, Sir Willmott notes a tendency to sentimentalize the news reports. This he considers objectionable because it represents a love of emotion for its own sake, manifested in a growing drift to "features," and feature treatment of the news. He does not object to proper *sentiment*, but finds that *sentimentality*, as distinct from the other, is not merely contaminating the domestic news reports, but also the foreign correspondence, which is a more serious matter because the spark of emotion is thus introduced into the tinder box of international relations and increases the possibility and danger of an explosion.

Much the same view as to the need for utter independence of thought on the part of the foreign correspondent was held by the late William Bolitho (Ryall), correspondent for the Manchester *Guardian* and the New York *World*. He contended that the correspondent should put aside all prejudice, stop all wishful-thinking, and, instead of letting his emotions dictate his judgments and his reports, that he should analyze his own prejudices, ruthlessly, so that he could discount them and thus come nearer impartiality. The next step was to learn to judge how others would act in the light of the prejudices and habits of thought that he was able to discern *in them*. This attitude Mr. Bolitho passed on to Walter Duranty, who attained fame as correspondent in Russia for the New York *Times*, and Mr. Duranty put it to use and acknowledged his debt to Bolitho.[9]

Even though the modern correspondent is writing much of the time about events and trends that are technical, the cannot ignore the human element involved in the news and encountered in getting the news. So he must be a diplomat, he must be tactful, he must learn how to persuade people to do things and tell him things, chiefly because he has won their trust, made them like him personality. He forms sincere friendships, but he must know how to play off one individual against another, or one group against another.

The best and most successful correspondents often win that reputation because they know how to deal with people. In contacts with officials the correspondent should, as one of the number has said, be sufficiently well informed himself so that he can *give* information as well as *ask* it. If he can do that regularly, he is sure of a welcome whenever he calls. Otherwise, he becomes a nuisance to be tolerated or to be "used." In fact, officials sometimes call, themselves, upon the correspondent who has something to give and who does not limit his interest in their affairs to mere receiving.

Yet, when persons, and especially persons in official positions, are more than naturally communicative, correspondents have learned that it is wise to verify all statements with extra care, lest they be made avenues for propaganda, or be used simply to help launch a "trial balloon."[10]

Similarly, correspondents find that they must exercise the greatest patience, and frequently ingenuity as well, on some stories which require long periods of waiting and physical inactivity.This is true, for example, of so-called "death-watches" set up when prominent persons are very ill, and it is true, also, of many conferences and meetings at Geneva or elsewhere.

The new correspondent at a post is instructed carefully in his work, if time and circumstances permit. He is given a few days to go about and become familiar in a general way with the city and its people, if his introduction happens to be under ideal conditions. Perhaps he may accompany an experienced correspondent, observe his methods, and meet officials of new importance. Then, the older correspondent permits the new man to act independently, but corrects his mistakes and makes suggestions when they are in order. Or the new man spends a sufficient time in the office, first handling copy, writing and rewriting dispatches, and otherwise familiarizing himself with the work and conditions. It requires more time to become accustomed to some countries than to others, certain situations are far more complex, languages more difficult, customs more involved, and general living conditions either more or less agreeable.

Political and economic circumstances in the country must be mastered by the correspondent, and any change from one country to another requires a new study. China and Japan, Russia and Italy probably are the most difficult countries for an American or British correspondent to understand. Two years is none too much to devote to learning what it is necessary to know to deal intelligently with the news in any one of them whereas six months to a year may suffice in London or New York, although no thorough knowledge would be possible even there in so brief a time.

It is the need for this long training which makes it desirable that correspondents be left at posts for considerable periods—three to ten years, or longer. Some have remained twenty-five years and more. If a correspondent does not enjoy living in a country, he should not stay there, but if he *does* enjoy it, his value is likely to increase with time, especially if he keeps his own national perspective. Under such circumstances, however, employers at home occasionally come to believe that the correspondent is so sympathetic to the point of view of the country in which he lives that he no longer sees affairs there with the perspective they want him to maintain. Sometimes there is a basis for the belief, but other times the attitude is unfair and dictated by local prejudices instead. It is true, however, that a correspondent needs to leave a country from time to time to refresh his viewpoint, and to keep his impartial outlook. This may mean a national change of scene as frequently as once in six weeks in some stormy countries, but certainly the intervals should be no greater than three years in any case.

There are times, of course, when a correspondent does not have the leisure to study a country or a situation. A crisis arises in some city or country remote from his usual base, and he must hasten to the new scene, round up the story as quickly as possible, and get it off. Then he will need to use his ingenuity and intelligence to the fullest extent.

Under such conditions, as a general thing, he spends time on the way to the scene of activity reading what he can about the situation he is to report. He tries to gain an understanding of both sides, if it is a controversy. This may mean reading books, reports, periodicals, newspapers. On arriving, he visits such persons and offices as he believes may be able to give him useful information. That probably means certain government offices, it means interviews with officials, with spokesmen for the opposition views, with local editors and journalists representing various groups, with some foreign diplomats and business men, or other resident foreigners who may be presumed to be neutral and yet to have some familiarity with local conditions. Thus he gathers his threads, and presently he is able to weave them together to form a tapestry picturing the situation. The clarity of the picture, and its accuracy, will depend largely upon his ability.

The foreign correspondent for the newspaper with a serious view of the news is constantly on the watch for several types of stories. A classification prepared, by way of suggestion, for representatives abroad for the Chicago *Daily News*, especially the non-American correspondent, indicates in general the kind of thing that concerns all correspondents of the better newspapers.[11]

(a) News events of truly international significance. . . .Be careful to avoid stories of merely local interest, especially local political stories, which seem big on the spot, but are of little consequence to our readers. In treating international news events, we should dwell particularly on their international significance,

especially as affecting the United States. [Or, in other cases, the people of the country where the report is to be published.]

(b) There is no part of the world in which the United States has not, at present, important interests—economic, moral, cultural, diplomatic, social, political. We should discover and analyze out these interests, whether actual or potential—and write about them.

(c) A story is frequently welcome explaining the national viewpoint of the country in which one is stationed—the national viewpoint, that is, regarding some truly international problem of great interest, but especially when this national viewpoint is interesting or significant in itself.

(d) Original interviews with well-known political, scientific, financial, industrial, artistic or literary personalities. It has, however, never been our policy to pay for interviews.[12]

(e) Scientific inventions, discoveries or movements, when they are of really international significance.

(f) Social problems and experiments, especially when analogous to our own social problems in America [or other countries where reports are to be published], and therefore apt to contain a lesson for us.

(g) Stories of the activities and the unusual experiences of Americans, especially of Chicagoans, living or travelling in Europe. [Again to be considered with appropriate changes for newspapers serving other communities.]

The easier it is to obtain and verify facts, the more accurately the press can report events. Journalists, particularly, have demanded freer access to information. One result has been the establishment by most governments of "press bureaus," "news departments" or "information sections," under the direction of "press officers" or "intelligence officers," to answer questions about the affairs of government, sometimes to arrange interviews, and to aid the press in general. Most of these bureaus have been organized since the Great War, during which period the need for information sources became especially obvious, not only as a service to journalists, but so that governments might be represented favorably and accurately in the press at home and abroad.

Helpful as these offices frequently are, each naturally is working primarily in the interests of its government. This is admitted and tacitly understood by all parties concerned. No such office will give out information unfavorable to the purposes or reputation of the government. The correspondent is obliged to find another, more impartial source for such data. This may be in a liberal or opposition press, at a foreign embassy, or it may come from an intelligent and communicative person of whatever connection.

Nowadays, at international conferences, for example, a correspondent usually is able to discover what happens even though a meeting is secret. Usually some one who has attended the secret session will talk, possibly because he is dissatisfied with the course of the negotiations, or more likely, because he is indifferent to the subject under consideration, or, again, because he is seeking to satisfy his own diplomatic purposes and reveals what has occurred on the understanding that his own anonymity is to be protected.

So it is that vague phrases, such as "it is learned on high authority," need not necessarily be regarded as evidence that the news report is of doubtful authenticity. Nor, on the other side, are official government denials of reports, or refutations by officials of statements or views attributed to them, necessarily to be accepted unquestioned. The public often is ready to doubt or discredit even the reputable press on such denials. But as between a responsible correspondent, interested primarily in presenting the facts, and a government bureau or official aware that a certain action or remark was inexpedient, or its announcement premature, which is the more likely to be dependable?[13]

The correspondent is an exile from his own people. Whatever the cynical may think, usually he is sincere in trying to give an honest picture of events or trends to stay-at-home persons. Thoughtful correspondents understand the responsibility they bear, and they accept it conscientiously.

Journalists, in organizing to advance their own interests and work, have thereby aided the entire press. Such organizations include particularly the Association of Correspondents

Accredited to the League of Nations, the Anglo-American Press Association in Paris, the Anglo-American Press Association in Vienna, the Anglo-American Press Association in Geneva, the Institute of Journalists and the National Union of Journalists in Great Britain, the Foreign Press Association in London, the Association of Foreign Correspondents in the United States, the National Press Club in Washington, the American Newspaper Guild, and the American Society of Newspaper Editors. Some of these groups have worked to raise journalistic standards, have dealt with local government officials, and have won their cooperation in simplifying news-gathering problems or clearing the news channels.

Press Associations

The Press Association of to-day had its origin in the handwritten news-letters provided in medieval times for individuals, for business firms, and for groups of nobles. Aside from governments, which needed information and which themselves distributed information in the routine of administration, bankers and traders found the greatest value in information services. In Europe and, later, in North America it was marine news and news of trade that brought the "reading room" into being as an essential part of coffee houses, and the more enterprising houses went to considerable trouble and expense to provide a good service of news.[14]

It was about 1725 that Edward Cave, inspector of the franks in London, and so able to use the mails freely, set up a system for the exchange of news between the London press and provincial newspapers. He sold the news service thus obtained for a guinea a week, and his news-collecting organization was fundamentally like that of a present-day press association. In the United States the earliest press associations were concerned more with obtaining foreign news and distributing it, than with domestic news, although they accomplished that exchange also. It was in 1827 that some New York newspapers formed a combination to defray the costs of meeting incoming ships to obtain European news.[15]

But the roots of the press associations go deeper in both England and America than these eighteenth and nineteenth century developments. Edward Lloyd had established a coffee house in Tower Street, London, in 1686 or 1687. He prospered, and the coffee house, situated in the center of the mercantile world of that time, became a center for business and social groups of a respectable and established character. It was a sort of club, and like some other early coffee houses, it also became a clearing-house for news and advertisements. The newspaper press was not highly developed at that time, but as the years went along it was the custom to have available in the coffee houses collections of newspapers, such as they were, not alone those published locally, but also newspapers brought from other countries.

This was particularly true at Lloyds, which was a center for seagoing men and for merchants and others with foreign trade interests, even as it became true somewhat later of coffee houses in New York and Boston. In 1696, partly to satisfy his customers, Edward Lloyd began the publication of a daily paper, *Lloyd's News,* which continued for seventy-six numbers, ceasing publication by government order on February 23, 1697. In 1713 Edward Lloyd died and in 1720 the business passed out of the control of his family, but continued under the same name, nevertheless. In 1734 the firm began the publication of *Lloyd's List,* which has continued ever since. It specialized in shipping news and built up a rather extensive foreign news service of its own, with thirty-two correspondents in twenty-eight ports sending both shipping news and general news. The service was in full working order by 1788, if not before, and later *Lloyd's List* achieved several journalistic "scoops."[16]

What Lloyd's meant to England, Samuel Topliff meant to the United States. As a young man he became proprietor of Gilbert's Coffee House and Marine Diary in Boston. The name later was changed to the Merchants' Reading Room, which was a sort of club where shippping news and general news was available to members through a file of domestic and foreign newspapers, and later through what was called *Topliff's Private Marine Journal,* consisting of seven large books in which were entered items of shipping information and of news brought in from foreign ports or from other ports in the United States.[17]

The Topliff service was well established by 1811, but Mr. Topliff's desire to see his patrons more adequately provided with news led him to set up what was the first real system for gathering foreign news for American use, and his system continued from 1820 to 1850. Henry Ingraham Blake, who had for years been a ship news reporter for the Boston *Mercury-Palladium*, began also to serve the Topliff coffee house with news. He would row out to ships entering Boston harbor, get packets of newspapers, ask questions of the Captain and other officers, and perhaps interview one or two passengers. Then he would bring the news to the coffee house, where it would be posted, and whence it would be forwarded to New York by pony express. The European vessels put in at Boston first, so Boston heard the news before New York.

Some newspapers commonly credited "Mr. Topliff's correspondent" for much of their foreign news. He sent news to them, and they may be assumed to have been among his subscribers, which meant that he was running a sort of press association, and possibly it should be considered the first in the United States. As the years passed the system for getting news improved and the service was extended. Topliff himself went to Europe in 1828 and spent a year in travel. His letters were published in American newspapers so that, in a sense, he was the first special correspondent for American newspapers.[18]

A venture somewhat like Topliff's was tried at Charleston, South Carolina, by Aaron Smith Willington. Meeting one incoming ship, Willington received the positive news that the Treaty of Ghent had been signed, ending the War of 1812 between the United States and Great Britain. This he announced to his reader on February 14, 1815, the treaty having actually been signed at Ghent on December 28, 1814. In the meantime, General Andrew Jackson had defeated the British forces at New Orleans on January 8, 1815. Some years later James Gordon Bennett, a recent immigrant from Scotland, found employment with Willington, starting a career that was to lead him to establish the New York *Herald* and usher in a new era in journalistic enterprise, as already described.

It was common enough for merchants and newspapers in Atlantic port cities to share the expenses of having some qualified person row out to newly arrived ships to get newspapers and information and then deliver the same to mercantile and editorial offices. This method was well developed before 1820. In about 1830 warmer competition between certain New York newspapers led to the use of clipper ships and schooner to meet the incoming ships farther at sea. One newspaper tried to outdo another until the costs of ship news collection threatened to outstrip any possible advantage that early publication of that news might involve. This expensive rivalry continued, nevertheless, for some years, but the costs to individual newspapers were somewhat mitigated, especially after 1837, by the formation of several so-called cooperative "harbor associations" sharing the expenses of meeting the ships and rushing the news to shore. Even so, however, some newspapers chose to act independently and, as they often were the more successful papers, they also were able to equip ever-faster boats.

In some instances a signaling system of bells or semaphores displayed prominently on masts was arranged in port cities. Lighthouse-keepers or others on the eastern headlands, seeing incoming ships, might signal the news on the land-semaphores. Then those who were to meet the ships went out into the bay or beyond. The news thus obtained was published in the New York or the Boston newspapers, which in turn were sent to inland cities.

Pony express services expedited the news, even so early as 1781, and regularly before 1830. They ran between Boston and Salem, Boston and New York, New York and Philadelphia, Baltimore and Washington. Some New York newspapers, notably the *Sun* and the *Herald*, used not only pony expresses but carrier pigeons and such short stretches of railroad as then existed, to rush the news from Washington and from Boston to New York. The rivalry in news collection was intense through the third decade of the nineteenth century in the United States. The advent of the telegraph brought a new phase of press rivalry in the following decade.[19]

In Europe the matter of news dissemination also was receiving attention. Individual newspapers had engaged correspondents on the Continent, or sent staff men there early in the nineteenth century. But the more systematic collection of news is associated with the names of Charles Havas and Julius Reuter.

Charles Havas established the Agence Havas, which has become both an important news agency and a successful advertising agency. Napoleon died at St. Helena on May 5, 1821; Paris heard about it on July 6th. Most persons did not mind the two months' delay, nor think much about it, being accustomed to such a time lag, but it suggested to M. Havas the need for improved news service. He was a native of Portugal, but had taken up residence in Paris. In 1825 he offered to supply certain Paris newspapers and government departments with extracts from newspapers published in England, Germany, Italy, Spain and Russia. While the news still would be late, the idea of such a daily service appealed to some nonetheless.

M. Havas ultimately found his sources of information insufficient for the needs of his clients, and he felt the need of assistance to keep up the service. So in about 1836 he engaged several translators, and used all the most advanced means to disseminate his news to government ministries, embassies, banks, and commercial houses. Newspapers, at that time, scarcely subscribed at all.

Although the Agence Havas generally is said to have been set up as a press agency in 1836, it was not until 1840 that it was firmly established, and only after 1845 did it prosper notably. In the latter year the agency opened a little office in the rue Jean Jacques Rousseau. To enrich his service of news after 1836, M. Havas had arranged to contribute news of France gratuitously to foreign newspapers in exchange for the free use of news from their columns. In this way the exchange of news between France, Belgium and England was developed to quite an extent. Correspondents were engaged in England, Germany, Italy, Spain, Belgium and Holland, while every effort was made to speed the messages.

It was in 1840, when M. Havas was in some financial difficulties, that he began to use carrier pigeons to transmit the news between Brussels and Paris every day. This method had been adopted at about the same time by Julius Reuter, a young bank clerk in Aix-la-Chapelle. Reuter had observed the eagerness with which bankers, brokers and merchants awaited the arrival, by mail coach or mounted courier, of the stock market prices from Brussels. He instituted a carrier pigeon service between Aix-la-Chapelle, the starting point of the

German communications system, and Brussels, which was in direct communication with Paris. So he was able to get the Paris Bourse prices over this gap in the communications system and into all the big German towns several hours before the regular mail service could bridge it. Reuter's enterprise was rewarded by generous patronage, enabling him to extend his service.

The carrier pigeon method enabled M. Havas to have the important news appearing in the London morning papers reach Paris in time for use in the evening papers there. The French press, and his other clients, were pleased, and his subscribers increased in number. After that the Havas agency grew rapidly. By 1845 it was necessary to establish sub-agencies in Brussels, Rome, Vienna, Madrid and even in the United States. After that date, also, the bureau began to develop quite rapidly as an advertising agency, differing in important respects, however, from the advertising agencies now known in Anglo-Saxon countries. The telegraph, cable and radio were adapted by the Havas agency as they became practicable and facilitated the handling of news.[20]

After M. Havas borrowed Reuter's carrier-pigeon idea for news transmission, the two men began to work together in providing a full exchange of news between Brussels and Paris, and in 1849 Reuter went to Paris to help Havas. In 1851 Reuter went on to London to establish his own agency there, but Reuters and Havas always have cooperated closely since that time.

The Agence Havas differs from the Reuters' agency in that it is an advertising agency, as well as a news agency.[21] After 1860 the Agence Havas offered to 200 French provincial newspapers, unable to afford a news service, a daily news review without cash payment, but it asked in exchange the exclusive right to a certain amount of advertising white space on the third and fourth pages, this space to be sold or disposed of by the Agence Havas as it saw fit. Havas then turned about and sold this space for its own advantage. Most of the papers accepted the plan, which since has been extended and altered so that some newspapers sell their advertising space to Havas for a flat sum. The agency, in addition to distributing the news, therefore controls about 80 per cent of the advertising space in French papers, both Paris and provincial, and acts as advertising representative, solicits advertisements and prepares advertising copy. This gives Havas a position of unique influence and importance in French journalism.[22]

After the coming of the telegraph, Havas obtained control from the State of special telegraph wires connecting its Paris headquarters with the editorial departments of practically all important newspapers in France. Ticker news services later were installed in some of these offices, as well as in some of the Paris newspaper offices. To others the news was delivered by mail or by messenger.

Charles Havas was succeeded by his son, Auguste, as head of the Agence Havas in 1860. In 1897 M. Charles Lafitte succeeded Auguste Havas and, in 1924, upon the death of M. Lafitte, M. Leon Renier became head of the agency. In 1925 the Agence Havas was capitalized at 50,000,000 francs (about $2,000,000). Its special wires extend about 3,500 miles, altogether, and the agency transmits approximately a million words a day. It deals quite largely in texts and official communications.

Julius Reuter opened a small office in London in 1851, the year in which the first cable across the Channel provided a wire between Paris and London. He hired an office boy to help him. At first he devoted his efforts to the transmission of Stock Exchange information and to obtaining clients for that service, but he was working on the idea of a daily news service to the press of London and the provinces.

Up to 1858 the London newspapers were receiving no regular service of news dispatches from the Continent. *The Times*, the *Morning Post*, and one or two other morning papers, had correspondents in Paris, Berlin, Vienna, Constantinople and some other capitals, but unless war was in progress or imminent, or unless there were other very important events to report, even those correspondents wrote very little or nothing. But Reuter had other ideas about the reporting of foreign news.

In Paris Reuter's chief agent was on confidential terms with the secretary of Napoleon III, another of his staff had entree to the French Government departments, a third handled assignments requiring careful work of special kinds, a fourth sought news and rumors appearing in newspapers published in all parts of the continent, a fifth prepared all the news matter for transmission, while a sixth actually sent it over the wire.[23]

This staff provided Reuter with a schedule of interesting and often exclusive news, quickly available.

Ultimately, late in 1858, M. Reuter was ready with his plan, and he approached Mr. John Walter of *The Times* first, but without success. Next, he chose to call upon Mr. James Grant, editor of the *Morning Advertiser,* then an important London paper. Mr. Grant has written of how, as a result of that call, the *Morning Advertiser* and other London papers, except *The Times,* gave M. Reuter's service a two weeks' trial at no cost to them. They tested his claim that he could provide a better service of foreign news at a lower cost (£ 30. a week to the *Morning Advertiser* instead of £ 40. for its existing service of dispatches). The trial satisfied all of the papers, which thereafter accepted his proposals and subscribed to his service. *The Times* followed suit a little later. Subsequently, Reuter extended the service to embrace other parts of the world, charging proportionately more, quite soon reaching £ 1,000 a year for morning papers, and £ 250 a year for afternoon papers, and the newspapers were compelled by competition to buy his service, even though sometimes at a cost greater than they wished to pay.[24]

The reputation of the agency was enhanced by its reports of the American Civil War and of the campaign of Solferino, but long before that it may be said to have been well established. Reuter himself ultimately became a British citizen, and the agency grew constantly in the extent of its news coverage under the name of Reuter's Telegram Co. Ltd., although known colloquially as Reuters, Limited.

M. Havas may be called the "father" of the modern news agency, but the Reuter agency became the most extensive and most important in the world. Reuter, like Havas, was quick to make use of the newest and best means of communication, and, in fact, Reuter financed the first section of the first cable from England to India. The Reuter agency organized virtually the only service of news from Africa, the Near and Middle East, and the Far East.

The Havas agency covered France, Italy, Switzerland, Belgium, Spain, Portugal, parts of Northern Africa and South America. The Wolff bureau, later formed in Germany, reported the news of that country and of other Central European countries, including Austria, Poland, the Balkans, the

Netherlands, and Scandinavian countries. In the years since 1914 North American agencies have extended their services to overlap those of the Agence Havas in France and Latin America, Reuter in the Eastern countries and of Wolff (now DNB) in Central Europe. These three European agencies and the Associated Press of the United States also formed an arrangement for the exchange of news, later joined by other associations.[25]

Just as Reuters later was to gain and retain great prestige by its one week's "beat" on the assassination of President Abraham Lincoln and by exclusive accounts of some of the engagements of the American Civil War, so, several decades earlier, American news agencies developed out of a rivalry to get and distribute European news first. The same competition actuated individual newspapers and, in some instances, they were so eager to offer their readers "exclusive" foreign news that they invented it themselves. This inventiveness gave rise to three notable "hoaxes" in the history of New York journalism alone.

The first was the so-called "moon hoax," perpetrated by Richard Adams Locke in the New York *Sun* in 1835. It was reported, in great detail and in the most plausible way, that a South African astronomer had discovered vegetable and animal life, buildings and winged people on the moon, all thanks to the marvelous capacity of a new telescope. To verify this report it was necessary to wait for slow ships in regular trade to go, not merely to Great Britain, where the accounts were said to have appeared in a scientific journal published in Edinburgh, but to South Africa, and return. During the long weeks intervening before the hoax was exposed, the subject was a matter of awe-stricken discussion in some quarters, although it was scoffed at in others, and Locke kept it going in several installments. So much interest attached to the articles that the *Sun* sold 19,380 copies on August 28, 1835, which was the largest circulation up to that time for any daily in the world. *The Times* of London then had 17,000 circulation.[26]

The second deception was Edgar Allan Poe's so-called "balloon hoax," in the New York *Sun* on April 13, 1844. It concerned a three-day trip across the Atlantic Ocean in a "steering balloon."[27] The third was the "wild animal hoax" printed by the New York *Herald* on Sunday, November 9, 1874. It told of events following an escape of the wild animals in the Central Park Zoo, New York.[28] No such escape had occurred.

The first stage in the development of press associations in the United States had been the information of rather kaleidoscopic harbor news associations in New York. With the advent of the telegraph, the field of competition was extended somewhat, for ships were met at Halifax, rather than at Boston or New York, and from there the news was rushed to Boston and New York newspapers by carrier pigeons or by combinations of pony express and telegraph, where it existed. The Mexican War, from 1846 to 1848, resulted in similar efforts for speeding news delivery from those Southern battlefields, usually by ship to New Orleans and from there overland by pony express and telegraph, wherever lines were to be found in operation.[29]

Peace was reached in the New York harbor rivalry with the formation in 1849 of the Harbor News Association. Instrumental in bringing about this truce was the fact that Daniel H. Craig of Boston was forestalling even the fastest of the New York newspaper boats.[30] He had arranged with correspondents in European countries to send him the latest news aboard the passenger steamships which began to make regular scheduled Atlantic crossings in 1845. His agents met the ships at Halifax and had carrier pigeons taken abroad. As the ships neared Boston, they released the pigeons, which flew to Boston, where Craig's assistants sent the news on by other pigeons to New York, and papers there subscribing to the service had a "beat" on the European news.

The New York newspapers that were being "beaten" tried to prevent Craig getting the pigeons aboard incoming ships, but they never succeeded in breaking up the system, so that in the end the *Herald* and the *Courier and Enquirer*, unable to combat him successfully, commissioned Craig to act for them in obtaining European news. Thus it may be said that Daniel H. Craig, who previously had been unsuccessful in starting a penny paper in Boston, was to sponsor the second news service in the United States, the first having been the Topliff service already mentioned.[31]

Most of the New York newspapers agreed to share the expenses of the Harbor News Association in 1849. Later, the Telegraphic and General News Association was formed on a similar basis to gather news from inland points. In 1856 these two Associations were merged to form the General News Association of New York. Out of this grew the New York Associated Press, a cooperative news-gathering organization of New York papers, something like the present City News Bureaus in Chicago and New York, except that it also sold to newspapers outside of New York the news collected by its member papers.

During the Civil War, particularly, other regional associations grew up, and after the War many of these continued the relationship already worked out. In 1872 the New York Associated Press was serving telegraphic news to more than 200 dailies in the United States, and it paid out more than $200,000 in the year for cable dispatches alone. By 1880 it served 30 per cent of all dailies in the country with both foreign and domestic news, at a cost of $500,000 a year.[32] This was the lineal ancestor of the present Associated Press, which is the oldest existing press association in the United States.[33]

Regional or sectional news agencies that grew up were based on a plan similar to that used by the New York association. There were the New England Associated Press, Southern Associated Press, and Western Associated Press. These came to cooperate so closely in the exchange of news as to form what was in effect one association, until internal rivalries and politics caused the Western Associated Press to break away in 1893. It set up as the Associated Press of Illinois, which soon grew so strong and so efficient that it drove the Associated Press of New York out of business and began to serve newspapers in all parts of the United States.

In 1900 the success of the Associated Press of Illinois was seriously threatened by a decision of the Illinois Supreme Court. The agency dissolved voluntarily as an Illinois organization, but reorganized itself under the Membership Corporation Law of New York State, a law intended to apply to social clubs, by which the organization was permitted to limit its membership. The Illinois Court had ruled that it must sell its news to all comers, whereas the Associated Press of Illinois felt that its chief advantage lay in being able to promise an exclusive news service to a newspaper in a certain community. Under the New York law it could, and can, do that, and membership may be restricted, just as in a social club. That is the present situation in the Associated Press and, therefore, the existing organization, while tracing its ancestry back to 1849, really was born in May, 1900.[34]

The new Associated Press extended its service not only throughout the United States, but to all other parts of the world. It set up bureaus in the most important capitals, opened foreign countries to modern methods of news reporting, and engaged literally hundreds of correspondents to "protect" it on events in their communities.[35]

It is not to be supposed that other press associations did not arise even in the nations served by Reuters, Havas, and the Associated Press. The histories of journalism reveal that some have been short-lived and others have merged with more vital organizations.[36] But some have survived and gained high respect.

So in the United States, there is the independent and strong United Press.[37] The Hearst-owned International News Service is enterprising, although more limited in its news coverage. In Great Britain the Press Association of the United Kingdom is a branch of Reuters devoted to covering news of Great Britain and Northern Ireland alone. The Central News and the Exchange Telegraph also are reputable agencies serving British newspapers.[38] In France there is the Agence Telegraphique Radio, which is allied to Havas, and some minor agencies.

In other countries press associations were developed, usually patterned after one of the first three—Havas, Reuters, or the Associated Press. Generally speaking, they make little effort to report the news outside their own countries but depend for such coverage upon affiliations with other agencies.[39]

Thirty principal news agencies, in as many countries, from an unofficial but effective World League of Press Associations for the exchange of news.[40] The original membership included Reuters (Great Britain), Havas (France), Associated Press (United States), Wolff (Germany), Westnik (Russia), Kokusai (Japan), Stefani (Italy), Fabra (Spain), and others. Westnik or the Petrograd News Agency became known as Rosta and later as the Tass agency under the Soviets. Kokusai in 1926 was trasformed into the Rengo agency and in 1936 it was known as the Domei agency. Wolff became known in 1933 as the Deutsches Nachrichten Buro.

Specially, the thirty members of the world league, or alliance, of press associations, country by country, with status of the agencies and the cities in which they have their main offices, now are as follows:[41]

Members of the World League of Press Associations

Austria	Amtliche Nachrichtenstelle (Official)	Vienna
Belgium	Agence Telegraphique Belge (Belga) (Semi-official)	Brussels
Bulgaria	Agence Telegraphique Bulgare (Official)	Sofia
Canada	Canadian Press, Ltd. (Cooperative, Independent)	Toronto, Ontario
China	Reuters (Branch of British Agency)	Shanghai
Czechoslovakia	Ceskoslovenska Tiskova Kancelar (Czechoslovak Press Bureau)	Prague
Denmark	Ritzaus Bureau (Ritzaus), (Dansk Telegrambureau) (Independent)	Copenhagen
Estonia	Eesti Telegraafi Agentuur A.S. (Eta) (Estonian Telegraph Agency Ltd.)	Tallinn
Finland	Finska Notisbyran	Helsingfors
France	Agence Havas (Semi-official)	Paris
Germany	Deutsches Nachrichten Buro G.m.b.h. (DNB), (Official)	Berlin
Great Britain	Reuters Ltd. (Independent)	London
Greece	Agence d'Athenese (Semi-official)	Athens
Hungary	Magyar Tavirati Iroda (Ungarishes Telegraphen-Korrespondenz Buro), (Hungarian Telegraphic Agency), (Semi-official)	Budapest
Italy	Agenzia Stefani (Official)	Rome

JAPAN	Domei Tsushin Sha Allied News Association), (Semi-official)	Tokyo
LATVIA	Latvijas Telegrafa Agentura (Leta), (Latvian Telegraph Agency)	Riga
LITHUANIA	Agence Telegraphique Lithuanienne (Lithuanian Telegraphic Agency)	Kovno
NETHERLANDS	Algemeen Nederlandsch Persbureau (ANP), (Official agency of Netherlands Daily Press Association)	Amsterdam
NORWAY	Norske Telegrambyra (Norwegian News Agency), (Independent)	Oslo
POLAND	Polska Agencja Telegraficzna (PAT), (Polish Telegraph Agency) (Official)	Warsaw
PORTUGAL	Agence Havas (Branch of French Agency)	Lisbon
RUMANIA	Agence Orient Radio (Rador), (Official)	Bucharest
RUSSIA	Tass (Telegrafnoje Agentstwo Ssojusa), (Telegraphic Agency of the Soviet States), (Official)	Moscow
SPAIN	Agencia Telegrafica Fabra (Official—Controlled by Havas)	Madrid and Barcelona
SWEDEN	Tidningarnas Telegrambyra (Telegram Agency of Newspapers) (Semi-official)	Stockholm
SWITZERLAND	Agence Telegraphique Suisse, S.A. (Schweizerische Depeschenagentur A.G.), (Swiss Telegraphic Agency)	Berne
TURKEY	Anodolu Ajnasi (Agene d'Anatolie) (Anatolian News Agency), (Semi-official)	Ankara
UNITED STATES OF AMERICA	Associated Press (Cooperative, Independent)	New York
YUGOSLAVIA	Agence Avala (Semi-official)	Belgrade

Almost every country represented in the world alliance has one or more news agencies in addition. The exceptions are the smallest countries, or countries under dictatorships or other arrangements wherein the press associations have been consolidated and made official or semi-official, or countries where no association exists.[42] It will be observed that no South American press associations are members of the world alliance. This is because South American news is covered by the United Press, Associated Press, International News Service, and Agence Havas, and finds its way into the news stream through these agencies. Domestic press associations are not developed in Latin America. The same is true of Australia, so far as concerns national associations, and of most other countries not represented. Although China has several press associations, a local branch of Reuters provides the news of that country to the rest of the world.

It may be said that there is a smaller, and quite new affiliation, including the United Press (United States), the British United Press (Great Britain and Canada), Agence Telegraphique Radio (France), and Tass (Russia). The French agency is allied to Havas, and Tass also is in the larger affiliation.

Although each of the agencies forming the "world league" originally was restricted, by mutual agreement, to the sale of news entirely in its own country or in well defined territories, that arrangement was "liberalized" at a London meeting in 1932, between the heads of Reuters, the Associated Press, Havas, and the Wolff agency. By this agreement any one of the agencies was permitted to sell its service independently to any newspaper or other clients wanting it in a country normally served by one of the other member agencies.

In practice, the four biggest agencies have arranged coverage of most of the world in the following way, with an exchange of news among them:

Associated Press.—Covers the United States, Central America, and cooperates with Havas to cover South America.

Havas.—Covers France, the French Colonies, Romanic countries of Europe, and cooperates with the Associated Press to cover South America, and with Reuters to cover the Near East.

Reuters.—Covers Great Britain and the British Empire, the Netherlands, the Far East, and cooperates with Havas to cover the Near East.

DNB.—Covers Germany and Austria.[43]

Among the other press associations of the world, not members of the league of agencies, but some of them very important, are the following:[44]

Other Leading Press Associations

ALBANIA	Albanian Press Bureau and Telegraph Agency	Tirana
AUSTRALIA	Australian Associated Press, Proprietary, Ltd.	Melbourne
	Australian Newspapers Cable Service	Sydney
	Provincial Press Association of South Australia	Adelaide
	Queensland Country Press Association	Brisbane
	Tasmanian Provincial and Country Press Association	Launceston
	Country Press Cooperative Company, Ltd.	Melbourne
	Victorian Provincial Press Association	Melbourne
	West Australian Provincial Press Association	Perth
	Australian United Press Ltd.	Sydney
	Australian Provincial Press Association	Sydney
	Country Press, Ltd.	Sydney
	New South Wales Country Press Association	Sydney
AUSTRIA	Korrespondenz Wilhelm (Semi-official)	Vienna
BRAZIL	Agencia Brasiliera (Independent)	Rio de Janeiro
	Uniao Telegrafica Brasileira (Independent)	Rio de Janeiro

CHINA	Central News Agency (Kuomintang Official)	Nanking
	Kuo Min (Chinese Semi-official)	Shanghai
	Shun Shih (Chinese)	Shanghai
	Domei Tsushin Sha (Allied News Association),[45] (Japanese)	Shanghai
	Agence Havas (French)[45]	Shanghai
	Reuters (British)[45]	Shanghai
	Transozean-Nachrichten (German)[45]	Shanghai
	Tass (Russian)[45]	Shanghai
	Associated Press (American)[45]	Shanghai
	United Press (American)[45]	Shanghai
CZECHOSLOVAKIA	Central European Press	Prague
	Radio Central	Prague
FINLAND	Suomen Tietotoimisto (STT), (Semi-official)	Helsingfors
	Presscentralen	Helsingfors
	Tyovaen Sanomalehtien Tietotoimisto (TST), (Social-Democratic)	Helsingfors
FRANCE	Agence Economique et Finaciere (Economic and financial news)	Paris
	Agence Fournier (Financial and political news)	Paris
	Agence Telegraphique Radio (Controlled by Havas), (Political and financial news)	Paris
GERMANY	Deutsche Diplomatisch-Politische Korrespondenz (Semi-official—political news)	Berlin
	Transozean-Nachrichten (Semi-official. For radio and overseas service)	Berlin
GREAT BRITAIN	British United Press Ltd.	London
	Central News, Ltd.	London

	The Central Press Ltd. (Correspondence and features for provincial and overseas papers)	London
	Exchange Telegraph Co. Ltd.	London
	Press Association Ltd. (Affilitated with Reuters for domestic news)	London
	British Continental Press	London
	London General Press (News of economics, finance, politics, science)	London
GREECE	Hellenic Press Association	Athens
HONDURAS	Asociacion de la Prensa Hondurena	Tegucigalpa
INDIA	Associated Press of India (Independent)	Calcutta, Delhi, etc.
	United Press of India (Independent)	Calcutta, Delhi, etc.
ITALY	Agenzia di Roma (Semi-official—political news)	Rome
	Agenzia Volta (Economic news)	Rome.
	Agenzia Telegrafica Orientale	Rome
	Radio Nazionale	Rome
JAPAN	Teikoku Tsushinsha (Imperial News Agency)	Tokyo
MEXICO	Agencia Noticiosa Telegrafica Americana (ANTA), (Semi-official, controlled by Havas)	Mexico City
MONACO	Agence Telegraphique	Monte Carlo
NETHERLANDS	Persbureau Vaz Dias	Amsterdam
	Persbureau Aneta (Colonial news service)	Batavia
	Nederlandsch Correspondentie-bureu (Semi-official)	The Hague
	Persbureau Aneta-Holland (Colonial news)	The Hague

NEW ZEALAND	United Press Association of New Zealand	Wellington
NORWAY	Avisernes Oslokontor A/S	Oslo
	Myres Pressebyraa	Oslo
POLAND	Agencja Telegraficzna Express (ATE)	Warsaw
	Agencja Eschodnia (EST)	Warsaw
	Iskra (Semi-official)	Warsaw
RUMANIA	Interbalkan	Bucharest
SOUTH AFRICA	Reuters Ltd. (Branch of British agency)	Pretoria & Cape Town
SWEDEN	Svensk-Amerikanska Nyhetsbyran (Swedish-American News Agency)	Stockholm
	Svensk-Internationella Pressbyram	Stockholm
TURKEY	Turkish Press Association (Independent, but recognized by the Government)	Ankara
UNITED STATES	United Press Associations (UP), (Independent)	New York
	International News Service (INS) (Hearst service)	New York
	Universal News Service (US), (Hearst service)	New York
	Federated Press (FP), (A labor service)	New York
	North American Newspaper Alliance (NANA)	New York
URUGUAY	Associated Press (Branch of American Agency)	Montevideo
	Circulo de la Prensa (Independent)	Montevideo
	United Press Associations (Branch of American Agency)	Montevideo

The larger press associations, especially in important centers such as London, Paris, and New York or Washington, maintain staffs organized as in a newspaper office, each with an executive equivalent to a city editor, or news editor, as he would be termed in Great Britain, assigning reporters to various events.

Apart from the feature services, which have arisen as adjuncts to the news reports, press associations are expected to deal primarily in pure facts.

The special correspondent, representing an individual newspaper or several newspapers, or a special syndicate, often writing under his own name, sometimes does much the same thing, but if he touches a story at all he frequently sends more detail and gives more emphasis to the interpretation.[46]

Certain press associations are not quite impartial, however. They serve governments or private interests. Some of them are subsidized by governments and are, in effect, agencies of those governments. This status sometimes is recognized, and the agency is frankly held to be "official" or "semi-official," but even some of those agencies which pretend to be "independent" are not beyond suspicion. They are, potentially at least, propaganda organizations. Some of these groups, as members of the world league, may feed into the news stream a certain amount of propaganda, despite the conscientious efforts of foreign agencies to keep it out.

It is not that governments necessarily pay money across the counter to persuade press associations to disseminate favoring news. But a properly disposed press association may enjoy favorable financial terms in its use of communication and transmission facilities. Or extremely generous payments may be made to the association for special service of news to out-of-the-way colonial-military, or governmental posts, or radio service to ships at sea and foreign countries. At the same time, payment for such services is not necessarily evidence that the association is "official," much less that it is engaged in distributing propaganda.[47]

It sometimes is assumed that because a government issues official statements and communiques which are distributed verbatim, through a press association, that such an association is clearly government-owned or controlled. This is not necessarily so. Press associations sometimes cooperate with their governments out of national loyalty. Reuters, Havas, the former Wolff agency of Germany, Stefani of Italy, the former Rengo agency of Japan and others have received exclusive news releases from their governments and in return have provided the governments with advance copies of incoming foreign dispatches before distribution. This sometimes has given government departments opportunity to re-word or revise dispatches to accord with the official viewpoint and, in some cases, to withhold the news completely until a time that seemed more suitable for its release.

There are occasions when this relationship of government and press is unfortunate. In France the Foreign Office prefers to have Havas communicate to the French press only those comments from foreign newspapers which are favorable to the actions or purposes of the French Government. Unless a French newspaper maintains its own foreign correspondents—and few do so—who can and will send other versions, readers may gain a totally incorrect view of foreign opinion on some subjects. Then, when events prove that they have been misled, instead of feeling annoyance with their government or the press, they vent their displeasure unjustly on the foreign peoples.

The same is true where a government maintains an absolute censorship over its press, as in Russia, Italy, and Germany. Opposition or unwelcome views never receive publicity in those countries unless with a propaganda purpose.

A phase of press association development has been the so-called "syndicates" dealing with long feature stories of the magazine variety, with fiction and short articles, puzzles, cartoons, et cetera, usually with emphasis on entertainment.

In the United States the syndicate idea seems to have begun with Henry Villard, who, as a reporter for the Associated Press in Springfield, Illinois, proposed a news-reporting system from Washington in 1881. He suggested a syndicate to gather and provide the same "political and other news by mail and telegraph to a number of papers in different parts of the country, geographically situated so that they would not interfere with each other by the simultaneous publication of the same matter. . . . My enterprise was to be a sort of supplement to the Associated Press. . . . It was indeed the beginning in this country of the news syndicates or agencies, of which scores now exist in Washington and New York. I think I am fairly entitled to be considered the pioneer in this business. . . ."[48] He went to

Washington and set up such a syndicate for reputed newspapers.

REFERENCES

1. Karl H. von Wiegand, "In Europe: Reporter vs. Correspondent," *Circulation* (Aug., 1925), pp. 12-13, 37; Sisley Huddleston, "Correspondent in Paris," *Blackwood's Magazine* (Sept., 1924), V. 216, pp. 321-31; Anon., "Your Mirrors of Europe" (by a Foreign Correspondent), *Sat. Eve. Post* (Dec. 9, 1922), pp. 5, 145-50.
2. There also is the type of correspondent who says, "I don't want facts; I want news." His editor wants from him, and he provides, stories which are less often comprised of authenticated facts than of rumors, suggestions of intrigue, perversions of the truth, reflections of prejudices, sensational statements and implications—in short, reports that make spicy reading, regardless of the harm they may do through poisoning the public mind. Such reports may be written without the slightest investigation, entirely from imagination, and they sometimes are so written, but reputable papers shun them.
3. E. S. Dithmar, "European Correspondent," *Bookman* (N. Y., May, 1904), V. 19, pp. 244-57. Washington correspondents have received grotesque orders from their editors, such as "We have information that there is something in the air. Get it and send us 1,000 words." "Get interview with President on local political situation. Tell him to make it short." "Please rush immediately names of all unknown dead soldiers from this state." J. Fred Essary, *Covering Washington*, pp. 56-57.
4. See Ch. I, pp. 8-9, for explanation of these terms.
5. Some Paris correspondents for newspapers in the United States have felt that their best efforts to present a fair view of France and French affairs have been nullified, on occasions, by an attitude held to be common in American newspaper offices. There, proprietors and editors, for some reason, consider the Paris correspondents to be pro-French, and so discount what they send. They sometimes neutralize accurate and good articles by the editing, the display, the editorials, and by reports from Washington.

   Washington correspondents have been sardonically termed "oracles of journalism" in the United States, and often they have been said to hold slightly anti-French prejudices. This is attributed to *(a)* lack of knowledge of Europe and the world from any sufficient first-hand experience, *(b)* traditionally uncordial press relations with the French embassy in Washington, and *(c)* absence of bureau heads with European experience.

6. In Block Foundation lecture at Yale University, New Haven, Dec. 8, 1931. Reported in *Editor and Publisher* (Dec. 12, 1931), p. 12.
7. Lord Northcliffe is credited with having said that a journalist should know how to ride a horse and wear a monocle. James Gordon Bennett said a special correspondent of the right kind should be "half diplomat, half detective."
8. In Europe any person of the slightest standing in the newspaper world is a "journalist." A "reporter," as American journalists of prominence often delight to call themselves, in self-conscious modesty, frequently is regarded in Europe and most other parts of the world as a mere keyhole-peeper, freelance tipster, gossip-monger and blackmailer. If a European journalist has a title, military, academic, or otherwise, he uses it, and, if he can claim to be a special editor of any sort, that is on his formal card. All the prestige that he can muster is scarcely enough to overcome an inherent distrust, dislike and, in some cases, contempt, for the press. Only a few exceptions are made.
9. Walter Duranty, *I Write as I Please*, pp. 93-106, 303-304.
10. Great Britain, for example, was anxious that the United States should view Gandhi and his actions in a light more sympathetic to the British policy. Knowing that the American people, like the British people, are prone to judge news on a sentimental basis, great care was taken that American correspondents in London should be "properly" informed on the Indian situation in which Gandhi was the central figure.
11. Derived from *Principles and Instructions of the Foreign Service of the Chicago Daily News* (see Anon.).
12. This suggests another problem of the foreign correspondent. In some countries, especially in Europe, public figures sometimes demand that they be paid if they grant an interview. By this requirement they save themselves from having to endure numberless interviews. As some of them are themselves writers, too, they consider that they are entitled to a return if they reveal their ideas instead of writing them and selling them as articles for their own profit.
13. Some light on the relations of the press with diplomats appears in: Richard Washburn Child, "International Show Windows," *Sat. Eve. Post* (Dec. 20, 1924), pp. 21, 105-10.

14. A concise summary of the history of press associations appears in: L. M. Salmon, *The Newspaper and the Historian*, Ch. 5; M. A. Shaaber, *Some Forerunners of the Newspaper in England*, 1476-1622; Victor Rosewater, *History of Cooperative News-Gathering in the United States*.
15. L. M. Salmon, *The Newspaper and the Historian*, Ch. 5.
16. Com. Frank Worsley and Capt. Glyn Griffith, *The Romance of Lloyd's: From Coffee-House to Palace*, Chs. 7, 12, 13.
17. The seven books were as follows: 1. General record of news, in which is recorded daily all information of a general nature, and such as is particularly interesting to the merchants of the place, as may be received from correspondents by land and water, and by arrivals at the port. 2. Record of all arrivals from foreign ports or places, with cargoes particularly specified to each consignee. 3. Record of all arrivals from other ports in the United States similarly noted as the second. 4. Record of all vessels clearing for foreign ports, time of sailing, etc. 5. Record of all vessels cleared for other ports in the United States. 6. Record of all arrivals and clearances from or for foreign ports in all parts of the United States, except Boston. 7. Record of names of all gentlemen introduced by the subscribers, the places whence they came, and the name of the subscriber introducing them. The place also boasted several maps useful to shipowner or merchant, and a good clock, among other things.

    Samuel Topliff, *Topliff's Travels*. Letters from abroad in the years 1828 and 1829. From the original manuscript. Edited with a memoir by Ethel Stanwood Bolton, pp. 67-68.
18. Victor Rosewater, *History of Cooperative News-Gathering in the United States*, pp. 5-8, 10.
19. D. C. Seitz, *The James Gordon Bennetts, Father and Son*, pp. 61-65, 90-93; M. E. Stone, *Fifty Years a Journalist*, pp. 204-18.
20. M. Eugene Legigan, *A'Agence Havas*. Conference a l'ecole des Sciences morales et politiques; A. G. Laney, "Havas World Power in News and Advertising," *Editor and Publisher* (June 19, 1928), pp. F.8-F.10.
21. The fact that the Agence Havas is devoted largely to the advertising business, and did not develop its service to the general press until after 1860, is the basis for a claim by the Reuters' agency to the distinction of being the first modern *news* agency. It began its service to newspapers in London in 1858.
22. "Most of the commercial advertising is handled by Havas. To alienate Havas may mean for a newspaper the loss of practically all its advertising revenue. This power of one advertising agency

is of tremendous importance for the press and for the public, for it is known that in several cases advertising patrons have objected to editorial policies and interfered directly or indirectly with them, stopped campaigns and tabooed topics." Pierre Denoyer, New York correspondent for *Le Petit Parisien*, speaking at the Princeton Conference on the Press in 1931. Anon., *Conference on the Press*, p. 129.

23. H. A. B., *About Newspapers: Chiefly English and Scottish*, pp. 115-17, quoting *Hubbard's Newspaper Press Directory of the World* (see Hubbard).
24. James Grant, *The Newspaper Press*, V. 2, Ch. 13.
25. Data on the Reuter service also appears in: Andrew Wynter, *Our Social Bees*, pp. 297-303. One of the earliest printed references to the Reuter service; H. M. Collins, *From Pigeon Post to Wireless*; J. D. Symon, *The Press and Its Story*, pp. 87-97; H. E. Wildes, *Social Currents in Japan*, Ch. 7. Presents a partial history of the Reuter service in Japan; Anon., "The Romance of Reuters in the Making," *The Graphic* (May 26, 1923), pp. 754-55, 780; F.D. Bone, "Reuter's Are Always Right: The History and Organization of Great News Agency with World-Wide Ramifications," *World's Press News* (July 4, 1929); Philip Schuyler, "Reuters' Connection with Old Jewry: Incidents in the History of a Great Agency. Reuters' Deeds Seen as Romance by Sir Roderick Jones," *Editor and Publisher* (Oct. 13, 1923); V. Prodzky, "Live Wires of Reuters," *World's Press News* (Mar. 31, 1932), pp. 14-15; Sir Roderick Jones, "The Romance of Reuters," lecture by Sir Roderick Jones at Hall of Institute of Journalists, London, Oct. 21, 1930. *Journal of the Institute of Journalists* (Dec., 1930), V. 18, pp. 223-24.

    Also the following four pamphlets published by the Reuter's Telegram Co. Ltd.: *A Note on Reuters.* (For private information only. Confidential); *International Conference on the Press.* "News Agencies and Their Work." Address by Sir Roderick Jones, K.B.E. (Chairman of Reuters), London, July 6, 1927; *Reuters.* Address by Sir Roderick Jones, K.B.E., before Cardiff Business Club, Cardiff, April 1932; *Reuters*, Address by Sir Roderick Jones, at School of Military Engineering, Chatham, Oct. 25, 1928.
26. F. M. O'Brien, *The Story of the Sun*, Ch. 3.
27. *Ibid.*, pp. 148-53.
28. D.C. Seitz, *The James Gordon Bennetts, Father and Son*, Ch. 13. A hoax that was inspired by mischief alone was that perpetrated upon the *Packet*, a weekly paper of Hull, England, in 1864. Through

a devious arrangement, the *Packet* received what seemed a bona fide message from the telegraph office announcing under the heading, "The War in Denmark," that "the enemy had taken Umbrage," and giving the geographical position of "Umbrage" in such a way as to place it somewhere in the middle of the North Sea, and noting its population and other data. The paper accepted the report as true, and printed it. William Hunt, *Then and Now. Fifty Years of Newspapers Work*, pp. 85-87.

29. F. M. O'Brien, *The Story of the Sun*, Chs. 6, 7. Illustrates rivalry for news among New York newspapers about the time of the Mexican War.
30. For further reference to Craig's service see: Frederic Hudson, *Journalism in the United States*, pp. 612-14; Victor Rosewater, *History of Cooperative News-Gathering in the United States*, Ch. 11; A. F. Harlow, *Old Wires and New Waves*.
31. M. E. Stone, *Fifty Years a Journalist*, pp. 204-18.
32. S. N. D. North, *History of the Periodical Press of the U.S.A.*, House of Representatives, 47th Congress, 2nd Session. Misc. Doc. Part 8, Dept. of Interior. Census Office. Census of 1880, p. 107. A full report of news transmission methods by the Associated Press and by newspapers appears on pp. 105-10.
33. Frederic Hudson, *Journalism in the United States*, Ch. 38. A more or less contemporary account of the history of the Harbor News Association and the New York Associated Press and rivals.
34. Inter-Ocean Pub. Co. *v.* Associated Press, 184 Ill. 438, 56 N.E. 822, 46 L.R.A. 568, 75 Am.St.Rep. 184; Victor Rosewater, *History of Cooperative News-Gathering in the United States*, Chs. 21, 22.
35. For data on the Associated Press see: Victor Rosewater, *Hisotry of Cooperative News-Gathering in the United States*. This book also traces the entire history of news gathering in the United States; M. E. Stone, *Fifty Years a Journalist*; M. E. Stone, *News Gathering*, a pamphlet published by the Associated Press; W. G. Bleyer, *Main Currents in the History of American Journalism*, pp. 402-404; Anon., "(AP)" (Associated Press), *Fortune* (Feb. 1937), pp. 88-93, 148-62.
36. The Laffan News Bureau, for example, was set up by the New York *Sun* in the late 'eighties, and continued as an independent bureau until 1916.
37. M. A. McRae, *Forty Years of Newspaperdom*, Ch. 7. Stephen Vincent Benet, "The United Press," *Fortune* (May, 1933), V. 7, No. 5, pp. 67-72, 94-104. N. D. Cochrane, *E. W. Scripps*.
38. H. Simonis, *The Street of Ink*, Ch. 15. Covers history and organization of Reuters, Central News, Exchange Telegraph Co.,

London News Agency; J. D. Symon, *The Press and Its Story*, pp. 87-97.

39. Sir Roderick Jones, *International Conference on the Press*, "News Agencies and Their Work." Address by Sir Roderick Jones, K.B.E., Chairman of Reuters, London, July 6, 1927.

40. The members of the World League are indicated in "The Press as a Factor in International Relations," by Paul F. Douglass and Karl Bomer. *Annals of the American Academy of Political and Social Science* (July, 1932), V. 162, pp. 265-68. Also in *Documents Relating to the Preparation of the Press Experts Committee* (Anon.). League of Nations Publication, C. 399, M. 140 (1928), pp. 12-13.

41. Compiled from *Associated Press Handbook, Political Handbook of the World, Europa* (see Anon.), and sources listed in n. 40, p. 65.

42. A conveninet source in which to find these and other press associations is the *Political Handbook of the World*. Published annually, it lists the most recent nomenclature and organization of the press of each country.

43. Paul F. Douglass and Karl Bomer, "The Press as a Factor in International Relations," *Annals of the American Academy of Political and Social Science* (July, 1932), Ch. 2. "The International Combination of News Agencies," pp. 265-68. This was before the Wolff agency had been reorganized as DNB.

44. Adapted from *Political Handbook of the World* (1937 edition). Unless otherwise noted, an agency is to be regarded as independent, at least nominally. If a nation is unrepresented on this list or on the previous list of associations forming the world league of news agencies, it may be assumed that it has no press association of its own, but is dependent upon press associations of other countries for its news service. Also, while some of these associations are important and devoted to providing a general service of news, many of them are concerned only with the news of a certain section or province, or with special kinds of news, such as news and interpretation of political and diplomatic affairs, news of business, etc., and some of them are little more than propaganda agencies.

45. China represents rather a special case for there a number of foreign press associations maintain independent offices, as indicated, due to the fact that the Chinese press associations are not well organized, nor are they always reliable or impartial in their handling of the news. The situation is similar in Uruguay, although on a smaller scale.

46. For example, the Associated Press sent 200 words from London about the Unemployment Commission report of Nov. 7, 1932.

The New York *Times* wanted more, so Charles A. Selden, its correspondent, sent 1,000 words and made page one. Such papers as the New York *Times* and *La Republique* of Buenos Aires are unique in the world of journalism because of penchant for details, but this very complete handling of the news is what they made their splendid reputations.

47. To avoid any such appearance of lending itself to propaganda purposes, the Canadian Press Association refused in May, 1920, to accept a joint British and Canadian Government subsidy increased to $50,000 or $60,000. The association, for about fifteen years prior to that date, had received a smaller subsidy, which was regarded as almost essential if it were to continue in business, but it had not "been very happy in the fact." John W. Dafoe of the Manitoba *Free Press*, so remarked at the Second Imperial Press Conference, Ottawa, 1920. Robert Donald ed., *The Imperial Press Conference in Canada, 1920*, pp. 168-69.

48. Henry Villard, *Memoirs of Henry Villard*, V. 1, pp. 153-54.

2

Handling the Language

I

AT an educational conference held in Vancouver, leader of the Canadian school system generally agreed that from half to three-quarters of their students in the first year of college were incompetent in grammar, syntax, and analysis of thought. What was notable in the discussion was that nearly every participant used the English language with uncommon force and precision. Any looseness or jargon heard there came from the three American guests, of whom I was one. Most of our hosts—Canadian teachers, principals, supervisors, and university instructors—had obviously gone through the mill of a classical education; the chairman made a mild pun involving Latin and was rewarded with an immediate laugh. Yet they declared themselves unable to pass on their linguistic accomplishment to the present school generation, and they wanted to know why.

In the United States the same complaint and inquiry has been endemic, commonplace, for quite a while. You come across it in the papers. You hear parents, school people, editors and publishers, lawyers and ministers, men of science and of business, lamenting the fact that their charges or their offspring or their employees can neither spell nor write "decent English." The deplorers blame the modern progressive school or the comics or TV; they feel that in school and outside, something which they call discipline is lacking, and they vaguely connect this lack with a general decline, aggravated by a "crisis." Like everything else, bad English is attributed to our bad times, and the past (which came to an end with the speaker's graduation from college) is credited with one more virtue, that of literary elegance.

The facts seem to me quite different, the causes much more tangled, and the explanation of our linguistic state at once more complex and less vague. For many years now I have been concerned with the art of writing and kept busy at the invidious task of improving other people's utterance, and I cannot see that performance has deteriorated. The level is low but it has not fallen. As a reader of history I am steadily reminded that the writing of any language has always been a hit-and-mass affair. Here is Amos Barrett, our chief source on the battles of Concord and Lexington: "It wont long before there was other minit Compneys. . . . We marched down about a mild or a mild half and we see them a coming . . ." and so on. An illiterate New England farmer? Not so, since he could write; he had been taught and in some way represents "the past." The question he poses is, how do people write who are not professionals or accomplished amateurs? The answer is: badly, at all times.

Writing is at the very least a knack, like drawing or being facile on the piano. Because everybody can speak and form letters, we mistakenly suppose that good, plain, writing is within everybody's power. Would we say this of good, straightforward, accurate drawing? Would we say it of melodic sense and correct, fluent harmonizing at the keyboard? Surely not. We say these are "gifts." Well, so is writing, even the writing of a bread-and-butter note or a simple public notice; and this last suggests that something has happened within the last hundred years to change the relation of the written word to daily life.

Whether it is the records we have to keep in every business and profession or the ceaseless communicating at a distance which modern transport and industry require, the world's work is now unmanageable, unthinkable, without *literature.* Just see how many steps you can take without being confronted with something written or with the necessity of writing something yourself. Having been away for a couple of weeks during the summer, I find a bill from the window washer, who luckily came on a day when the cleaning woman was in the apartment. He has therefore scribbled below the date "The windows have been cleaned Wed. 12:30 P.M. Your maid was there to verify the statement"—perfectly clear and adequate. One can even appreciate the change of tense as his mind went from the job just finished to the future when I would be reading this message from the past.

Call this bad writing if you like, it remains perfectly harmless. The danger to the language, if any, does not come from such trifles. It comes rather from the college bred millions who regularly write and who in the course of their daily work circulate the prevailing mixture of jargon, cant, vogue words, and loose syntax that passes for prose. And the greater part of this verbiage is published, circulated, presumably read. A committee won't sit of its drivelings are not destined for print. Even as interoffice memo goes out in sixteen copies and the school-children's compositions appear verbatim in a mimeographed magazine. Multiply these cultural facts by the huge number of activities which (it would seem) exist only to bombard us with paper, and you have found the source of the belief in a "decline" in writing ability—no decline at all, simply the infinite duplication of dufferism. This it is which leads us into false comparisons and gloomy thoughts.

II

The apparent deterioration of language is a general phenomenon which is denounced throughout western Europe. One had only to read the catalog of the British Exhibition of 1951 to see the common symptoms in England. Sir Ernest Gowers's excellent little book of a few years earlier, *Plain Words,* was an attempt to curve the universal disease in one congested spot, the civil service, which is presumably the most highly educated professional group in Britain.

In France, the newspapers, the reports of parliamentary debates, and the literary reviews show to what extent ignorance of forms and insensitivity to usage can successfully compete against a training obsessively aimed at verbal competence. And by way of confirmation, M. Jean Delorme, a native observer of the language in French Canada, was led to declare the classic speech "infected" on this side of the Atlantic too. As for Germany, a foreign colleague and correspondent of mine, a person of catholic tastes and broad judgment, volunteers the opinion that "people who cultivate good pure German are nowadays generally unpopular, especially among the devotees of newspaper fiction and articles. The universal barbarism of language has already gone well into the grotesque."

So much for the democratic reality. But great as has been the effect of enlarged "literacy," it does not alone account for what is now seen as linguistic decadence. The educated, in fact the leaders of modern thought, have done as much if not more to confuse the judgment. For what is meant by the misnomer "pure speech" is simply a habit of respect toward usage, which insures a certain fixity in vocabulary, forms, and syntax. Language cannot stand still, but it can change more or less rapidly and violently. During the last hundred years, nearly every intellectual force has worked, in all innocence, against language. The strongest, science and technology, did two damaging things: they poured quantities of awkward new words into the language, and this in turn persuaded everybody that each new thing must have a name, preferably "scientific." These new words technical or commercial, were fashioned to impress, an air of profundity being imparted by the particularly scientific letters k, x, and o = Kodak, Kleenex, Sapolio. The new technological words that came in were sinful hybrids like "electrocute" and "triphibian," or misunderstood phrases like "personal equation," "*n*th degree," or "psychological moment"—brain addlers of the greatest potency.

The passion for jargon was soon at its height, from which it shows no sign of descending. Every real or pseudo science pours new verbiage into the street, every separate school or ism does likewise, without shame or restraint. We can gauge the result from the disappearance of the dictionary properly so called. Consult what is in many ways the best of them, *Webster's New World Dictionary*, and what you find is a miniature encyclopedia filled with the explanation of initials, proper names, and entries like "macrosporangium" or "abhenry," which are not and never will be words of the English language.

Under the spate of awe-inspiring vocables, the layman naturally feels that he too must dignify his doings and not be left behind in the race for prestige. Common acts must suggest a technical process. Thus we get "contact" and "funnel" as workaday verbs—and "process" itself: "we'll process your application"—as if it were necessary to name the steps or choices of daily life with scientific generality. I know a young businessman who makes jottings of his business thoughts; when he has enough on one topic he *folderizes* them.

What is wrong with all this is not merely that it is new, heedless, vulgar, and unnecessary (all signs of harmful vice in a language) but that jargon swamps thought. The habit of talking through cant words destroys the power of seeing things plain. "I'll contact you to finalize the agreement." What does it mean? The drift is plain enough, but compare: "I'll call at your office to sign the contract." The former raises no clear image or expectation, the latter does. Moreover, the former smells of inflated ego, it fills the mouth in a silly bumptious way.

But who cares? Why fuss?—good question both. Nobody cares much because we all think it's the deed (or the thing) that counts, not the words. This conviction, too, is a product of modern technology, and its effect is great though unremarked. The power of words over, nature which has played such a role in human history, is now an exploded belief, a dead emotion. Far from words controlling things, it is now things that dictate words. As soon as science was able to chop up the physical world and recombine it in new forms, language followed suit: and this not only among scientists making up new vocables, but among the supposed guardians of the language, the poets and men of letters. It is highly significant that around 1860 writers deliberately began to defy usage and turn syntax upside down. Lewis Carroll and Edward Lear made good fun with it; "obscure" poets such as Rimbaud sought new depths of meaning. There was in this a strong impulse to destroy all convention, for Victorian moralism had made the idea of conventionality at once suspect and hateful. The revolt succeeded and its spirit is still alive; novelty hunting is now a linguistic virtue; or to express it differently, common influence is at work in Jabberwocky and James Joyce, in the scientist's lingo and in the advertiser's "Dynaflow," "Hydramatic," or

"Frigidaire"—which end by becoming household words. In short, modern man is feeling his oats as the manipulator of objects, and he shows it in his manhandling of words.

This helps to explain why the predominant fault or the bad English encountered today is not the crude vulgarism of the untaught but the blithe irresponsibility of the taught. The language is no longer regarded as common treasure to be hoarded and protected as far as possible. Rather, it is loot from the enemy to be played with. squandered, plastered on for one's adornment. Literary words imperfectly grasped, meanings assumed from bare inspection, monsters spawned for a trivial cause—these are but a few of the signs of squandering. To give examples: the hotel clerk giving me a good room feels bound to mention the well-known person whom "we last hospitalized in that room." Not to lag behind Joyce, the advertiser bids you "slip your feet into these easy-going *leisuals* and breathe a sigh of real comfort.

Undoubtedly these strange desires are often born of the need to ram an idea down unwilling throats. We all fear our neighbor's wandering attention and try to keep him awake by little shocks of singularity, or again by an overdose of meaning. Unfortunately, novelty hunting proceeds from the known to the unknown by a leap of faith. "It was pleasant," writes the author of very workmanlike detective stories, "to watch her face and find his resentment *vitiate* as he made excuses for her."

III

The notable fact is that all this occurs in printed books, written by writers, published (usually) by first-rate firms that employ editors. In speech, the same blunders and distortions come from educated people. It is all very well to say, as one expert has confidently done, that "what certain words really mean is moving toward what they seem to mean," the implication being that after a while everything will be in place. Actually, this leaves meaning nowhere, if only because we're not all moving in steps. The *New Yorker* spotted a movie theater sign on which "adultery" was used to mean "adulthood." From an English periodical I learn that some new houses "*affront* the opposite side of the street." If Mrs. Malaprop is going to become the patron saint of English, what is going to prevent "contention" from meaning the same thing as "contentment" or the maker of woodcuts from being called a woodcutter?

There is no getting around it: meaning implies convention, and the discovery that meanings change does not alter the fact that when convention is broken, misunderstanding and chaos are closed at hand. True, the vagaries of those who prevent good words to careless misuse seem more often ludicrous than harmful. This might give us comfort if language, like a great maw, could digest anything and dispose of it in time. But language is not a kind of ostrich. Language is alive only by a metaphor drawn from the life of its users. Hence every defect in the language is a defect in somebody.

For language is either the incarnation of our thought and feelings or a cloak for their absence. When the ordinary man who has prepared a report on sales up to 30 June rumbles on about "the frame of reference in which the coordination campaign was conceived," he is filling the air with noises, not thoughts.

For self-protection, no doubt, the contemporary mind is opposed to all this quibbling. It speaks with the backing of popular approval when it says: "Stop it! You understand perfectly well what all these people mean. Don't be an old purist looking below the surface and meddling with democratic self-expression." To haggle over language is quibbling, of course. All precision is quibbling, whether about decimals in mathematics or grains of drugs prescriptions—fairly important quibbles. The question is whether in language the results justify the quibble. Well, the public is here the best judge, and it is evident that as a consumer of the written word, the public is always complaining that it cannot understand what it is asked to read: the government blanks, the instructions on the bottle or gadget, the gobbledygook of every trade, the highbrow jargon of the educators, psychiatrists, and social workers, and—one must also add—the prose of literary critics. The great cry today is for improved communication, mass communication, the arts of communication, and yet under the pretext of being free and easy and above quibbling, those who do the most talking and writing indulge themselves in the very obscurities and ambiguities that cause the outcry.

They are abetted, moreover, by another offspring of the scientific spirit, the professional student of language. In his modern embodiment, the linguist takes of the view that whatever occurs in anybody's speech is a fact of language and must not be tampered with, but only caught in flight and pinned on a card. This is "scientific detachment," and it has gone so far that under its influence in many schools all the categories of grammar, syntax, and rhetoric have been discarded. The modern way to learn English or a foreign language is to absorb a phrase-by-phrase enumeration of all that might conceivably be said in ordinary talk—a directory instead of a grammar.

This brings us back to our first difficulty, how to teach the millions the use of their mother tongue *in composition*. We have made nearly everybody literate in the sense of able to read and write words. But that is not writing. Even those who profess disdain for the literary art and the literary quibbles respond automatically to good writing, which they find unexpectedly easy to read and retain, mysteriously "pleasant" as compared with their neighbors' matted prose. The linguists themselves pay lip service to "effective" speech, approving the end while forbidding discrimination among the means.

Now many thousands of people in the United States today exercise the discrimination; there is amid the garbage a steady supply of good writing, modestly done and published—in every newspaper and magazine, over TV and radio, in millions of ads and public notices, in travel booklets, and printed instructions on objects of daily use. Good writing is good writing wherever it occurs, and some of the impugned comics which are supposed to defile the native well of English in our young are far better than acceptable.

It is therefore idle and erroneous to condemn "the newspapers" or "the radio" en masse. Here too one must discriminate, and the failure to do so is one cause of the trouble—the strange cultural trait whose origin I have sketched and which makes us at once indifferent to our language, full of complaints about it, and irresponsible about mangling it still more. In these conditions people who write well learn to do so by virtue of a strong desire developed usually under necessity: their job requires lucidity, precision, brevity. If they write advertising copy they must not only make it fit the space but make the words yield the tone.

Tone—that is the starting point of any teaching in composition. What effect are you producing and at what cost of words? The fewer the words, and the more transparent they are, the easier they will be to understand. The closer the ideas they stand for and the more natural their linkage, the more easily will the meaning be retained. Simple in appearance, this formula is yet extremely difficult to apply, and even more arduous to teach. You cannot work on more than one pupil at a time and you must be willing to observe and enter into his mind. On his part, the discipline calls for a thorough immersion in the medium. He must form the habit of attending to words, constructions, accents, and etymologies in everything he reads or hears—just as the painter unceasingly notes line and color and the musician tones. The would-be writer has the harder task because words are entangled with the business of life, and he must stand off from it to look at them, hearing at the same time their harmonies and discords. It is an endless duty, which finally becomes automatic. The ideal writer would mentally recast his own death sentence as he was reading it—if it was a bad sentence.

IV

Now such a discipline cannot be imposed from without, and not everybody needs it in full. But its principle, which suffices for ordinary purposes, should be made clear to every beginner, child or adult. Unfortunately, the school system, even when progressive, makes writing an irrational chore approached in the mood of rebellion. The school does this in two ways: by requiring length and by concentrating on correctness. I know very well that correctness was supposedly given up long ago. The modern teacher does not mention it. But if the teacher marks spelling and grammatical errors and speaks of little else, what is a child to think? He gets a mark with the comment "imaginative" or "not imaginative enough" and, most often, "too short," and he is left with no more idea of composition than a cow in a field has of landscape painting. How *does* one judge the right length and get it out of a reluctant brain? Nobody answers, except perhaps with the word "creative," which has brought unmerited gloom to many a cheerful child. Who can be creative on demand, by next Tuesday, and in the requisite amount? In all but a few chatterboxes, mental paralysis is the only result.

Meanwhile the things that are teachable, the ways of translating the flashes of thought into consecutive sentences, are neglected. They have been, most often, neglected in the teachers themselves. How do *they* write or speak, what do *they* read? If they read and write educational literature, as they often must for advancement, are they fit to teach composition? And what of the teachers of other subjects, whose professional jargon also infects their speech—what is their countervailing effect on a child to whom a good English teacher has just imparted a notion of the writer's craft? Suppose the teacher of a course on family life has just been reading *Social Casework* and his mind is irradiated with this "Familial societality is already a settled question biologically, structured in our inherited bodies and physiology but the answer to those other questions are not yet safely and irrevocably anatomized." Unless this is immediately thrown up like the nux vomica it is, it will contaminate everybody it touches from pupil to public—in fact the whole blooming familial societality.

The cure is harsh and likely to be unpopular, for it must start with self-denial. It can be initiated by the school but it must not stop there. As many of us as possible must work out of our system, first, all the vogue words that almost always mean nothing but temporary vacancy of mind—such words as "basic," "major," "overall," "personal," "values," "exciting" (everything from a new handbag to a new baby); then all the wormy expressions indicative of bad conscience, false modesty, and genteelism, as in: "Frankly, I don't know too much about it"—a typical formula which tries through candor and whining to minimize ignorance while claiming a kind of merit for it; finally, all the tribal adornments which being cast off may disclose the plain man we would like to be: no frames of reference, field theories, or apperception protocols; no texture, prior to, or in terms of; and the least amount of coordination, dynamics, and concepts.

After the vocabulary has been cleansed, the patient is ready for what our Canadian friends at the Vancouver conference deplored the lack of in the modern undergraduate: analysis of thought. To show what is meant and let criticism begin at home, I choose an example from an educational report entitled "The English Language Arts." It begins: "Because language arts or English is so—" Stop right there! What are language arts?—A perfectly unnecessary phrase of the pseudoscientific kind which tries to "cover." Besides, "language arts or English" is nonsense: ever hear of another language? Moreover, "language arts . . . is" doesn't sound like a happy opening for a report by and to English teachers. Let us go on: English is so what? Well, "language arts or English is so intimately connected with all knowledge and all living, it is the subject which most often bursts the dikes separating it from others." What do you mean, language is *connected* with living? And how does English connect with *all* knowledge and *all* living? Is the practical knowledge of the Russian engineer intimately connected with English? Do the amoebas speak English? And if this intimacy does exist, then what are these dikes that separate English from other subjects? Are these subjects not part of "all knowledge" with which English is connected—or rather, of which it too is a part?

Cruel work, but necessary if anything akin to thought is to arise from the written word. The Neanderthal glimmer from which the quoted sentence sprang is irrecoverable but its developed form should run something like this: "English, being a medium of communication, cannot be confined within set limits like other subjects; to the peoples whose speech it is, all theoretical knowledge, and indeed most of life, is inseparable from its use."

V

Standardizing the Daily

Various causes have contributed to that standardization of the American daily newspaper which is one of the most discouraging features of the press today. In the first place, your newspaperman is, as I have elsewhere pointed out, what the children call a "copy-cat". He watches his rivals and more distant contemporaries like a hawk. If any one of them hits upon a single new feature, be it comic strip, or picture page, or cross word puzzle, or advice to the unhappily wed, all the rest of them follow suit. Original ideas are scarce and they are not copyrighted. Hence the rush to imitate. Especially is this true in the case of a successful daily. Immediately its success is assured everybody else similarly situated hastens to imitate type or make-up. Observe the New York dailies and see how they follow the *Times* in their first page "stories."

Take the case of the *Herald Tribune*. It has made great gains sine it took over the *Herald*, affording a rare case of one newspaper really holding the bulk of the circulation which it purchased. It has now become an excellent newspaper, for which the credit goes primarily, it is believed, to the present managing editor, Arthur S. Draper, and the willingness of Mr. and Mrs. Reid to abandon the old narrow partisanship of the news pages. But when you come to analyze the *Herald Tribune* there is not a single original feature of importance. The powers that be on the *Herald Tribune* decided to go after the *Times* on its own lines and they have profited thereby because that meant getting out a daily with lots of news in it—even to the printing of long speeches and cabled documents of importance—but it involved only slight originality save for the distinctive types and headlines used.

The fact is that few of the present generation of journalists set any store by beauty of type and appearance. That passed with the coming of mass production. Hearst hastened its demise with the screaming whole-page heads six inches deep of his flamboyant period of 1895-1900. That he would become quieter and more conservative was inevitable. But competitors and observers all over the country imitated him in order to increase sales. Today the headlines are everywhere approximately the same save for those fine old Southern dailies which have escaped the economic pressure and the competition which have gone so far to standardize the Northern and Western press. There are still exceptions in the North, like the Baltimore *Suns*, the Cincinnati *Enquirer*, and the Boston *Transcript*, but in the main the owners of the press have themselves decreed the drift toward standardization. Professor Henry E. Birdsong, who teaches journalism in Temple University in Philadelphia, tells me that when his beginning students stumble upon the *Enquirer* or *Transcript* they are excited by what they consider these *new* departures. For many years the Philadelphia *Record* had its special size and typography. Two years ago it was taken over by a new owner and now it is practically impossible at a distance to tell whether one is looking at a copy of the *Ledger* or the *Record*. The latter's management sees no sales value in originality of type and make-up.

I know of only one case in recent years in which a daily has deliberately chosen an original first-page make-up and attractive new typography—the New York *Morning Telegraph*, which, as a sports daily, is out of the ordinary competition. The most outstanding case of a newspaper which has kept its old and original format is the Cincinnati *Enquirer*, or *Enquirer*, as they call it out there. Its appearance has not been changed in forty or fifty years; it is the only paper left, as far as I know, which carries its one-column heads, sometimes ten lines deep. In its attention to local, suburban, and nearby communities it is almost unique, and it appears to have an amazing vitality and vigor.

It is hardly necessary to dwell upon the standardization of our dailies resulting from the development of our great news services. That speaks for itself. It is the most normal and defensible of all the standardizing tendencies; indeed, it is a justifiable as it was inevitable. The 1,200 members of the Associated Press naturally carry exactly the same news, but as the lesser dailies become more prosperous the drift toward differentiation by means of special cablegrams and telegrams and exclusive correspondents at once sets in. As soon, however, as these special features become costly there is the inevitable temptation to syndicate them in turn.

Today, when one travels through the country on a Sunday on a fast train and buys successively the Buffalo, Cleveland, Chicago, Indianapolis, Toledo, and St. Louis Sunday papers it is hardly possible to tell which city is represented in a given mass of printed pages without carefully scanning the page headings. One finds the same "comics", the same Sunday magazines, the same special "features" in almost all of them and, of course, in most of them precisely the same Associated Press news. I have looked through the Sunday editions of nine big Eastern and Mid-Western papers and I found "Little Orphan Annie" in seven of them, and she doubtless graces hundreds of others. "The Gumps," I am sorry to say, are not so popular, as they appear only five times. I was shocked to find "Mutt and Jeff" in only three of them, and "the Katzenjammer Kids", once the leading American comic, in only two. A cursory examination of the Philadelphia *Enquirer*, for example, reveals twenty features that have appeared in the other eight newspapers, and probably as many more have appeared in other Sunday issues not included in this study. The special services of the New York *Times, Herald Tribune, American*, and the other New York dailies are as widely syndicated as possible. The truth is that our people, in or out of journalism, facing the same problems, having great economic stakes in the existing order, are bound to react in the same way if they do not happen to be infected by the germ of liberalism or radicalism. The newspaper profession has turned out to be a business and as a result there was bound to be standardization of the mentality of owners and editors which had its effect upon the editorial pages and news pages, too.

So we have a steady waning of individualism of the daily, marked first by the disappearance of the great editor whose personality shone through its pages—men such as Watterson, Medill, the Bennetts, Godkin, Dana, Greely, Raymond, Nelson—and then by the extinction of the typographical originality. You could tell the *Tribune* of Horace Greeley, the Springfield *Republican* of the Bowleses, the old Boston *Post*, the *Evening Post* of Godkin, as far as you could see the format. They were distinctive institutions bearing the impress of owners and editors. Now they have nearly all yielded to the tremendous pressure every owner is under to increase circulation in order to get more advertising at higher rates, in order, in turn, to meet his steadily increasing costs. No wonder he turns to syndicates, to combinations, or to special services. What more natural, too, than to wake up your pages just like one of the New York dailies, with your editorial pages, "opposite-editorial" pages, society and sports pages in the same relative positions? The appearance of the tabloid is, of course, a variation from the old standardized type of daily, but it is significant that the tabloios themselves imitate one another with complete fidelity.

In the sports pages above all others the opportunity for standardization is of the best. But here we have the offset that there is a tremendous thirst for the views of the distinguished commentators on sports who are paid very large salaries and are bid for by rival dailies because they carry with them, as they migrate from one daily to another, a following of "fans" whose numbers run into the thousands. Read the leading dailies in the East and see how much alike their financial pages are. As for the editorial pages, standardization is at work there with a vengeance. The same "columnist" and the same editorial cartoons may appear in a dozen or many more dailies, and the same half-columns of medical advice and the same personal gossip from Washington. I have personally received as many as sixty clippings of an editorial commenting upon some words of mine from as many small dailies all over the Union—all of which had received the editorial from the same source and accepted its facts and comment, without subjecting them to any critical examination whatever. The Newspaper Enterprise Association, one of the leading syndicates of the country, sends out daily about five editorials. It is the belief of the managers that 80 to 90 per cent of 800 to 900 newspapers they serve use one or more of these "canned" editorials a day.

As for the syndicates, they play an ever-increasing role. For example, the Newspaper Enterprise Association which is a Scripps-Howard organization, spends $2,225,000 annually on its service. Of this, $500,000 goes for pictures only, to obtain which quickly no expense is spared. Thus, to rush to New York a few photographs of the stranded German airplane which was the first to cross the Atlantic from east to west it hired a special train as well as airplanes—the modern press photographer in his daring outranks the special correspondents of old. Sometimes the N.E.A. has spent $12,000 for a single picture; sometimes it hires a whole fleet of airplanes to distribute its photographs. This Association offers three kinds of service—the difference being in the quantity of matter offered. It sells, besides editorial matter, foreign correspondence of the gossipy, "feature" variety, and letters from Washington, comics, radio, aviation, and other features.

On the other hand, the North American Newspaper Alliance is most eager to let one know that its chief aim is to get away from standardization. It serves no chain of newspapers, only independent dailies, and but one in each city. It is not interested in factual, but in interpretative articles. Most of its clients belong to the Associated Press and like that organization, the Alliance is cooperative and non-profit-making. It is especially strong in financial and business articles, is distinctly dignified, believes itself "conservatively liberal," and also supplies "women matter", news of Hollywood (daily!), and is able to purchase such costly features as articles by H.G. Wells and G.B. Shaw. It gives plenty of attention to sports and "comics."

There is, of course, another side to syndication which, in all fairness, must be set forth. Without the syndicate small-town newspapers would be much duller and much less informed than they are. They could not print any news pictures; they could not broaden their pages; they could not have much—if any—news of New York, Washington, or other centers; their foreign features would probably almost disappear, except in so far as they were brought to them by the news associations. Some of the syndicated Washington and European correspondence is of genuine educational value.

Most of the modern manufacturing inventions tend to standardize the dailies. In speaking of the new teletypesetter, which he is developing, Mr. Frank E. Gannett recently said:

> The teletypesetter automatically will make necessary greater care in the preparation of all copy. Our wire services will be compelled to edit their stuff better and will undoubtedly give newspapers a complete, carefully written story instead of bulletins, flashes, leads, subleads, kill-leads, and all the other corrections that now come to the telegraph editor in a jumbled fashion. The teletypesetter will, of course, work toward standardization. It will be necessary for newspapers that intend to go in a circuit to standardize their grammatical style, width of column, and the size of type used. It will also tend to standardize our news services. . . .

Moreover a complete newspaper page has already been transmitted by radio from San Francisco to the General Electric

Company laboratory in Schnectady. When this process is perfected I cannot see why the great Eastern and Mid-Western dailies cannot reproduce their issues on the Pacific Coast or anywhere else and put them on sale at once. This development, too, will make for standardization and for the further aggrandizement in wealth and influence of our most powerful and prosperous dailies. Indeed, in the *Technological Review* for December, 1929, John J. Rowlands goes so far as to predict a master newspaper, to be issued in New York and transmitted by wire and air to a thousand newspaper offices for immediate reissuing—which will certainly hasten the day of the control of public opinion by a few men or one master-capitalist.

Whether this comes or not, there can be no doubt that standardization of the press will continue to increase as the years pass.

3

News and New Technology

THE new technology is faster, cleaner and much freer of error than the old technology, and can avoid multiple handling of type. It therefore needs less people, and less space, and less expense. The current doctrine in the US is known as 'capturing the original keystrokes,' (*i.e.* those of the journalists and ad takers), in word perfect form, so that the successive stages of re-keyboarding under the old system (principally at the Linotype or other linecaster machine) can be eliminated, along with the proofreading function. But there are still snags, especially at the plate making stage.

On the following page there is a flow chart showing the old process and the new process. These are then described more fully, with comment. This description of how the new technology compares with the old can be skipped by those who know, and by those who do not need to know: most of the following chapters make reasonable sense without detailed knowledge of the process, although with it their point should be clearer. Some of the detail may reflect US rather than UK practice: but if so, the variation is small. Much of this chapter is an abbreviated version of part of a report on the newspaper business by Dirks Brothers, the New York stockbrokers, to whom acknowledgement is made.

The Old Technology

Descriptive phrases for the old methods of printing are 'hot lead' or 'hot type,' derived from the fact that molten lead is used to form lines of type. The descriptive phrase for the new method is 'cold type.' The key to the 'hot type' method is the Linotype machine and its variations. The process with 'old technology' is this:

1. Copy is produced in the newsroom and advertising department and sent to the copy desk in the composing room.
2. The copy desk is a routing service. With a lengthy news story, for example, the copy cutter will slice the copy into segments of a few paragraphs to be distributed to different typesetters. The object is speed—six typesetters can produce a story in a fraction of the time it takes one typesetter.
3. Linotype and headline casting machines are the next step in the process. A Linotype is a large, awkward-looking typesetting contraption with mechanical arms, cases of matrices (molds), and a keyboard. It was invented in 1884 by Ottmar Mergenthaler. An operator sits at the keyboard and taps out lines of type. When he hits a key, a matrix for the appropriate letter ejects from the matrix case and falls into a form. The operator inserts spaces so that the line of type is 'justified', *i.e.* extended to the end of the line. He also hyphenates words at the end of the line. When the operator has assembled the line of matrices in the form, he pushes a lever that causes molten lead to be injected into the matrices, creating a line of type. A man manually operating a Linotype typically can set three to five lines of type per minute, and depending on the skill of the operator, an error might be made every 10 or 20 lines of type. In recent years the introduction (but not in Fleet Street!) of tape punching, and subsequently the introduction of computers, has greatly improved the speed of the hot-metal processes. With tape, an operator sits at a typewriter-like machine that punches holes in paper tape; the tape is then fed into a device that reads the tape and drives the Linotype machine. Freed from a manual operator, a Linotype can produce 10 to 15 lines of type per minute.
4. Once a news story or advertising matter is set in lead type, a proof sheet is made from it.

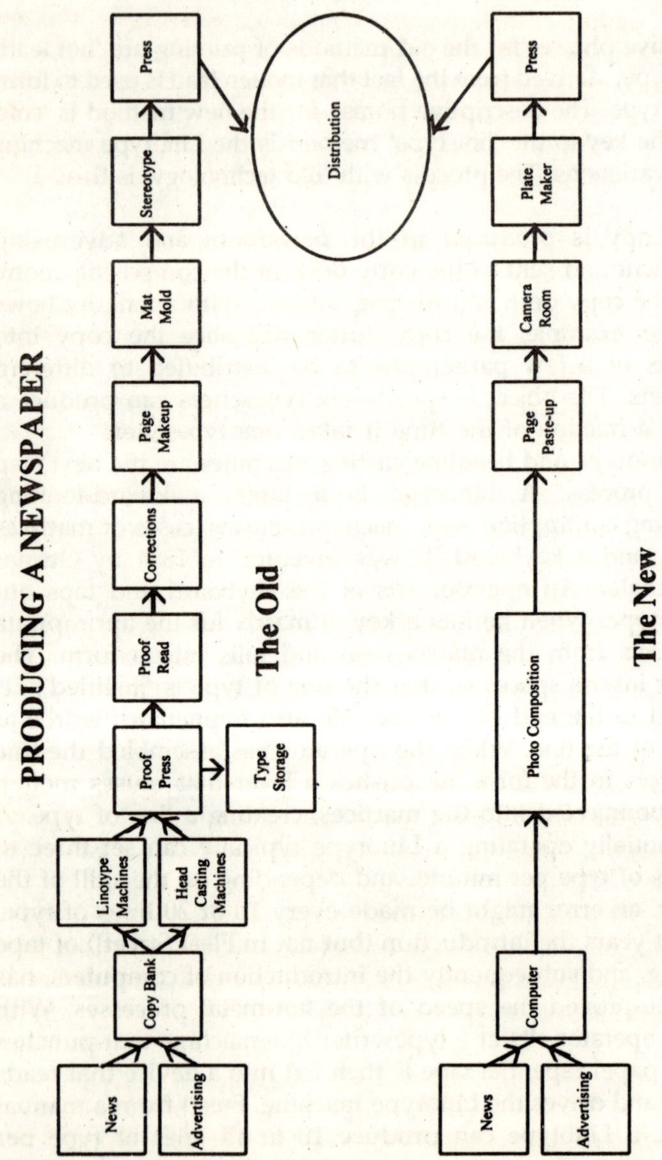
PRODUCING A NEWSPAPER
The Old
News
Advertising
Copy Bank
Linotype Machines
Head Casting Machines
Proof Press
Type Storage
Proof Read
Corrections
Page Makeup
Mat Mold
Stereotype
Press
Distribution
The New
News
Advertising
Computer
Photo Composition
Page Paste-up
Camera Room
Plate Maker
Press

5. Proofreaders go over the proofs line by line to search out errors. Once the errors are noted on the proof, it is sent back through the line-casting process so that corrected lines may be set and substituted for the bad lines.

6. The type is then sent to page make-up. There it is carefully fitted into page forms, an operation that required extensive cutting and fitting. Zinc engravings of photographs and previously assembled display advertisements are added. When finished, the page form is a reverse metal version of the newspaper page as it will come off the press.

7. A moist, artboard-like mat is placed over the page form before installing the form in a mat-molding machine. The mat holder is a large, heavy machine that applies great pressure on the mat, pressing it down onto the page form. The results is a mold of the page.

8. The page mold is curved and dried in a mat former, trimmed, and then is placed in the stereotype machine, which forces molter lead under high pressure into the mold. This produces a semi-cylindrical plate, weighing about 40 pounds, that is mounted on a press cylinder.

9. A continuous roll of paper is fed through the press and is printed directly with the plate.

10. Finally, newspapers roll off the press, to be stacked and bundled. Then the bundles are loaded onto delivery trucks for distribution.

The process is labour-intensive, requiring operators for machines, proofreaders, and some people just to lug type around from place to place. There are redundant manipulations of copy, particularly in the keyboarding and proofreaders process. Moreover, many different skills are required, and an assortment of unions—each jealous of its prerogatives—has grown up over the years. The hot-type printing process is cumbersome, dirty, time-consuming, and above all costly, although in its way it works, and works well.

The New Technology

Just as the Linotype machine is the key to the old, hot-type printing system, so the photocomposition machine is the key to the new, cold-type system. 'Cold-type' is used as the descriptive phrase because in this process molten lead is not used: rather, print images are generated photographically on paper. An important element in achieving the high speed and efficiency of photocomposition is the computer.

An equally important use of new technology is under way in newsrooms and advertising departments. Electronic devices are either taking over or enhancing the traditional use of typewriters, *i.e.*:—

(a) VDU or VDT (*acronyms for Video Display Unit or Terminal*): The video typewriter has a standard keyboard, but instead of paper there is a cathode ray tube—like a small TV screen—on top of the typewriter. A reporter or ad writer types out copy as before, but what he composes appears on the tube. If he wants to change something he just types over it; the words disappear and the new ones take their place. He can roll back copy on the screen to review or change earlier portions. When he is satisfied, he pushes a code button and the copy is transmitted electronically to the computer. Some VDUs, instead of feeding electronically to the computer, produce a paper tape with the copy information on it. This then is fed to the computer. Other more elaborate and expensive VDU's can be used to lay out advertisements.

(b) OCR (*acronym for Optical Character Reader or Recognition*): With an OCR (often called a 'scanner') a reporter or ad writer composes at an electric typewriter. If typed sufficiently well, his copy can be fed directly into the OCR; otherwise, a typist must prepare cleanly typed copy. With OCR, a scanning light reads the copy and creates either an electronic version of the copy that is transmitted to the computer, or a paper tape that is fed to the computer. With both of these concepts, the object is to insert the copy into the computer, where it is justified for left and right margins and stored. A newspaper that uses video screens in its newsroom may also want to install optical scanners there and in other departments to handle advertising copy, wire copy, or syndicated matter that comes to the newspaper already typed out.

(c) Another newsroom function affected by the new technology is editing. Using the same or a more elaborate video display screen, an editor taps out a code to call a particular

story from computer storage. The story is reproduced on the VDU's display screen, and the editor revises and rearranges as he wishes using the keyboard. When finished, he sends the story back to the computer, which digests the changes and readies the copy for the photocomposition machine.

(d) Central to the advantages of this technology is that it in effect eliminates proofreading. Under the old method, an editor could send perfect copy to the composing room only to have errors committed by the typesetting machines and operators. This made an elaborate proofreading system mandatory. With the new equipment, the editor, having read a story carefully, can send presumably perfect copy to the computer and on to the photocomposition machine confident that it will be reproduced with near perfect accuracy. The error rate with this new method is about one in 250,000 lines.

The next step in the new process is the computer, which has taken over several of the functions of the old composing room. Computers store copy electronically, a function that previously occupied large areas in the composing room with trays full of lead type. Computers justify the margins of lines of type, a procedure previously laboriously performed by a linotype operator, and they make the changes and corrections ordered by the editors. Importantly, the computer does all of these things—distributing copy from point to point, incorporating changes, justifying—in a matter of seconds.

The photocomposition machine has revolutionized the basic method of getting words into print. The sophisticated photocomposition machines of today can be driven by several methods: a keyboard, electronic impulses from computers, punched paper tape, or magnetic tape. Essentially what a photocomposition machine does is to translate the input into a printed readout of the original copy. The copy reappears in column form just as it will finally appear in the newspaper. There are many sizes and types of photocomposition machines. Speeds range from 25 lines per minute for less sophisticated machines up to several thousands of lines per minute for high-priced, computer-driven models. Photocomposition machines take the place of Linotype and headcasting machines and the operators needed to run them. Because of their high accuracy, they eliminate mechanically caused typesetting errors, thus contributing to the elimination of the proofreading process.

With the new technology, the laborious page make-up function is replaced with page paste-up. Working with scissors and paste, a make-up man assembles the printed-out columns from the photocomposition machine onto a page form. He also applies the photographs and the advertisements. When he is through, he has pasted up the complete newspaper page as it will look when it rolls off the press. (Some of the latest photocomposition machines will print full pages, rather than just columns, so eliminating page paste-ups.)

In the camera room, a photograph is taken of the page paste-up. The result is a negative of the page, which is sent to the plate-making department.

At this point, the flow chart should diverge into two streams, depending on whether the plate is to be made for a web offset press or for a letterpress plant. The basic point is that the cold-type page paste-up and the negative made from it are *flat* surfaces, while a letterpress printing plant demands a *raised* surface to print from. For a long time, there was no really satisfactory way of converting from a flat to a raised surface. The magnesium and zinc plates available for this purpose can be expensive and time-wasting to produce although they are used here and there, often for part only of a newspaper. So for a long time photocomposition was linked more or less exclusively to web offset printing, which does not demand a raised surface, but works on the principle of creating areas on the printing plate that either attract or repel ink. It meant that photocomposition was long confined to the small circulation newspapers to which web offset printing was also for long confined, because of low speed and tricky start-up period.

This posed a dilemma for the large circulation letterpress houses. Printing presses are vastly expensive items (far more expensive than photocomposition equipment and its associated computers and input devices) and last a long time: so they could not and would not throw them away. But they also wanted to take advantage of the cost saving associated with photocomposition. How?

Research quite recently provided an answer, an 'interface' between flat photocomposed page paste-ups and raised printing surfaces, in the form of 'shallow relief printing plates,' otherwise known as polymer or plastic plates. Basically these plates are layers of relatively soft photosensitive plastic, parts of which are hardened by exposure through the page negative, leaving the rest to be washed away in a bath, so creating a raised printing surface. The plastic plate is flexible, and is then bent into a semi-circle to fit direct onto a press cylinder.

There are still problems with plastic plates, however. One is that they are still expensive and slow to make compared to stereo plates. Another is that the quality of reproduction of half tone pictures, as opposed to type areas, is still poor. Acceptability of plastic plates does therefore still depend on how valuable time is (is it an early feature page or a late news page?) and on a calculation about the savings from photocomposition versus the extra costs in plate making (it is all too easy to lose in plate making the time and money saving in composing). Some newspapers have adopted a compromise position, making a plastic plate but then using it, not as a direct printing plate but as a pattern plate, that is, using it to make traditional stereo plates. This can be a successful, if interim, arrangement.

Automatic stacking, typing, and loading machines have been developed that greatly simplify the distribution process. American newspaper dispatch departments are different to British ones because of the large number of pre-printed advertising inserts, often for specific sections of the newspaper's distribution area, that have to be inserted into the main paper after it is printed and folded, especially on Sundays. This can be a very labour intensive business (as indeed is the normal handling of British papers in the warehouse, even without special inserts).

The Americans have been developing automated dispatch systems, and progress in this area of newspaper operations is further evidence that it is the whole range of newspaper activities, and not just the composing room, that is 'under attack' in terms of technological development and elimination of jobs. Pioneering work on computer controlled semi-automatic loading has been done in Houston, Texas, with the computer directing which bundles containing which combination of inserts go to which delivery van for distributing to which area or areas of the city. This work is being followed up by Gannett and other newspapers, and the *Washington Star*, for example, has recently ordered a big automated mail room system from Harris Corp. for on line insertion of pre-printed inserts. Here then is yet another example of further parts of the newspaper operation falling within the ambit of the computer, showing how the computer is gradually moving into a central role in US newspapers.

Need for Technological Change

Some US publishers can, and some cannot, produce more or less dramatic figures showing the savings in labour costs resulting from new equipment. But the further you get into this technological revolution, the less labour there is left to save. However, the revolution has now gone so far, and built up such a momentum, that there is now no alternative path. The main job is to get to the end of the path with the maximum speed and minimum waste of money. A bonus, in the eyes of many US managements, is that by that time, they believe, they will be rid of the constraints of the printing craft unions, which will have vanished along with the technology that created and defined them.

If you talk to executives of Media General, the Richmond, Virginia newspaper groups that publishes a local morning and local evening paper and a financial daily, and has had a seminal influence on the introduction of new technology in the US, they produce dramatic figures for the financial savings from photocomposition and its associated equipment. Previously, they had 185 skilled printers working in their composing room, earning about $200 a week in 1971 and (if they were still there) perhaps $230-240 now. However, the figure is now down to 140, and it is an entirely different group of people, originally unskilled and now trained, if at all, on the job, earning $125 a week. The savings from the change were $800,000 in the first year alone, and are now running at $1.25 million a year. The cost of the equipment was $900,000.

To many print works managers and newspaper publishers, these are dreamy figures. They show with startling clarity *(a)* that the name of the game in new technology in the US has been the elimination of expensive manpower *(b)* that those savings are, or could be, immediate and substantial. The production director at the American Newspaper Publishers Association says bluntly 'technology is useless without eliminating people.'

At Norfolk, Virginia, the composing room of the local newspaper group is down in less than 3 years from 230 to 130, and is expected to go down to below 80 in time (some 7 extra typists elsewhere have to be offset against these figures). The *Washington Post*, the *New York Times*, the *New York Daily News* and the *Detroit News* have each recently shed about 100 skilled printers through one means or another. And so it goes on.

One skilled printer may earn, say $12,000 a year. One Video Display Unit costs, nowadays, about $8,000. People are getting more expensive as time goes on and electronic equipment less expensive. The economics of replacing skilled printers at that wage level (plus their overhead costs like pensions and social security) with video screens used by journalists, advertising men and others who are on the paper's staff anyway, are therefore obvious. Similarly, an OCR configuration, including the special typewriters need to go with the basic OCR machine, might cost $50,000. You do not need to displace many printers at a real cost of perhaps $15,000 a year each to justify that capital expenditure. Another revealing comparison is with the current cost of a single hot lead line caster machine—from £12,000 to £24,000 depending on specifications—and you might need 20 to 100 or more of them to produce a paper, depending on its size.

There are other savings attached to the new technology: it needs far less space, and that saves on building costs and building rentals; it is cleaner and quieter, and makes for much pleasanter working environments; it does not go on strike (well, not usually); and you can write it off against tax in many cases. And how, US publishers look forward to a not too distant day when the composing room, once the greatest user of labour in a newspaper, and its biggest cost centre apart from newsprint, becomes totally automated, eliminating printers, skilled or otherwise, from all areas except the press room itself and perhaps the plate-making section (although that too is on the automation schedule), and the maintenance department.

This fundamental point does however need some qualifications and comments, although they do no invalidate it.

1. Many plants in the US were substantially over-manned in the first place, due to make-work rules, management hiring policies, etc. In principle, savings on manpower could be made without needing new technology as the justification; indeed, in many places they have been made. However, in many other places they have not and where savings have been made, they have not gone as far as they could do on a strict definition of need. Therefore new technology is in most cases the necessary catalyst and occasion for achieving or attempting to achieve these reductions in manpower. What is more, the new technology opens up the possibility of taking this process much further than is possible with traditional technology.

2. In this situation, it is not surprising that the initial cuts in manpower made to coincide with the arrival of new equipment should appear so dramatic in at least certain instances. However, this can only be done once, or perhaps twice. By definition, it cannot go on indefinitely, as stages two, three, four, etc. of the automation process come and go. In other words, manpower savings may be and are clear and sufficient justification for new investment in the early rounds, but it may be rash to assume that they always will be.

3. Anyway, not all papers can necessarily show these labour savings even in the early rounds, even though they may have other justifications for the investment. For example, it is not uncommon to find labour savings in the composing area (which are usually quite real) offset to one degree or another by increases in staff elsewhere—say, in the editorial department, to cope with the extra work load created there by the new technology in the composing area: or in the press room, where the company has switched to web offset at the same time, and is still getting used to it: or in maintenance areas, to cope with the sometimes temperamental new machinery: or simply overall, in coping with new machinery that may have been unwisely chosen, badly programmed, or improperly prepared for, creating the need for many hands to make it work. (In questioning a manager about his 'savings' it is usually advisable to ask him about total staff numbers as well as composing room staff—he may neglect to tell you, since the composing room is

often looked at, rightly, as a separate cost centre but disregarding consequences elsewhere.)

4. There is anyway another more or less explicit justification for investment in new technology in the minds of many US newspaper managers, even if it does not produce overall staff cost savings. That is that it weakens and may in time destroy the printing craft unions, in particular the International Typographical Union, the big composing room craft union, by lessening their numbers and substituting less skilled non-unionised labour or at least members of more amenable unions. Put another way, it has enabled management to re-assert that managerial control over the plant, in terms of recruitment, manning standards, and choice of equipment, which it had previously lost to the tightly organised craft unions. This in itself, in the eyes of many US publishers, is quite sufficient justification for the new technology.

5. It is therefore a mistake to look at pure numbers—it also matters *who* you employ. Is he (or she) skilled or unskilled, earning a high wage or a relatively low wage, unionised or non-unionised? Even if a plant does not show big overall savings in pure numbers, it may on closer inspection be using different, cheaper and more amenable people, as a result of using new equipment.

6. Reduced labour costs may be the carrot that leads a newspaper management down the path of new technology. But it is not long before that management has no alternative but to follow the path. You cannot go back to hot lead. In the US, as we have noted, they are not making hot lead machines any more, and in many areas even now it is hard to find men who still know how to work them. The task soon becomes one of elaborating and improving your cold-type system, of moving on to the next generation of more sophisticated electronic machines. Even in the US it is still too soon to quantify the total overall cost of carrying out the switch from hot lead to a total cold electronic system. The revolution has simply not got that far yet and anyway, the labour savings may be mainly loaded towards the beginning of the change-over, and some of the biggest costs loaded towards the end of it, with the arrival of 'total systems' of electronic newspaper production. Yet these final and most expensive steps may be quite unavoidable, for

technical or competitive reasons. The final sums may look different from the interim ones.

7. Realising this, many US publishers are now pausing, consolidating, taking breath, and trying to work out where they want to get in, say, 10 years from now. This will influence all their investment decisions from now on. This pause is no doubt also influenced by the current business recession, which has caused new investment decisions to be postponed. But from now on, the real influence on the pace of automation may in many instances be the total financial position of the newspaper, in terms of what it can afford, rather than the narrower question of labour costs.

8. One last caution. Composing room costs are only part of total newspaper costs. How big a part depends on, for example, how big a circulation the paper has and therefore how much (expensive) newsprint it uses. Typically, composing room costs are in the range 10 per cent to 30 per cent of total costs. So saving, say, a third of 10 per cent of costs is not going to make a paper rich overnight. But it is argued that big cost items like newsprint are something you cannot do anything about: composing room costs are something you can and therefore should tackle—it may make the overall difference between showing a profit and not showing one.

US publishers are in the grip of an irreversible process: maybe the unions are too. Publishers on the whole welcome it, for the reasons stated, and also because many of them feel that they have got to become an electronic medium. Paper, they feel, may become an impossible medium to use, for conservationist and ecological reasons, as well as prices. One day, they argue, their distribution system may have to be by TV cable and electronics, rather than by newsboy and on paper, bringing an interest convergence of the two at present technically distinct media of newspapers and television.

That is a long term view. But here and now the US newspaper industry almost certainly owes one of its most important developments to the availability of cheap photocomposition systems, requiring little labour and allied to web offset printing: and that is the big growth of small circulation local or suburban weekly papers, often with circulation well below 10,000—indeed the average is under

5,000. In about 1960, the total circulation of the US weekly press was about 17 million. It is now about double that, spread over something like 7,600 titles (these figures are for 1973, and may of course have declined a bit since then, with the fall in advertising revenue, but the basic phenomenon is clear). Nearly 90 per cent of these small papers are printed by web offset, which almost certainly means a similar percentage photo-composed. It is estimated that an investment of $250,000—300,000 would buy enough plant to start a local weekly paper—well within the borrowing scope of a local businessman or group.

In other words, the base of the US newspaper pyramid has been expanding quite fast, even if its middle and upper layers may have shrunk. The more successful weeklies have tended to go twice or thrice weekly, even convert to dailies. So there is a groundswell of activity at this level which is important, both for the overall structure of the US press, and for the evidence it provides that new technology can and does promote the foundations of new, if relatively modest, newspapers.

Management and Unions

British newspaper managers have usually said that they would modernise and automate 'if the unions would let us,' and only now are they facing up to the industrial relations problems involved. The American union situation was, from the managerial point of view, often worse than in the UK. But they have managed to get through the 'union barrier.' However, the means used by American managements to do this were often foul rather than fair, by confrontation rather than conciliation, and it is questionable whether they are desirable in the British context. However, they have placed the biggest and toughest US print union, the ITU, in a parlous position where it is fighting for its very survival. The most remarkable omission from the American scene is any attempt at systematic joint consultation, before the event, between management and unions over automation: but such consultation has also been remarkable for its absence in this country until recently, and even now is very limited. At least American employers have now learnt the need to co-operate between themselves, if not with the unions, over labour matters.

The struggle between unions and managements over modernisation and automation in America began about 25 years ago: patterns of confrontation set in very early, reflecting union-management attitudes throughout US society. In the author's opinion, many employers deliberately and from the first sought confrontation, as soon as they felt they had the power to do so (either technically, through new technology, or legally, through the Taft-Hartley act and 'right-to-work' laws in various states) leaving the unions little alternative except tame surrender or bloody-mindedness. Employers on the other hand would certainly argue that given the character of the unions they themselves had little choice except tame surrender (leading perhaps to eventual demise of their business through excessive labour costs) and bloody-mindedness.

American employers will add that the reason why Florida in general, and the *Miami Herald* in particular, were such trail-blazers in new technology, was that they 'had no unions.' This is only partly true. Florida did have unions, and so did Miami. But the earliest seminal event in the post-war saga of new technology in US newspapers was the series of strikes at the *Miami Herald* in the late 1940s over the introduction of new machinery. Thanks to the availability of cheap alternative labour and restrictive labour laws, the management won these strikes and eliminated the unions from the *Miami Herald* organisation. This seems to have set the pattern for Florida as a whole, where the print unions certainly do still have some members in some locations, but where their will or wish or ability to object to changes instituted by management is virtually nil.

This meant that when photo-composition came on the scene in the 1960s, Florida was in the unique position of having both the managerial freedom to introduce it as and when it liked, the electronic expertise to install it, deriving the necessary personnel from the space programme centred on Cape Canaveral, and the cheap labour to operate it in place of expensive journeymen printers (as the 'Sunshine State.' Florida has attracted millions of immigrants from other states and from Cuba). So the photo-composition revolution set in , with Florida showing the rest of the US how it could be done.

The second seminal event, and the one which has had the most immediate influence on current attitudes and behaviour, was the strike at the Richmond, Virginia, newspapers in 1971. Although it clearly follows the earlier Florida pattern, it is worth recounting here in detail, for all that it shows about managerial policy and union reactions all over the US since that date.

Richmond, Virginia

The company is called Media General, and it publishes a morning and an evening paper, in a local monopoly situation. In about 1970, it decided to launch a new paper, a financial daily with a strong emphasis on financial data, analysis of stock and share prices, and market reports. To make it pay—and to work out the figures—it needed an advanced computer and photocomposition set-up, having been up to then a conventional hot lead house. It set up a separate company to publish the financial daily, with non-union people to work the new equipment. A dispute broke out with the typographical union, and in 1971 the union struck.

The critical part of the story is what happened next. The management, which had expected the strike and laid its plans, brought new photo-setting equipment into the main newspaper area. They brought lorries in past the picket lines and loaded the hot dead linecaster machines onto them and drove them out of the plant and simply sold them, mainly for scrap. Meanwhile, management and advertising people, helped by secretaries and others who were simply recruited off the street, set about working the new photo-setting equipment. The papers did not lose an edition. The first photo-set copies were late and they were terrible to look at for several months. But they came out.

The union had of course walked out in the belief (well founded in the days when there was only hot lead) that the paper could not be got out without them. Its members then had to watch the management literally scrapping the machinery that had been their livelihood. The pickets could not stop other workers coming and going into the plant, under state labour laws. Also, the unions in the plate-making and printing press areas are quite separate, and stayed at work, partly because labour laws in the US make sympathy strikes difficult, and partly because inter-union relations are often strained.

Of the 180 or so men who walked out, less than 10 ever came back to work in the building. The power of the union at Richmond was broken, and since then the paper has relied on cheap non-union female and male labour with a high turnover (30-35 per cent a year) to do most of the composing work. There are two other similar but smaller strikes over the same issue, at about the same time, also in the Southern states. The union lost all three battles, as, it is fair to comment, it was almost bound to do given the relative simplicity of the new technology, and the US labour laws.

Since then (despite limited strike action in New York and Dallas last year) neither the Typographical Union nor any other union has ever risked a full scale confrontation with management over new technology in the US. Conversely, management have almost everywhere adopted the same basic tactic—get in the new equipment, train some management or other non-union people to work it, then give the union an ultimatum 'the new equipment goes live on such and such a date: if you don't work it, we will.' This tactic, whatever the objections to it, has eventually worked. The last bastions against the total switch of the US newspaper industry to electronic and photo-setting methods fell last year with the signing of the new labour contracts in New York and Washington. It is unfortunate, to say the least, that 5 of the original 8 New York area newspapers had to die, partly because of strikes over the automation issue, before this new accord was reached. Some employers argue that some of these titles could have survived if the 'Richmond tactic' had been used earlier in New York to beat the union: the union feels that in those earlier years it was bound to retaliate when confronted with that type of managerial attitude.

That said, there is no doubt that both in New York and Washington the newspaper managements faced a labour situation which was both difficult and in any rational business (which the Press is not) indefensible. Because these two cities offer the best parallels with Fleet Street, in terms of size of publications, strength of unions, competitive situation, and complexity of issues, it is worth examining in detail the experience of the *Washington Post* and the *New York Times*. In both cases it is important to understand one feature of US labour contracts which is mercifully absent from this country, and which made the labour situation in these and many other US cities even more difficult to tackle than it is said to be in Fleet Street. That feature is the phenomemon of 'reproduce' or 'bogus copy'.

Under labour agreements that seem to have been universal among large US cities of the North and East and date back many decades, the Typographical Union has had the right to re-set any material that comes into the newspaper already set. This applies mainly to advertisements which come in as an already made-up block. In the UK the rule is that the composing room staff get paid *as if* they had done the original setting of this material: in the US they actually do (or did) the re-setting in order to get the money, even though the original in-coming block may have already been used in the paper. This 'make-work' rule, as employers have dubbed it, loomed larger and larger as successive booms in advertising followed each other in the post-war years of economic prosperity. The consequences, in the case of the *Washington Post*, were startling.

The *Washington Post*

Some 15 years ago, the *Post* was the junior paper in Washington (to the *Washington Star*). Then it began to outstrip its rival, coinciding with the great boom in advertising revenue of the 1960 and early 1970s. One result of this otherwise pleas phenomenon was that the amount of 'reproduce' material w for re-setting by the composing room staff grew and gre the backlog had by 1973 grown to the staggering tota 40,000 pages—all of it technically work waiting to be became really serious when taken in conjunction union rule—if there was work to do in the pl journeyman printer arriving in town could, as staff and do it, or at least do other work so tha in principle, free to do it.

The result was almost hilarious. The lost control of its staff numbers, impri two rules in the union contract whic employers, had signed. It watched in dismay as journeymen printers, many of them displaced from Richmond, Virginia, and other places where there had been dispute or loss of work, came to Washington and simply attached themselves to the *Post*, without the *Washington Post* being able to do anything about it. In only about 3 years, the composing room staff grew from 500 to nearly 800.

It was then that the management decided to act. They brought in Mr. John Prescott from the *Miami Herald* (of course) to take charge of the newspaper division, and the management then set about the task of achieving a new labour contract that would *(a)* do away with 'bogus' copy for good and all, *(b)* reduce the number of employees, and *(c)* pave the way for new technology. There followed about 14 months of often acrimonious bargaining with the local union, during which wildcat strikes and sabotage occurred and threats were made to the life of Mr. Prescott (although no one claims that the majority of the employees concerned would or did condone such tactics). However, there was no all-out strike. The *Washington Post* followed the by now classic tactic of getting in new photosetting equipment and training non-union and management personnel to work it, as a precaution against a strike. But they had one other factor on their side: they are a rich and varied organisation, and could and did also spend money to get out of their predicament.

The main features of the new labour agreement that came into force in the autumn of 1974 are:

1. the 'bogus copy' system was brought out, at a cost of $2.6 million;
2. a special 6 months scheme offering voluntary retirement on advantageous terms;
3. management to have control of recruitment;
4. management to have the right to introduce new equipment;
5. a job guarantee for those who do not leave under the special retirement scheme.

This is an expensive package. But between 1974 and the nd of January 1975 over 100 printers left under the special scheme, some of them taking as much as $50,000-$60,000 with them, as a result of the special payments and their entitlements under the profit sharing scheme that the *Washington Post,* until this last contract, had operated. Such men, often around 60 years of age, are now well off beyond any possible previous expectations. The management expects wastage and retirements to take the numbers in the composing room down to nearly 400 within 5 years (bearing in mind the high average age of printing staff here as elsewhere in the US—about 55). It is now planning a comprehensive switch to 'cold type' methods, with its ultimate aim being the 'total system' represented by the NSDG computer project.

The *New York Times* and *Daily News*

A feature of the Washington situation during the negotiation of the last labour contract was that for the first time the two main employers in the city, the *Washington Post* and the *Washington Star,* joined forces and negotiated together, that is presented a united front to the union. This feature was repeated in New York during their 1974 negotiations of a new labour contract, when the *New York Times* and the *New York Daily News* (but not the *New York Post*) joined forces. In both cities, they had learnt the lesson of previous negotiations, when a single union picked off divided employers one by one. While important in Washington, this assumed greater significance in New York, with its sad history of newspaper closures due in part of strikes and disputes over new equipment. The previous labour contract had, in the eyes of the *New York Times* and other papers in New York, virtually prohibited new technology, although the union insists that its intention was not to prohibit it, but to ensure that the employers consulted the union in due time about its installation. But whatever the reason, New York a year ago was as backward technically as Fleet Street is today—a vast hot metal operation with large and expensive skilled staffs to make it work.

The story of the New York negotiations last year was long and complex, and full of typically New York dramatic stories, like Mr. Bertram Powers, the Typographical Union leader in New York, symbolically stamping on and breaking a printing plate produced by the new processes—it had to be symbolic, because Mr. Powers is not a young man and has a gammy leg.

The *New York Times* and the *Daily News* set up a joint training centre over the river in New Jersey, where they trained non-union staff (secretaries, managers, circulation people) in the use of photo-setting equipment, away from the eyes of the union. They also installed photo-setting equipment in their respective offices, but on different floors from the main composing areas. Both did dummy runs and assured themselves that in the event of a strike they could produce a paper of sorts. (Mr. Powers incidentally maintains that he knew all along that this equipment was there, and that he was meant to know, because his men had to pass that way at the *New York Times* between composing room and staff canteen.) The two companies then began their negotiations.

Here the critical factor was that by adroit manoeuvering (hailed by other employers as a masterpiece of its kind) the two employers managed to isolate the New York Typographical Union *both* from the other unions in their plants and from the national headquarters of the ITU. There is not much love lost between the ITU and some of the other unions, in New York at any rate, and many of the other unions—the pressmen, the stereotypers and engravers, the electricians, engineers, the journalists' union—felt strongly that it was high time the ITU in New York came to terms with automations, especially given the previous newspaper closures and loss of jobs in New York. The ITU headquarters took a not dissimilar view; nationally, the union had decided that it neither could nor wanted to fight automation, and was busy elsewhere making the best deals it could to ensure the survival of the union under the new conditions.

Consequently, the other unions in New York continued to work normally when the ITU staged various forms of protest action during the negotiations: ITU headquarters refused to sanction an official strike in New York. To cap it all, when ITU members at the *Daily News* refused to handle the new equipment and tried to stop the paper coming out at all by action that fell short of a full strike, the management then proceeded to use the non-union people it had trained, and its new equipment, to put out a paper without the union: a poor paper, it is true, but a paper nevertheless. Not long afterwards, agreement was reached.

It was not, however, in any sense a walkover for the newspaper companies. It is quite fair to say that the union got most of what it wanted for its members. It got a ten year guarantee of no redundancies both for its full time members working at the two papers, and for the so-called 'substitutes' who from time to time took over from the regular staff men, until such time as a staff job came vacant. As the average age of ITU members in New York is over 55, this meant in effect a lifetime guarantee of jobs for most of the men affected. Also, the union got jurisdiction over large sections of the new equipment which is to be installed, as specified in a map of the expected new configuration placed in the back of the new labour agreement. There were, as in Washington, special early retirement schemes which over 100 men on each newspaper took advantage of.

The managements got what they principally wanted—freedom to introduce new technology, and to determine their own staff levels, subject to the jobs guarantee (the same achievement as in Washington). Both employers are now laying their plans for fairly rapid transition to photo-composition and electronic system. They, and the union, are aware that much of the new equipment specified in the labour agreement may itself be obsolete and not needed in ten years, making valueless the jurisdictional rights obtained by the ITU in this agreement. But the fact remains that the ITU has won a valuable 10 year breathing space in which to take stock and plan for the future.

Apart from the belated cooperation between newspaper companies, and their readiness to train non-union labour to outflank the union, what stands out most from this narrative is the simple vulnerability of the union to the new photo-setting equipment. It is vastly simpler to use than hot metal machines, and the computer parts of the operation are anyway run by specialist computer men.

But it is not only in the composing room (contrary to a lot of received opinion) that this attack on traditional skills and training requirements is being made. Many people say that the pressroom is still a skilled area, where men are needed with the proper training and experience—therefore, union men. Indeed, in many US newspapers, even where the ITU had lost its grip in the composing area, the pressmen's union is still strong. But there are one or two instances which suggest (and I put it no higher) that this is not necessarily so, and that the pressroom may one day be under the same attack as the composing room (although of course it employs far fewer people in the first place). Certainly Mr. Powers of New York ITU thinks so, and there is evidence to support him.

Dallas Morning News

At the *Dallas Morning News*, the pressroom men went on strike in the spring of 1974, over a manning levels dispute, believing that this would stop the paper. But the management, having been given notice of the strike, took the now familiar course and began training non-union people to work the presses. These people, with only a month or two's experience, moved in when the pressmen walked out, and got the paper out. They have continued to do so, and the pressmen and their union have not since been re-admitted into the building. The matter is still in the American arbitration procedure: but the lesson is there.

Army Times

At the *Army Times* offices outside Washington, where a group of local weekly papers are also produced, the staff is entirely non-union (and has been since the offices moved out of the centre of the city specifically for this purpose). The new staff are all trained on the spot, and they rotate among jobs—operating the photo-setters, pasting-up, and working the presses. Of course, there is always a proportion of the men in the press room who have been doing it for several years. But the rotation principle apparently works. There is one other instructive feature of the *Army Times:* it is now about 50-50 black and white, and about 50-50 men and women, whereas before it was all white, all men. This phenomenon—the end of union organisation meaning more jobs for women and blacks—is a familiar pattern in US newspaper offices. That may be good for women and blacks: for the employers it certainly means cheaper labour.

American circumstances are in certain important ways different from the UK. But what surely stands out is *(a)* that a firm collective approach is more fruitful for the general good of the industry, and *(b)* that it is neither desirable nor probably possible in the UK to treat unions and their members as cavalierly as has been done in many parts of the US, even though some union attitudes are deeply conservative and have to be overcome somehow.

4

Global News Network

WHILE the *statistics* of news communication are rather forbidding, they carry implications that are great indeed. Who shall say whether some obscure incident in Europe or America or China may not hold the key to new possibilities for mankind, to changes perhaps no more remote than next year, or next week? Yet, if the cost of transmitting a dispatch between Europe and America is $25, and the cost for a message of the same length between China and Europe or America is more than $100, it is clear that the editor who has a budget to observe will give his readers rather less news about China. But history, in the making, recognizes no such budgetary limitations.

How the World Grew Smaller

What power over the thoughts of the peoples of the world are hidden in the ownership and control of transmission facilities! Does the land that owns the cables rule the world? Certainly the nation whose radio towers receive from and send to far-away parts of the earth never can be ignored in international relations! It is too well informed; its own voice informs too many others.

Only a century ago, the nations lived in comparative isolation. Mail alone carried intelligence between peoples, and between men at home. There was then no telegraph, no cable, no telephone, no wireless. There was no newspaper comparable to those of to-day, and most persons on the globe feared and were ignorant of what was beyond their physical or mental horizons. In the statistics of communication, therefore, concerned with miles of wire and costs per word, a great romance is hidden, and its conclusion no man knows even now.

One of the longest cables the telecommunication, laid from the Caribbean to Central America, carried across the Isthmus of Panama, and down the west coast of South America. Known as a "back-door cable," this resulted in more favorable relations between the Americas, and was followed by better business conditions, closer news contacts, and an offset to European cultural expansion in Brazil, Argentine and Chile, particularly. At about the same time, the cable was completed from San Francisco across the Pacific.

Italy put down cables in the Mediterranean; the Netherlands extended cables to its East Indian colonies; and Japan laid cables connecting points in the Far East. Denmark did not take part in the competition for cable advantages but, as already noted, it did build a telegraph line from Copenhagen, across Russia and Siberia, to Shanghai, the line known as the Great Northern route.

In 1920, as a post-war move, there was held at Washington an International Conference on Communications. It resulted in some changes, particularly in the ownership of more than 15,000 miles of German cables. The two German Atlantic cables, running from Emden via the Azores to New York, were assigned to the care of the five principal subscribers to the League of Nations, to whom the revenue from their operation was to accrue.

The chief controversy was over control of three cables centering on the former German island of Yap, called the "cable crossroads of the Pacific." President Wilson wanted the island to be neutralized, but Japan ultimately won a mandate over it, while recognizing the United States' claim to equal cable and radio rights there. Control of the three cables centering there was divided. Japan got the Yap-Shanghai line; the United States obtained control of the Guam end of the Yap-Guam cable; the Netherlands got control of the Netherlands Indies end of the Yap-Menado (Celebes) cable. This meant that, for the time, cable communication between Shanghai and San Francisco passed through a Japanese control point, which strengthened the Japanese position, and weakened the position of the United States in China. Great Britain, which was opposed to the expansion of the United States interests in the Far East, supported the Japanese in this dispute, which had been carried over from the so-called Peace Conference at Versailles to the Washington Conference on Communications in 1920, to the Washington Naval Conference in 1921-1922, and ultimately to another conference in 1922.

In 1919, prior to the later conferences which resulted in only minor adjustments, chiefly in the German holdings, the onwership of the world's submarine cables was vested in interests of the following nationalities:

GREAT BRITAIN	51	per cent of the total
UNITED STATES	26.5	
FRANCE	9	
GERMANY	7.5	
DENMARK	3	
SPAIN	1	
ITALY	1	
JAPAN	1	
	100	

Thus it is apparent that three states control more than 86 per cent of the cables serving the 65 or so countries comprising the world family.[1] This concentration of control would permit those national authorities to exert a great influence on international communications.

To be sure, national governments always hold actual or potential control of the land lines operating within their frontiers. If not already owned, these lines are at the disposal of military and other officials. Local governments also control the rights of foreign companies or governments to land cables on their shores, and may grant, withhold, renew, or revoke the licenses of foreign companies doing a local communications business. This right to revoke licenses has been used on occasions as a club to force foreign cable companies to exercise an unofficial censorship on outgoing messages, lest by failing to do so they permit unfriendly messages to go, and suffer the penalty of losing their franchises, so sacrificing their investments in equipment as well as the company's good will.

Apart from submarine cables, there are nearly 7,000,000 miles of land lines in the world. They are divided by continents as follows:[2]

NORTH AMERICA	40 per cent	(Those in Canada and the United States are privately owned.)
EUROPE	36 per cent	(Many of the European lines are government-owned.)
ASIA	12 per cent	(These are all government-owned and operated.)
SOUTH AMERICA	6 per cent	(Some of these lines are financed and owned by foreign interests.)
AFRICA	3 per cent	(Same as above.)
OCEANIA	2.53 per cent	(Same as above.)
	99.53 per cent	

Telephones, which have long been of use in news gathering, and which, since 1927, have come to be used increasingly for long-distance communications to and from all parts of the world, require more than 115,000,000 miles of wire to service the 35,000,000 more or less, instruments in the world. These telephones, two-thirds of which are privately owned and operated, are distributed as follows, again by continents.[2]

NORTH AMERICA	66 per cent	(59 per cent in the United States)
EUROPE	29 per cent	
ASIA	3 per cent	
OCEANIA (Including Australia and New Zealand	2.5 per cent	
SOUTH AMERICA	1 per cent	
AFRICA	.5 per cent	
	100 per cent	

Long-distance circuits, growing more common, linking the most distant places, often in the form of radio telephone, began with a Berlin-Amsterdam circuit in 1896, and continued as follows: Berlin-Paris, 1900; Berlin-Copenhagen, 1903; Paris-London, 1910; Paris-Madrid, 1912; Paris-Amsterdam, 1913; Berlin-Milan, 1914; Berlin-Sofia, 1915, and Berlin-London, 1926. After the Great War the use of the long-distance telephone increased as technical improvements were made in its operation. Transocean communication by radio-telephone began in 1927, when the London-New York circuit was opened. Following that, New York, London, Paris, Buenos Aires, Tokyo and other places were linked by telephone.

In the field of wireless telephony, the United States was able by 1930 to reach 86 per cent of all the telephones in the world, and the same was true of Great Britain. Since then, the percentage has increased.

The new forms of communication employing radio principles, as developed since 1920, have made political control of the cables somewhat less important and have made Great Britain's near monopoly of the cables correspondingly less important, strategically. Radio communication is cheaper than cables so far as concerns equipment. The servicing is easier and cheaper. It can be used more freely. It reduces costs of transmission. It prevents a nation being bottled up when cables, telephones, and telegraph lines are cut, apart from the development of devices to garble or break up radio waves deliberately. It permits direct communication between sender and receiver.

The United States held the key to the successful operation of radio communication in its control of the so-called Alexanderson high-frequency alternator, a wartime invention. Although the Marconi system was successful, it was not then reliable in all weather conditions. Neither was the system using the Alexanderson alternator, in the beginning, but that device did make it possible for messages to bridge much greater distances with more certainty and increased strength of signals.

British interests tried to buy the alternator at the end of the War, but the United States Government interfered to prevent the sale abroad. Granted to the Radio Corporation of America, for use in transmission, it was so powerful a trump card as to force the Marconi Company, long supreme, to sell its interests in the United States. Then the Radio Corporation of America, controlling the former Marconi contracts in the United States, was able to conclude its own traffic arrangements with Great Britain, France and Germany. In this way, the Radio Corporation of America came to represent a power in world communications comparable to British cable preeminence.

The Radio Corporation offered service across the Atlantic at lower-than-cable rates, the first reduction in the trans-Atlantic rates for twenty years. It also revised the Pacific rates downward. It extended service to 49 countries and reduced the time for transmission very greatly in certain instances.

There was a general improvement in trans-Atlantic communications, beginning in about 1923. Better cables were laid by the long-established Commercial Cable Co., and also by the Western Union Telegraph Co. The International Telephone and Telegraph Corporation, an organization financed by J. P. Morgan & Co., built up telephone systems in Latin America and in Spain, and then invaded North America to form a powerful communications group, embracing the Postal Telegraph-Commercial Cable System and All-America Cables. The Western Union Telegraph Co. remained as an independent and very strong organization. The same was true of the Radio Corporation of America. But there was talk of a merger of all three groups.

The result of this threat in Great Britain, was a merger of cable and wireless interests to present a solid front. To help in this move, there came the "beam" or directional wireless, developed by the British Marconi Wireless Telegraph Co. and put into use in 1924. It had the effect of a reflector behind the transmitting apparatus, permitting wireless broadcast to concentrate most strength over a rather narrow segment, roughly, a "beam." It gave far stronger signals from the same power, and was preferable in some respects to the cable, especially over distances exceeding 2000 miles. Using the "beam" wireless, the British Government sponsored an Empire communications system linking London with Canada, Australia, South Africa and India. As it developed, the beam system was to be adapted for wireless telephony and rapid facsimile transmission. In 1927 it had reached a point where 200 words a minute could be transmitted from London to Australia.

The new beam system could handle an increased traffic at rates lower than the cables.[3] Used experimentally in 1926-1927, it cut into the cable business and caused friction between the beam system, which was government-owned, and the British Marconi interests (although they had developed the system) and the British cable companies, privately owned, and even with the government-owned cables in the Atlantic and Pacific.

This situation led to the summoning of the Imperial Wireless and Cable Conference in 1927-1928, at which there was concluded a merger of all British communications companies under the title of Cable and Wireless, Ltd., with an operating subsidiary called Imperial and International Communications, Ltd., the present so-called "Imperial," "Eastern," "Empiradio" and "Marconi." It began operations in 1928 over the so-called "Red Network," a cable and wireless system linking all parts of the Empire without once touching non-British soil. This had been an ideal cherished by the British Government since 1910, but even so, its formation did not entirely allay British alarm at American communications plans and accomplishments.

The British merger had been inspired not only as a means of matching a strong British communications organization against an American, but as a means of providing and assuring an adequate service to knit the Empire. This was demanded with particular insistence by newspaper editors and publishers at every Empire Press Conference. Lower cable rates also were held to be one of the greatest Empire needs, as a means of encouraging the interchange of news and so building a sense of Empire solidarity, and it was urged that a flat rate of one penny a word (2 cents, U.S.) should apply to press messages transmitted between any and all parts of the Empire.[4]

General Routing and Rates for Press Messages

The transmission of news has become a matter of routine in most world centers. Only extraordinary events, such as wars, adventures of prominent persons, cataclysms of nature, or mishaps involving passenger ships, planes, or trains, send reporters rushing to remote or far places without regard for expense or difficulty. At such times the facts and the pictures become all-important. And it is then that difficulties may arise owing to the disorganization or lack of transportation or transmission facilities.[5]

International conferences, attracting swarms of reporters, perhaps to small towns, sometimes tax the available communications facilities, as well as the housing facilities, but because the needs of the press on such occasions usually have been anticipated, the difficulties are not serious, even if they exist to all.[6]

As technical problems have been solved, an increasing volume of news matter has been transmitted by radio or wireless, terms used synonymously, both by long wave and short wave. Between cities in Europe, and between London and continental cities, the long-distance telephone is used a great deal, sometimes almost to the exclusion of the telegraph, particularly by London newspapers. At prearranged times a correspondent calls his home office, or perhaps a bureau of his paper at a point nearer the home office, which relays the message. Transoceanic telephone calls have become increasingly common in transmitting or gathering news.

There is a growing exchange of news between continents and countries. News entering the United States, as an example, increased two and one-half times between 1916 and 1929, while outgoing news quadrupled in that period.[7] The greatest flow of news as between continents is between Europe and North America, with the flow westward more than twice the flow toward Europe. Between Asia and North America the cost of transmission over the single existing cable line has been high, which long tended to keep down the volume except at moments of crisis. The development of improved communication by radio and, above all the reduction of press rates, relieved the situation considerably and has increased the flow of news across the Pacific.

The relations between Asia and Europe have been closer, because they are linked by two land lines, as well as by coastwise cables passing through the Indian Ocean, the Red Sea and the Mediterranean. In fact, much of the news of Asia that reaches North America has gone by way of Europe, since that route sometimes is both quicker and more economical.

South America, once linked closely to Europe in a news way, in the years since the beginning of the Great War has established more intimate news relations with North America. Latin America now receives more world news by way of the United States than by way of Europe, although the French Agence Havas is attempting to recapture its former preeminence in that field.[8]

Both Africa and the Antipodes are, as yet, minor factors in the exchange of news, although Australia is in regular news communication with Great Britain.[9]

A considerable volume of news and editorial matter continues to go by mail. It is called "mail copy." Matter that is not urgent or extremely timely may go that way as a measure of economy. Perhaps, if statistics were available, it would be found that the mails continue to carry most of the news volume.

Much depends upon what one considers to be news. If news ceases to be news 12 hours or 24 hours after it occurs, the implication is that only *events* can be so considered. But that is not true. In the first place, anything is news until it becomes known, and if the mail brings the first information on some subject to a whole population or even a portion of the population one year late, or five years late, or even more, that information is still news.[10]

But, in addition, news can be considered to reside in trends, interpretations and analyses as well as in events. There is much background matter or advance matter that also can be mailed, in the case of an anticipated event, such as a conference or a royal wedding or a coronation.

A curious sort of pride in presenting only events of the minute-before-last prevents some newspapers from using mail copy. When they do so, sometimes they put a current date on it, even though that is unethical. Or they may omit the date entirely, with results that sometimes are confusing. But some newspapers, emancipated from such false emphasis on timeliness, present mail copy as just what it is, bearing dates anywhere from a few days to a few weeks old, and no one is the worse for it.

The *Christian Science Monitor* probably uses as much mail copy as any newspaper in the world. The New York *Times*, the New York *Herald Tribune*, the New York *Sun*, the Chicago *Daily*

News, The Times of London, and other first class newspapers in the United States, Great Britain, and other countries, follow this procedure. Press associations also send out what they call "news letters" or "clip sheets" containing items and articles for publication, and these services provide some of the most interesting and useful matter in the newspapers.

When the telegraph, the cable and the telephone were new, the charges for their use were high. It cost $5 or £1 to cable a single word across the Atlantic. To-day the "press rate" is 5 cents or $2\frac{1}{2}$ pence. Yet publishers object that even these rates ought to be lower, and particularly that the rates across the Pacific and between Europe and Australia or New Zealand should be reduced.[11]

The transmission facilities of the world are not perfect, but in the areas where most of the news is being exchanged it is rare for any serious mechanical fault to delay news transit.[12] In the years immediately after the Great War a correspondent, when possible, allowed five hours for the transmission of a message from Paris to New York. Radio competition and the improvement of cable communications reduced the transmission time to minutes, rather than hours, and in some cases to seconds. If one company cannot handle a message promptly, another can; if the cables can promise nothing, there is the radio; if the Paris-New York cables are busy, the message may be relayed to London by wire or telephone and sent from there by cable or radio. Or news originating in Shanghai, for example, may reach New York by way of Moscow and Copenhagen, instead of direct to San Francisco, across the Pacific.

Such round-about routes for news transmission may puzzle the layman. But it is *time*, not distance, that governs when deadlines approach. The routes are constantly being tested by press associations, newspapers, and their correspondents to get faster, more efficient, less expensive transmission.

A regular and ever-present obstacle to quick and certain transmission of virgin news is censorship, whether in wartime or in peace. Censorship on outgoing dispatches is possible where governments control transmission facilities, as they do in most countries; or where they are able to exercise an indirect regulation.

Because the press uses the cables so much it receives a special "press rate," lower than other rates. This means a saving on much traffic, but if immediate transmission is required, and at times of crisis, the press pays the regular rate and even the "urgent" rate, which is still higher, to obtain the fastest service.

The press rate between London or Paris and New York in 1936 was 5 cents or $2\frac{1}{2}$ pence a word, as already noted. Between South America and New York the rate was 14 cents a word, but this was cut to 5 cents a word late in the year. From South America to Europe the rate was 20 to 25 cents a word; this also was cut to 8 to 15 cents. Before the Great War all rates were higher. Even in 1936 the Tokyo rate on an "urgent" message was $2.16 a word. The Shanghai-San Francisco regular press rate then was 25 cents a word, San Francisco-Manila, 12 cents with a 6 cents deferred rate; and San Francisco-Honolulu, 6 cents, with a 3 cents deferred rate. The same rates applied to radio dispatches in 1936.

In addition to the San Francisco-Shanghai cable, there was the British-owned cable in the Pacific, reaching from Vancouver, British Columbia, to Australia, New Zealand and, indirectly, to Hong Kong. It offered a 1922 press rate of 5 cents a word from Canada to Australia, as contrasted to a 27-cent rate then in effect from San Francisco to Shanghai. The British Government encouraged the interchange of news between parts of the empire and, through its ownership of certain communications facilities, it was able to provide a rate of $7\frac{1}{2}$ pence (about 15 cents) a word between London and Melbourne, which was a low figure, considering the distance.

The rate for communication between London and portions of the Empire so far away as Australia had long remained high, causing concern to editors and others who wished to keep Australia informed concerning affairs at the center of the Empire, with a view to maintaining Empire loyalty and unity unimpaired.

When the Eastern Extension Co. put in a cable to Australia in 1872 the transmission rate over the 15,000 miles was £9.9.0 for twenty words. In 1875 the single word rate was reduced to 10/8d. The first time that the press was considered entitled to a special rate was in 1886, when the word rate for ordinary messages was reduced to 9/4d, and a press rate set at 2/8d a word. In 1891 this was further cut to 4/- a word for ordinary messages and 1/10d a word at press rate. Some years later this was reduced further to 3/6d for regular and a proportionate press reduction. In 1930 the press rate was 6d a word by cable, and 4d a word by radio.[13]

In some instances the British and Dominion Governments have given financial assistance to the press and press associations in meeting expenses for cable news transmission. Although this assistance has been necessary to insure any considerable transmission of news, it has bothered some editors and officials, as implying that the press is thereby placed under a certain obligation to the government which grants it this subsidy, and such aids and guarantees have lately been declined in certain instances.

There do remain portions of the Empire which cannot receive news direct from Great Britain by cable or wire, although the wireless is reaching most of them now. The desire to serve them gave impetus to the development of Reuters' wireless news service, which began from Leafield in 1923, and now is serving newspapers throughout the world, broadcasting from Leafield and Rugby by a beam system direct to Montreal, Cape Town, Bombay, Cairo, Shanghai, Tokyo, and other foreign and Empire points.

Because the rates are so high between the Far East and the United States, the volume of news exchanged has been somewhat restricted. And one reason those rates are so much higher has been that there is only the one cable across the Pacific between San Francisco and Shanghai, and that an old one. It can carry only about 100 letters a minute, whereas newer cables across the Atlantic can handle 2500 letters a minute. But, as it would cost $10,000,000 to $16,000,000 to lay a new Pacific cable, there has been hesitation about putting it down, especially with the radio threatening to make cable lines obsolete.[14]

The advent of the radio, in fact, had much to do with breaking the rate schedule from its previous high level. It brought a threat to the cable, more especially in the Pacific area. In 1920, also, the New York *Times* set up its own wireless station to receive foreign news, and the Chicago *Tribune* in 1920 and 1921 was receiving news by wireless direct from Bordeaux, France.

Beginning in 1921, dispatches from the United States to newspapers in Honolulu or Manila could be sent by the United States Navy radio. Congress granted special authorization in 1920 to make this possible. The rate was 6 cents a word to newspapers in Manila, 3 cents a word to those in Honolulu. But that did not link the United States directly with China or Japan. It was necessary to pay additional cable or wireless tolls between Manila and Shanghai or Tokyo, bringing the cost up to 24 to 27 cents a word between San Francisco and Tokyo or Shanghai. Beginning in 1922, the Navy radio also began to carry eastbound dispatches, linking Manila with San Francisco, and correspondents in China or Japan could radio or cable their messages to Manila for relay.

The traffic across the Pacific was limited, except in times of crisis or on other rare occasions. But the United Press, shortly after the Great War, began to send a general report of world news to Nippon Dempo Tsushin Sha, a Japanese press association with which it had an exchange arrangement until Nippon Dempo was absorbed by Domei in 1936. It sent a fairly complete news report to the *Mainichi* in Osaka and to the *Nichi Nichi* in Tokyo. The Associated Press in 1922 was sending an average of 1000 words a day from San Francisco to Honolulu, and about 800 to Manila by the Navy radio. It also sent a daily report, totalling about 5000 words a month, to Kokusai (later to become known as Rengo, and now as Domei), the Japanese news agency with which it had exchange arrangements. Other press messages by Navy radio in 1922, as sent from San Francisco to Honolulu, totaled about 3000 words daily; and about 2500 words daily between Honolulu and Guam, and between Guam and Manila.

In 1922 Congress granted a renewal of the press privilege of using the Navy radio, that renewal to continue until June, 1925. Only news messages were acceptable, commercial messages being barried. The Navy radio had stations at San Francisco, San Diego, Seattle, Honolulu, Guam, Manila, Peiping and Pribiloff Island. The press authority was renewed again in 1925, and once more in 1927. When the question of further renewal arose in 1929, however, the Radio Corporation of America, which had become strong, entered a petition that the service to the press be discontinued, since the commercial system was offering a service which, while somewhat more expensive than the Navy radio, was purported to be reasonable.

The Radio Corporation had been operating a service in 1922 between San Francisco and Tokyo, by way of Honolulu, but high rates kept the schedule low. It transmitted a daily news report of about 250 words from San Francisco to Tokyo for the Trans-Pacific News Service, a group organized by B. W. Fleisher, American publisher of the *Japan Advertiser* in Tokyo, to provide news to papers in Japan and China, and to offer an interpretation of Far-Eastern affairs to Occidental papers. It also carried some Associated Press and United Press Messages. The press business carried by the Radio Corporation was to increase later.

The Radio Corporation of America, in addition to its service from San Francisco to Tokyo, was able to provide radio communication with points in China, Manchuria and Korea through its Japanese connections. Its press rate in 1922 was 27 cents per word, and $2.16 per word for urgent messages which had to go through at once. This was lower, however, than the cable rate, which was then 32 cents a word for press matter, and $2.88 per word at the "urgent" rate, and it was not much higher than the combined rate for Navy radio plus radio from Guam or Manila to Tokyo or Shanghai.[15]

The Federal Wireless Company, an American-owned corporation, in 1922 was planning to erect a radio station in Shanghai for trans-Pacific communication, with smaller stations at Shanghai, Peiping, Canton and Mukden. It required months of negotiations and months to construct the Shanghai station.[16] A resolution at the Washington Naval Conference had prohibited the use of any government radio station in China, Japan or other Far-Eastern country, and this prevented any cooperative agreement to carry the news to or from those countries by existing government radio.[17]

A trans-Pacific of 9 cents a word for the press was advocated by some North American publishers, and the United Press, represented by its then president, Karl A. Bickel, constantly urged a low Pacific rate. In this, support was found in some Japanese and Chinese press circles. Pending the actual reduction in the rates, which was blocked by political and commercial considerations on both sides of the Pacific, the American press was growing to depend more and more on the Navy radio.

Permanent right to use the Navy radio was sought as early as 1925, but it met opposition not only from the growing Radio Corporation of America, as already noted, but also from the Commercial Cables Co., operating the single trans-Pacific cable line.

At length, early in 1925, as a result of negotiations between the United Press and General James G. Harbord, president of the Radio Corporation, an agreement was reached by which the press rate between the United States and Japan was to be reduced from 27 cents a word to 10 cents a word, with a proportionate reduction in rates to and from China. But the Japanese Government declined to approve the plan on the ground that the cable and radio facilities of Japan were not yet great enough to handle the increased volume of business that might be expected to follow so drastic a reduction. At length, in the autumn of 1925, a rate of 22 cents a word was set.

As the radio rate was reduced, cable rates also came down. Beginning in the summer of 1926 the Commercial Cable Co. announced a deferred rate on press service between North America and Manila, Shanghai and Hong Kong. The existing rates had been: New York to Manila, 33 cents; New York to China, 35 cents; San Francisco to Manila, 27 cents; San Francisco to China, 29 cents. The new "deferred" rates however, were set as follows: New York to Manila, 17 cents; New York to China, 20 cents; San Francisco to Manila, 14 cents; San Francisco to China, 17 cents.

After the disappointing attempt to reduce the radio rate in 1925, it was cut to 18 cents in 1927 and in 1929 it was brought down to a rate which permitted a more liberal transmission of news to and from the Far East. This was a new "deferred" radio press rate of 9 cents a word between North America and Japan. But the "urgent" rate from Japan to San Francisco remained at $2.16 a word. Nor was there any change in the rates from Chinese cities—Shanghai, Peiping, Nanking, Hong Kong—or from Singapore. They continued to range from 12 to 25 cents a word. The same rates were applied to the cable transmission westward, between North America and the Far East.[18]

It was in 1929 that the Radio Corporation of America contested further use of the Navy radio by the press. The matter was referred to a hearing of the Federal Radio Commission, and in the end the Radio Corporation was victorious. In the following year that organization set in operation its new commercial radio station at Shanghai, providing direct wireless communication across the Pacific and opening the way for speedy transmission, which was to be much appreciated in 1931 and 1932.

Following the break-down of world currencies in 1929 and 1930, the rates for cable and radio messages across the Pacific, as well as elsewhere, were upset again, due to confusion in monetary exchange. The Madrid radio-telegraph conference of 1933 resulted in a sharp increase in "urgent" rates for cables.[19] This was most serious in the Pacific because, as it worked out, it meant that rates were raised very high again, which proved especially burdensome to North American press associations and newspapers because they could not take refuge in such government aid as some other press associations enjoy.

It was in 1920 that the New York *Times* erected a wireless receiving antenna on the roof, with a receiving set in the building. Here it intercepted reports from ships, and occasionally a distress call gave the *Times* an early lead on a potential story of trouble at sea. Somewhat later, the Hearst newspapers constructed a similar receiving station in New York.

The chief American initiative in converting the wireless into an important adjunct of the world press system for news gathering to have been that of the Chicago *Tribune.* On Oct. 14, 1920, the *Tribune* radio station, 9ZN, in Chicago, received its first news dispatch direct from Europe, through the Lafayette wireless station at Bordeaux, France, erected there by the United States Government during the War. It was a receiving station only, at the Chicago end. Similar receiving stations were put into operation by three other newspapers, the New York *Times,* the New York *American* and the Philadelphia *Public Ledger*. They received news dispatches from great arc sending stations at Bordeaux and Lyons, France, and at Nauen, Germany.

Because these receiving stations could not reply direct to the sending stations, it was agreed in advance that the sending station would send out the call, as for 9ZN, at a given time, say 9 P.M. Chicago time. The Chicago *Tribune* operator would be ready at that hour to receive messages, in Continental code, and the stories would be on the cable editor's desk half an hour later, ready to be prepared for publication. If static spoiled reception at a certain point, however, the operator was able to get a repeat by wiring a poweful U.S. Navy radio station at Great Lakes Naval Training Station, a few miles north of Chicago, and that station would "break" Bordeaux and have the missing portion repeated.

For almost three months the Chicago *Tribune* received all of its dispatches from continental Europe in that way, weather permitting. For the *Tribune,* that totaled about 3,000 words daily. The system saved hours of transmission time, as compared to the then-existing system of commercial cable and wireless, and cost about 30 per cent less.

Early in 1921, the Lafayette station passed into the hands of the French Government, which reached an agreement with the newly formed Radio Corporation of America by which all dispatches intended by North America must be handled at the American end by the Radio Corporation and by Western Union, with which it had arrangements for land transmission. After that, the *Tribune* messages were so handled, through Radio Corporation and Western Union. This proved to be slower than the previous arrangement and, lacking a set filing time to send the press messages, the dispatching took place at periods often unsatisfactory so far as concerned meeting newspaper deadlines.

Although their radio stations were no longer officially recognized, the *Tribune* and the three other papers which had made the original arrangement in 1920, continued to listen to the transmission of their news dispatches from Bordeaux and to take them direct and use them as before. The duplicates, as handled commercially, would come along several hours later, so meeting the requirements of form, but by that time the intercepted messages often were being read in early editions of the papers.

At length, however, the various restrictions and complexities of this system induced the four newspapers in the original group to set up a cooperative wireless station at Halifax, Nova Scotia. They formed a Canadian Company, the News Traffic Board, Ltd. This station, operating from six to nine hours a day, beginning in February, 1922, received press messages from Great Britain and from continental Europe, sent by the British General Post Office wireless transmitting station at Leafield, near Oxford.

This station attained a considerable speed, amounting to twice that of the cable at the time. It was not always free of interference due to weather conditions, however[20] and messages had to be relayed at all times from Halifax to Chicago by telegraph. As the old-line telegraph companies were not anxious to aid this competitive communications group, there was frequent transmission delay, overland, and an attempt was made late in 1926 to triple the usual press rate for such messages. Competition, however, between the Western Union, which usually carried the traffic out of Halifax, and the Canadian Pacific Telegraph Co., allied with the Postal Telegraph Co., brought down the rates again after three nights.

Commercial radio companies also were attempting to improve their mechanical services in all countries. The Marconi Companies in Great Britain and Canada put into operation the first "beam" wireless system on Oct. 21, 1926, providing direct transmission between London and Montreal, taking only one minute for the message to pass from the Central Telegraph office in London to the office of the Montreal *Star*.

Radio rates generally are slightly lower than cable rates. The Atlantic rate, for example, is about $4\frac{1}{2}$ cents, instead of 5 cents a word, which is the cable charge.[21]

Broadcasts of the news for radio listeners began very early in the nineteen-twenties. There was some experimental handling of the news in that way, as well. During the political conventions of June and July, 1924, in the United States, some newspapers prepared their news reports in part upon the basis of the broadcasts heard from the convention halls.

In November, 1923, the Reuters' organization in Britain began a Reuterian toll service of commercial messages to all parts of Europe by wireless from Leafield. At length the service was operating entirely around the clock, and it was considered essential to use the Rugby broadcasting station, also. At stated times, news would be broadcast, as well as commercial information, and stations all over Europe and in some other parts of the world would listen in.

In Europe there is only two hours difference in the time between London and Constantinople, extreme points. All commercial messages, as so broadcast, were of use in the Bourses and produce exchanges. In some places where it was received in Europe, the service would be re-broadcast for the benefit of other places where the sets would not pick up the original broadcast. Improvements in broadcast methods later enabled the service, by "beam"system and short wave, to reach the far parts of the world with news and commercial information, on a toll basis and otherwise. So the Reuterian service became the largest of its kind, and made a special effort to provide a supply of news to Empire papers in Canada, Australia, New Zealand, and South Africa particularly. In addition, the service was picked up and used in Hong Kong, Shanghai, and other Far-Eastern places, where quotations on silver, rubber, and other products set the standard for local trade.

In Russia a radio transmission of news started before 1926. At that time a graduate of the Moscow School of Dramatic Expression spoke the news, as provided by the Tass agency, into a microphone in Moscow. In 168 Russian newspaper offices, some of them 3000 kilometers away, the news was taken down, word by word, for use. This relatively inexpensive system for news distribution, without telegraph or telephone wires, was one of the things that helped the Russian press develop as rapidly as it did.[22]

The Wolff agency in Germany began a wireless broadcast of news over an internal wireless telephone system, and later this became a world broadcast of news by means of the Transozean-Nachrichten, a service reaching South America, the Far East, and ships at sea through the Nauen wireless station.

A Helvetian wireless news service reached Swiss newspapers. The Havas agency, despite the Reuter beginning in 1923, has been quoted as asserting itself to be the first big news agency to try to develop radio transmission of the news. In 1931 the Havasian service began to broadcast news to Northern Africa, to South America, and to the Orient. This service continued and was extended in the years following, with an effort to increase the number of places reached. The preparation of this news is a matter of interest to the French Foreign Office. By 1933 the service had a powerful station at Pontoise, near Paris, operating 21 hours a day. It was provided to newspapers at a lower rate than that for cable news because, so it was pointed out, there was no expense for the maintenance of cable facilities.[23]

News service also was being sent to South America by Agenzia Stampa, an Italian organization.

The radio telephone, put into operation in 1927, was used in 1930 by the New York *Times*, the Associated Press and International News Service to get first-hand accounts of developments in the revolution that occurred in Argentina.[24] London newspapers used it at times to telephone to the United States; it was less common for American newspapers to telephone Europe. The first news story radio-telephoned from Europe to Japan went over the air on March 12, 1935, when Webb Miller, European news manager of the United Press, read a dispatch in London to a representative of the Nippon Dempo agency in Tokyo, but by 1937 the Pacific was bridged between North America and Japan, not only by radio telephone, but also in the radio transmission of photographs.[25]

The long-distance land-line telephone continues to be widely used by the press in every country, while in European countries, particularly, correspondents serving British newspapers telephone their dispatches to London regularly. In the same way, European correspondents for newspapers in the United States sometimes telephone their dispatches to a control bureau, or relay point, usually London or Paris, to be edited and sent along.[26]

The telephone sometimes is combined with a radio recording device, or a sort of dictaphone, to speed up news handling and reduce expense. In this system, correspondents telephone their dispatches, which, instead of being taken down by stenographers, are recorded on the dictaphone. This permits the correspondent to speak more rapidly into the telephone, and so saves toll charges on time consumed. The record later is played back at a lower speed, enabling the message to be typed out and used by a London paper, or skeletonized, retranscribed and sent on to the United States.[27]

The development of short wave radio brought new progress in transmission methods. Its first important use for news handling began when Admiral Richard E. Byrd made his first expedition to the South Polar regions, from 1928 to 1930, as already described. Russell Owen, New York *Times* reporter who accompanied the expedition, sent his stories by short wave radio almost nightly over the 10,000 miles from Little America, where the expedition established a base, to the *Times* building in the heart of New York. The short waves carried his reports at 1,200 words an hour. The New York *Times,* through its syndicate arrangements, relayed his stories to 40 American and Canadian newspapers, and to 17 foreign newspapers, published in Sydney, Antwerp, Prague, London, Milan, Osaka, Rotterdam, Mexico City, Oslo, Copenhagen, Stockholm, Helsingfors, Buenos Aires, La Paz and Cartagena. Only occasionally did weather conditions make reception difficult.[28]

The New York *Times* made another mark in the use of short wave radio for news handling when, on Feb. 17, 1933, it intercepted for publication a 15,000-word Manchurian report of the League of Nations' Committee of Nineteen, broadcast to the world from Geneva. The report was the longest in words ever handled by the *Times,* and it took the longest time, keeping two operators simultaneously busy from 9 A.M. until 7.22 P.M. New York time.[29]

The short wave radio brought a new development, also, in the general use of wireless for transmission of news across the Atlantic. Early in 1928 the United States Federal Radio Commission set aside 20 radio wave bands for trans-Atlantic press communication.

The American Publishers' Committee had been erected on the foundation established in 1922 by the News Traffic Board, Ltd. Mr. Joseph B. Pierson, former cable editor of the Chicago *Tribune,* had been active in establishing the original trans-Atlantic wireless transmission of news dispatches in 1920, and he was trustee of the American Publishers' Commission on Cable and Radio Communication. By 1928 there were other newspapers receiving press dispatches through the News Traffic Board's Canadian station. When the Federal Radio Commission notified newspapers that it was going to hold general hearings on the matter of using short wave radio, and on the specific allocation of the wave bands, Mr. Pierson brought together nine newspapers, later joined by the Scripps-Howard newspapers and others, making twelve newspapers and press associations, to form a committee and to represent the interests of the press before the Commission.

This group was organized as the American News Traffic Corporation. Members were the Chicago *Tribune,* the United

Press Association, the Los Angeles *Times,* the San Francisco *Chronicle,* the New York *Herald Tribune,* the New York *World,* the *Christian Science Monitor,* the New York *Times,* the Scripps-Howard newspapers, the Consolidated Press Association, the Philadelphia *Public Ledger,* and Universal News Service.

To this group, on Dec. 22, 1928, was granted 40 clear short wave radio channels, 20 of them for intra-continental use and 20 of them for inter-continental use. It was required by the Federal Radio Commission that newspapers agree to open their stations to all newspapers and press associations without restrictions, the newspapers taking part on the understanding that the American News Traffic Corporation was to be a public service corporation.[30]

At length, after six months of controversy over the allocation of the wave lengths, there was organized in July, 1929, a $1,000,000 corporation called Press Wireless, Inc., erected on the foundations of the American News Traffic Corporation, with Mr. Pierson remaining as trustee for the press. To this group, organized as a public utility corporation, were allotted the 20 transoceanic wave bands, while the 20 transcontinental wave bands were reserved to the press for latter assignment, probably to Press Wireless, Inc. This newly formed corporation would assign various wave lengths, in requisite numbers, to newspapers and press associations, and generally would act to provide a *bona fide* service to the press of the United States on an equitable basis permitting any accredited correspondent to file dispatches.

The Hearst newspapers protested this arrangement, as they had the original allocation,[31] and the case was referred to the Court of Appeals of the District of Columbia, with an answer to the Hearst objections filed by the Federal Radio Commission.

In March, 1930, the 20 transcontinental short wave bands, which had been held by the Federal Radio Commission, were at last granted to Press Wireless, Inc. This grant was attacked by the Radio Corporation of America Communications, Inc., a subsidiary of the Radio Corporation of America, which appealed to the District of Columbia Court of Appeals, on the ground that the assignment of all frequencies in the short wave band to Press Wireless, Inc., and commercial organizations, stood in the way of developing a "truly national system of domestic communication" by the Radio Corporation of America, which it was contended would best serve the public interest. It held that the Radio Corporation of America was more fully able to comply with the standards set down by the Federal Radio Commission.[32]

By that time, however, Press Wireless, Inc., had started to operate on the transoceanic bands, beginning Sept. 15, 1929. Its rate was lower than any other communications route and, although transmission was not always reliable at first, it found active interest among publishers in the United States and in some other countries. Five American newspapers made up the original membership. They were the Chicago *Tribune,* the Chicago *Daily News,* the *Christian Science Monitor,* the Los Angeles *Times* and the San Francisco *Chronicle.* Purchase of stock in the corporation was open to all American newspapers on the same general terms as those given the five newspapers holding shares at the time. It was, and it remains, a public service corporation in a legal sense, obliged to accept for transmission and reception the press dispatches filed by any correspondent or newspaper, provided the subject matter involved is intended for publication in the press, and provided payment is guaranteed.

Radio stations were erected near New York, Chicago, Boston, Los Angeles and San Francisco. These five stations were in operation by April, 1930, handling about 15,000 words a day, which was considered just a beginning.

Independent wave bands, beyond the 40 granted to Press Wireless, Inc., went to Universal Service Wireless, a Hearst organization serving all Hearst newspapers. This grant was made in December, 1929. In 1931 the Hearst newspapers formed the American Radio News Corporation and received permits and licenses, despite the protest of Press Wireless, Inc.[33]

In January, 1931, the Federal Radio Commission granted permission to Press Wireless, Inc., to erect 19 short wave stations for national and international press communications purposes. This marked the conclusion of the litigation in the District of Columbia Court of Appeals over the assignment of the 20 national wave bands and seven of the international wave bands.[34]

By September of 1931 direct wireless transmission of news from Paris to the United States had begun. A powerful transmission station in France was placed at the disposal of American correspondents, as well as a station in England. Most of the dispatches were received in the United States either at Needham, Massachusetts, or Little Neck, Long Island, New York, and distributed from there. Dispatches from the United States and Canada, intended for the French press and other continental destinations, were transmitted from Hicksville, Long Island. By 1932 about 15,000,000 words of press material were being transmitted annually from continental Europe to the United States, and about 3,000,000 words from the United States flowed toward Europe.

In a general way, these figures imply that the American newspaper reader has more information at hand about European affairs than the European reader has about American affairs. This may be taken to indicate a growth in Americans' interest in world affairs. Newspapers do not believe there is any widespread or strong interest in foreign affairs, but they know that there is an *increasing* interest. The average better-type American newspaper to-day prints far more news from Europe, and from other parts of the world, than it did in 1913, and infinitely more than it did in 1900.

What has happened in the United States also has happened in other countries, in greater or less degree, for the entire world is becoming aware of itself as a unit, rather than as an agglomeration of diverse peoples without common interests, evidence of nationalism to the contrary notwithstanding.

In this change from arid provincialism to rich cosmopolitanism the unfolding communications system of the world plays a part so vital that even such statistics as must be used to tell its story cannot quite obscure its vast importance.

REFERENCES

1. G. A. Schreiner, *Cables and Wireless;* J. Saxon Mills, *The Press and Communications of Empire;* Charles Hodges, *Background of International Relations,* Ch. 22.
2. These figures all are extracted from G. A. Schreiner, *Cables and Wireless;* J. Saxon Mills, *The Press and Communications of Empire;* Charles Hodges, *Background of International Relations,* Ch. 22.

3. Press rates, as cited by Sir Basil Blackett, Chairman of Imperial & International Communications, Ltd., at the Fourth Imperial Press Conference, London, June, 1930. See the report of that Conference, and also the Company's reprint of the speech, *Empire Communications and the Empire Press.*

LONDON to:	1913	1930	
	Cable	Cable	Radio
AUSTRALIA	$7\frac{1}{2}$d	6d	4d
SOUTH AFRICA	$3\frac{3}{4}$d	$2\frac{3}{4}$d	$2\frac{1}{2}$ d
INDIA..............................	4d	3d	$2\frac{1}{2}$ d
CANADA (eastern provinces).	5d	$2\frac{1}{2}$ d	$2\frac{1}{2}$d
WEST INDIES.................	$1\frac{1}{2}$d	$7\frac{1}{2}$ d	$7\frac{1}{2}$d

4. Robert Donald, ed., *The Imperial Press Conference in Canada, 1920,* pp. 167-68, 173-74. (This is the second Imperial Conference).

See also: Anon., *A Parliament of the Press: The First Imperial Press Conference, 1909;* H. E. Turner, ed., *The Imperial Press Conference in Australia, 1925.* (This is the Third Conference.) H.E. Turner, ed., *The Fourth Imperial Press Conference, 1930.*

J. Saxon Mills, *The Press and Communications of Empire.* (A Survey based upon reports and addresses at the Imperial Press Conference of 1920).

The Fifth Imperial Press Conference was held at Capetown in 1935.

5. Examples include the Riff War in 1926, the Ethiopian campaign in 1935, the Japanese earthquake in 1923, the Russo-Japanese clash along the Chinese Eastern Railway in 1929, the landing of the German transatlantic plane, *Bremen,* at Greenley Island, Labrador, in 1928; the emergency landing of Admiral Byrd's trans-Atlantic plane at Ver-sur-Mer, France, in 1927; the forced descent of the Graf Zeppelin in the south of France in 1929, the Japanese invasion of Manchuria in 1931, and others. At such times enterprising reporters sometimes have used their wits to obtain exclusive control of all transmission facilities, tying them up long enough to insure that their own reports, at least, would be published first. See: Vernon McKenzie, *Behind the Headlines: Journalistic Adventures of Today.*

6. The League of Nations, both at Geneva and in the conferences held under its sponsorship in various parts of Europe, has

supervised press facilities so expertly as to make the reporter's work comparatively easy, so far as concerned matters of transmission. The facilities at the London Economic Conference of 1933 represent a case in point. Such conferences have set new records in the number of words dispatched. Political gatherings, sensational court trials, and great sports events also have resulted in heavy files.

7. M. M. Willey and S. A. Rice, *Communication Agencies and Social Life*, pp. 171-72. The Willey-Rice study is a part of a more comprehensive study of "Recent Social Trends in the United States" made under the direction of a Committee appointed by President Hoover. See Part II, "The Agencies of Point to Point Communication," Chs. 10-13, pp. 104-54. Also Ch. 14, pp. 156-77.
8. It was estimated in 1931 that Latin America received from North American press associations about 30,000,000 words annually, of which 10,000,000 consisted of news of the United States. C.S. Smith, "News Makes the Americas Better Neighbors," *Quill* (Oct., 1931), pp. 6-7, 15-16.
9. E. W. Sharp, *International News Communications,* Univ. of Missouri Bulletin (Univ. of Missouri), Vol. 28, No. 3. Vol. No. 45. Journalism Series; Guy Innes, "Cabling the News," *Journalism: By Some Masters of the Craft* (see Anon.), pp.135-43.
10. The excavations of the tomb of Tut-ankh-amen was big news three thousand years after his burial. The discovery of the remains of Andree, the Arctic explorer, with his records and equipment, in the north of Canada was news 33 years after his disappearance while making an attempt to reach the North Pole by balloon. These stories, and many others, were news even though so many years had elapsed since the events which they represented. The Great War had been in progress for many months before that fact became known to the residents of some islands and isolated parts of the world, and to those persons it was news, even though it had become history in Europe itself.
11. At every Imperial Press Conference stress has been put upon the need for cheaper cable rates, with an insistent demand for a rate of 1d (2 cents) a word anywhere within the Empire. See reports of the Conferences. See also: Victor Rosewater, *History of Cooperative News-Gathering in the United States*. Chs. 6, 7, 8, 25, deal with the development of the telegraph and cable rates. The World Press Congresses, at Honolulu in 1921, Geneva in 1926, Mexico City in 1931, also have urged the lower press rates. The League of Nations, too, at its Conference on the Press, has given its endorsement to the lower rate. See also: Keith Clark,

International Communications: the American Attitude; James M. Herring and Gerald C. Gross, *Telecommunications: Economics and Regulations.*

12. Useful summaries of the world communications systems, usually with special reference to news transmission, include the following: G.A. Schreiner, *Cables and Wireless.* A guide to cable and wireless communications, with special data in Ch. 6, "The Press and International Communication," pp. 158-89. The Appendix lists cables under government administration; the privately operated, government operated, and government subsidized cables; and the book contains a map of world cable communications, all as of 1924; L. B. Tribolet, *The International Aspects of Electrical Communications in the Pacific Area.* A study of cable and wireless communications in the Pacific area, as of 1929. It gives consideration to national ownership of communications lines and the propaganda values inherent in those ownerships; Charles Hodges, *The Background of International Relations,* Ch. 22, "The Nerves of World Politics," pp. 467-85. A description of the world system of communications, as of 1931, with reading references; F. J. Brown, *The Cable and Wireless Communications of the World,* 2nd rev. ed. Includes the history of the press rates up to 1930; J. Saxon Mills, *The Press and Communications of the Empire.* A survey based upon reports and addresses at the Imperial Press Conference of 1920, and published in 1924; Keith Clark, *International Communications: the American Attitude;* O.W. Riegel, *Mobilizing for Chaos,* Chs. 2, 3, 4, pp. 18-107. Some of the problems inherent in control of world communications.

13. Robert Donald, ed., *The Imperial Press Conference in Canada,* p. 172; Sir Basil Blackett, *Empire Communications and the Empire Press.* (Reprint by Imperial and International Communications, Ltd., from the report of the Fourth Imperial Press Conference held in London in 1930).

14. It took as much as a hundred hours for a cable message to reach Tokyo from Washington during the naval conference in 1921, so Japanese correspondents discovered, whether sent at regular or at press rates. That was too slow, but if a message was to go at the "urgent" rate it then would cost $3.24 a word, which was excessive. From Tokyo to San Francisco, the time and expense were nearly as great.

Walter Sammis, "Phonetics and Easy Communication Japan's Greatest Needs," *Editor and Publisher* (Dec. 24, 1921), pp.

17, 33; L. B. Tribolet, *The International Aspects of Electrical Communications in the Pacific Area.*

15. A good summary of trans-Pacific communications facilities, as they were in 1922, is presented by: John R. Morris, "Navy Radio Must be Speeded to Win Far-East Business," *Editor and Publisher* (July 1, 1922), p. 6.

16. Much of the foregoing data is from a bulletin published by the Pan-Pacific Union, and quoted in *Editor and Publisher*. See: Anon., "Pacific News Volume Is Increasing", *Editor and Publisher* (Oct. 14, 1922), p. 24.

17. Anon., "Government Radio Barred in China by Arms Parley Agreement," *Editor and Publisher* (Feb. 11, 1922), p. 6.

18. The New York *Times*, with an excellent foreign news service, expended more than $500,000 on cable and radio tolls in twelve months ending in August, 1927. Although the rates were 5 cents a word for news from London and $5\frac{1}{2}$ cents a word from Paris at that time, with slightly higher rates from Berlin and Rome, the press rate from Tokyo was 21 cents, and from Shanghai it was 31 cents then. This made news from London, as published, represent a cost of about $50 a column, while the news from Tokyo would represent a cost of more than $200 a column, and that from China, between $300 and $350 a column. See editorial in New York *Times* of Aug. 26, 1927. Quoted in *Editor and Publisher*, Sept. 3, 1927. By 1932 the New York *Times* was receiving about 4,000 words daily from the Far East, a great increase due to critical events in Manchuria and China, attending the Japanese invasion. The cable costs alone averaged $500 a day for a time. One of the most expensive days was Feb. 3, 1932, when tolls for matter sent from Shanghai, Tokyo and Manila totaled $685.20. Of this total, $532.80 represented news from Shanghai; $131.04, news from Tokyo; and $21.36, news from Manila. *The Little Times*, house organ of the New York *Times* (Feb. 25, 1932), p. 4.

19. A. G. West, "Increased Cable and Radio Rates to be Resisted in Congress," *Editor and Publisher* (Dec. 30, 1933), p. 24; A.G. West, "Storm of Protest Follows Rise in 'Urgent' Rate on Cables," *Editor and Publisher* (Jan. 13, 1934), p. 38.

In the latter reference, the following rates to and from New York are cited, as of that date:

PRESS RATES	*Cents per word*	URGENT PRESS	*Per word*
To London	5	To London	23
From London	7.80	From London	34
To Berlin	7	To Berlin	25
From Berlin	11	From Berlin	38
To Tokyo (full)	22	To Tokyo	82
To Tokyo (deferred)	13	From Tokyo	82
From Tokyo	13		
To Shanghai (full)	24		
To Shanghai (deferred)	16		

Above rates, all via Commercial Cable. If via Radio Corporation of America (RCA) of Western Union, "urgent" rate was 88 cents to or from Shanghai, while to or from Montevideo it was 13 cents, or if "urgent", 52 cents.

20. Information from an address by Joseph C. Northrup of the Chicago *Tribune* at the Medill School of Journalism, Northwestern University. Reprinted in *The Trib*, house organ of the Chicago *Tribune* (Feb., 1922), pp. 1, 4-6; also in *The W-G-N* (Anon.), pp. 101-103, 152.
21. See note 3, page 106, for other examples of relationship between cable and radio rates.
22. Reported by H. V. Kaltenborn, in an address at the Press Congress of the World, Geneva, in September, 1926. See: Walter Williams, ed., *Press Congress of the World in Switzerland*, pp. 57-61.
23. John W. Perry, "France Plans Propaganda Drive in U. S.," *Editor and Publisher* (April 15, 1933), pp. 7, 34; Anon., "Radio News Takes Europe's Rivalries to South America," *Christian Science Monitor* (Aug. 30, 1933), pp. 1, 7.
24. John F. Roche, "New Radiophone Feats by Newspapers," *Editor and Publisher* (Sept. 20, 1930), pp. 16, 66.
25. Anon., "News Story Phoned London to Japan," *Editor and Publisher* (March 16, 1935), p. 29; Anon., "First Radio Picture Across the Pacific," *Editor and Publisher* (April 17, 1937), p. 90.

26. G. H. Archambault, "Phone Supplants Wire in Europe," *Editor and Publisher* (April 13, 1935), pp. 8, 11; Anon., "(AP)" (Associated Press), *Fortune* (Feb. 1937), pp. 88-93, 148-62.
27. Described by Frederick T. Birchall of the New York *Times,* in an address at Columbia University, New York; Anon., "Foolish to Fight a Censor—Birchall," *Editor and Publisher* (Nov. 3, 1934), p. 4; Douglas Dies, "Rebel Phone Censors Have a Sense of Humor (Sometimes), Says UP Man," *Editor and Publisher* (Sept. 26, 1936), p. 16.
28. R. L. Duffus, "Covering the News of Frozen Antarctica", New York *Times* (Feb. 10, 1929), Pt. 10, p. 4; Anon., "Owen, From Antarctic, Tells Story as Easily as Nearby District Men," *Editor and Publisher* (Feb. 16, 1929), p. 18; John F. Roche, "News of Byrd's Flight Flashed to New York in Split Second," *Editor and Publisher* (Dec. 7, 1929), p. 8; J. W. Perry, "Byrd Story Made Radio History," *Editor and Publisher* (June 21, 1930), p. 12; F. E. Meinholtz, "*Times* Station Made Radio History in 1930," *The Little Times,* house organ of the New York *Times* (Jan. 22, 1931).
29. Anon., "N. Y. *Times* Set Radio Record in Getting 15,000-Word Report," *Editor and Publisher* (Feb. 25, 1933), p. 8.
30. The origins of this plan are told by: George H. Manning, "Publishers Propose Ten Companies to Control Press Radio Channels," *Editor and Publisher* (Dec. 1, 1928), p. 26; Anon., "Joe Pierson Wins Short Wave Radio for U.S. Inter-Press Telegraphy," *The Trib,* house organ of the Chicago *Tribune* (Feb. 1929), p. 5.
31. Anon., "W. R. Hearst Files Protest to Proposed Allocation of Radio Wave Bands," *Editor and Publisher* (Feb. 9, 1929), pp. 5-6; G. H. Manning, "Ask Annulment of Radio Allocations," *Editor and Puolisher* (Mar. 9, 1929), p. 15.
32. Anon., "R.C.A. Seeks Press Wave Bands," *Editor and Publisher* (April 5, 1930).
33. A general history of the formation of Press Wireless, Inc., appears in: Ben Kartman, "Dailies Fighting for Freedom of Air to Improve Exchange of News," *Editor and Publisher* (April 12, 1930), pp. 5, 46. James M. Herring and Gerald C. Gross, *Telecommunications: Economics and Regulation,* pp. 90, 300.
34. G. H. Manning, "Press Wireless Given Permit for Network," *Editor and Publisher* (Jan. 24, 1931).

5

Computers in the Newsroom

Introduction

THE eighties have been widely regarded as the decade in which the marriage between the computer and communication technologies has prospered and has delivered a "child," commonly named as Information Technology or simply as IT. The wonderful exploits of this young IT are found in all walks of life. It is not surprising, therefore, that it should also have greatly benefited the news-industry, including news agencies and newspapers whose source of raw material (news) is inherently global and whose prime activity is timely delivery of a processed version at the breakfast tables next day.

Like in any other field, the productivity of a news-agency or a newspaper in its day-to-day business operations can be considerably enhanced by use of IT. We will, however, confine ourselves to activities having direct bearing on news making. Among these, the three major activities which can yield maximum productivity increase through automation/ modernisation are: reception and transmission of news, editing and processing of the news for content, style, etc., and errors are preparation of the final copy using computerised typesetting equipment.

The use of computer as well as communication is almost 25 years old. Phillips (1) traces the use of computers for typesetting to 1962. Data communication as applicable today to the news-industry is a more developed form of message switching or store and forward messaging. Message switching systems existed even before 1962 and were used by leading news agencies at that time. The technology required for editorial assistance, which is commonly called word processing is, however, a later phenomenon and had to await appropriate computing techniques and products such as terminals, time sharing and micro processors, which developed rapidly but only in 1970s.

Since the news-industry represents a very big market in financial terms and is important as the fourth column of the establishment, it has always been identified as a potential area of business by the computer industry. Major computer companies such as IBM, RCA and DEC, etc. have been early in the field. Oddly, one does not identify either in the past or present a single major vendor offering a comprehensive system meeting all the three needs of collection, processing and printing of news.

Communication

In the developed world, the data communication scene is so advanced that an organisation, newspaper and news-agencies included, can be connected through a couple of physical links representing several virtual links to a public switched data-network (PSDN) and through that network to virtually all other organisations around the world. Services such as electronic mail, which is an advanced form of message switching is but one among many services that can be availed of by the organisation through a PDSN. Considering that the arrival, usage and extensive connectivity of VIKRAM, the Indian PSDN, is a couple of years away, it is more relevant that we review the role of communication in news-handling from an Indian perspective.

With minor exceptions, the means of data-communication employed by news agencies and newspapers in India consist of dedicated point-to-point teleprinter (TP) lines and telex machines. Both operate at 50 bands per second and in five bit Baudot code. These channels have low throughput (*i.e.,* low volume of text carried) compared to high speed data channels.

But, this is not a bottleneck and is quite commensurate with the volume of news carried and the tariffs that are applicable to TP/telex in Indian environment. Further, developing countries such as India do not possess a large number of inter-city circuits. Employing a data-circuit in spite of the proven adequate of a teleprinter circuit is both nationally wasteful as well as cost ineffective.

The news arrives at a news agency or newspaper centre over telex from correspondents and stringers (telegrams are also received on telex). Teleprinter lines bring news from other news agencies, its own news offices in other towns and its editing centres in other metro cities. As for the outward flow of news, (transmission), a newspaper transmits items only to its offices and publishing centres in other cities. A news agency, on the other hand, earns its money primarily through transmission. It may feed within hundreds of newspapers, in the same and other cities, and even a few news agencies abroad. Since the transmission to newspapers in the same city does not warrant individual control, the actual number of teleprinter channels connected to an integrated computer and communication system in a news agency centre may be very high. Nonetheless, it can be as high as 64 as in the case of Press Trust of India's New Delhi editing centre.

From the communication point of view, any system installed or to be installed at a news agency or newspaper centre must meet the following objectives:

(a) Reception of incoming news without any loss.
(b) Tolerance for signal distortion in incoming news.
(c) Tolerance for header deviations in incoming items.
(d) Immediate generation and transmission of an acknowledgement to the sender, whenever an item is received on the channel.
(e) Intimation of header errors to the sender so that he can re-transmit the item after connection. Alternatively, a list of header errors may be generated at the receiving centre. It will allow manual editing of such 'rejected' items, without to and fro re-transmission.
(f) Hourly or half-hourly generation of reports prepared channel-wise and sent on respective channels so that the

other side is informed about the items received and items sent from the centre.

(g) Queuing of items released for transmission, channel-wise and priority-wise.

(h) Display of the channel status and the status of incoming and outgoing traffic. The latter is represented by the transmission 'queue.'

(i) Control over incoming and outgoing traffic through commands such as opening and closing of channels and starting and stopping of channel diversions.

(j) Ability to monitor incoming data or outgoing data on a channel to detect any corruption. Also ability to initiate test, transmission so that the other side can monitor channel stability/corruptions.

The teleprinter and telex channels are not computer compatible (*i.e.,* not RS232 asynchronous) and, hence, cannot be readily and directly connected to a computer. Even otherwise it is necessary to provide isolation and amplification to meet P and T requirements before a channel can be connected to a computer. For this purpose, special circuits called LTU (Line Terminating Units) are employed which make these channels RS232 compatible.

This still does not solve a problem of channel connections. An otherwise suitable computer may not have required the large number of RS232 ports. This problem is solved by designing a micro-processor—based front-end unit called multiplexor. Such a multiplexor allows data reception and transmission from upto 16 teleprinter/telex channels through a single RS232 port operating at 4800 bps in the host mini computer. A 64-channel system requires only four such ports of the host computer leaving the other ports for connecting editing terminals, printers, etc.

The multiplexor and host computer change information in the form of ASCII packets. (The format and protocol of these is of proprietary nature.) Being micro-processor-controlled and because it has a memory, the front-end multiplexor performs three very desirable functions besides that of port reduction; (a) per channel character level processing which is of real-time nature and thereby reducing the real-time criticality and load of the host computer, (b) buffering the inflow and outflow of characters allowing flow control, and (c) conversion between Baudot and ASCII. While the multiplexor is principally a device for connecting large number of low speed channels, a few data channels of 300 to 2400 bps can also be connected to it.

Since data on such channels is directly RS232 compatible and in ASCII code, both these conversions are bypassed in case of such channels.

Editing

The process of refining a raw news item into a publication matter is extremely complex. On-field study of a newsroom operations does impart a certain insight into it.

Some of the news input, particularly coming from correspondents and other editing centres, may be so well written that no further work is required other than keeping track of these items in terms of their importance and the space they will merit in the local stringers may be in non-conforming style and, hence, it has to be virtually re-written. All shades in between also exist. Thus, the final news item may be the result of minor or major editing of the original item and may possibly involve merging of items on the same even from different sources.

Sometimes, incoming items have to be killed for want of sufficient information, sufficient reader interest or lack of space. A major event may be covered in several parts either connected or disjointed. One must also remember that news items have their own dynamics and can develop either rapidly or slowly. It is necessary for the editor to remember the threads of various developing stories and assign them to his sub-editors to work on. Likewise, the chief reporter also does a similar task and attempts to optimally assign reporter resources available to him.

While word processing as is commonly understood and as can be accomplished through popular packages such as Wordstar does remain essential to the editing task, the facilities that an integrated news-system must provide go beyond mere editing. The system must be able to categorise stories by content, by work-station, by person who is dealing with it at the moment, by stages of processing, etc. The system should also produce directory displays of the news ensemble in desired categories.

DUPLEX HOT STANDBY CONFIGURATION FOR NEWS SYSTEM

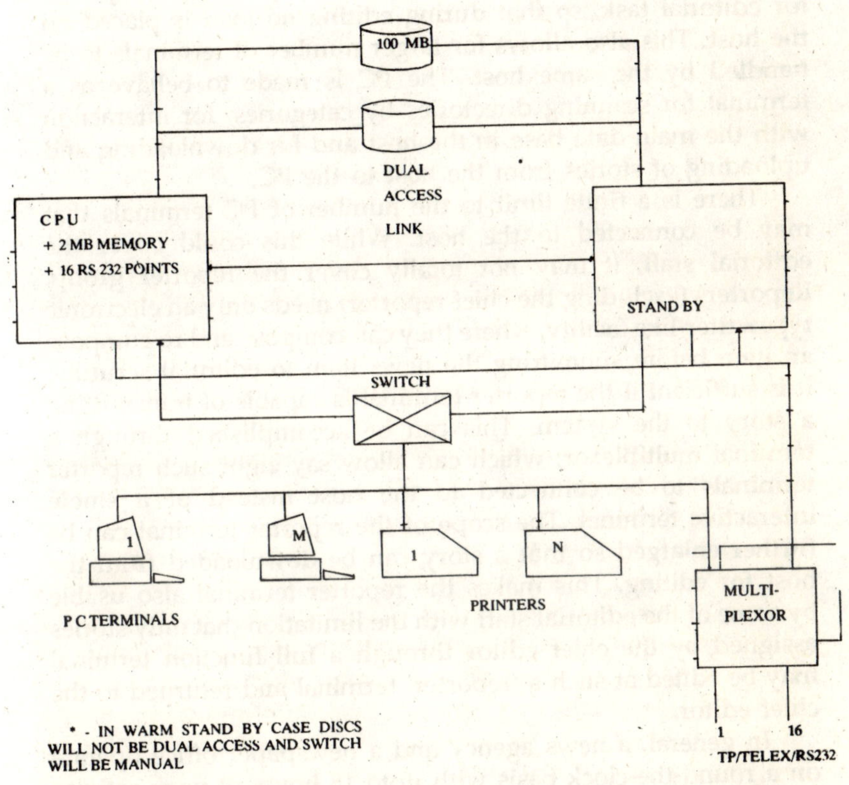

* - IN WARM STAND BY CASE DISCS WILL NOT BE DUAL ACCESS AND SWITCH WILL BE MANUAL

Before the advent of personal computers, it was common to have the host computer share the load of communication as well as of editing. Indeed, the system designed by us three years ago for the Press Trust of India had followed this approach. Today, it is more cost-effective to deploy personal computers for editorial task, so that during editing no load is placed on the host. This also allows for larger number of terminals to be handled by the same host. The PC is made to behave as a terminal for scanning directories by categories, for interaction with the main data base in the host and for downloading and uploading of stories from the host to the PC.

There is a finite limit to the number of PC terminals that may be connected to the host. While this could cover the editorial staff, it may not totally cover the reporter group. Reporters (excluding the chief reporter) needs only an electronic typewriter-like facility, where they can compose and re-compose an item before submitting the news item to editorial scrutiny. It is sufficient if the reporter terminal is capable of transmitting a story to the system. This can be accomplished through a terminal multiplexor, which can allow say eight such reporter terminals to be connected to the host instead of a single interactive terminal. The scope of the reporter terminal can be further enlarged so that a story can be downloaded from the host for editing. This makes the reporter terminal also usable by some of the editorial staff with the limitation that only stories assigned by the chief editor through a full function terminal may be edited at such a 'reporter' terminal and returned to the chief editor.

In general, a news agency and a newspaper office operate on a round-the-clock basis with upto 18 hours of peak activity during a day. The inherent nature of a news-room work demands continuous operation. A gap of more than a hour can be catastrophic. Thus, reliability and uptime are important specifications for a news systems. Ideally, a fault-tolerant computer is needed for this application but due to their high cost an equivalent duplex (i.e., two-computer) system, operating as one active and one hot-standby pair, is minimally needed. The duplex system becomes more cost effective if it operates in a load sharing mode. It can support twice the number of terminals provided a graceful degeneration is acceptable. In the event of the failure of one system only half the terminals, which are considered essential and of priority will continue to work while the non-essential terminals will have to wait for the other system to come up. Figure on p. 117 shows components of such a system.

Typesetting

Whereas a news agency delivers its products by transmitting it to the newspapers, a newspaper has to additionally go through another critical step of typesetting and page layout before the newspaper can be printed and delivered to customers. Typesetting may also be used by a news agency such as The Press Trust of India, which publishes daily and weekly feature services in areas such as science, agriculture, etc., to groups of select audiences.

Typesetting has rapidly advanced in the last few years through the combination of personal computer and laser printer creating a vast market for what is known as Desk-Top Publishing (or simply DTP). While DTPs are ideal for small volume publishing and provide cost effective in-house typesetting to medium and large organisations, it is not adequate in terms of throughput and quality required in newspaper publishing at least for the present. The typesetting requirements of newspapers such as *The Times of India* virtually requires a mainframe computer for composing news and classified advertisements and an equally powerful, top-of-the-range typesetter to produce print-ready copy.

It appears cost effective not to integrate the typesetting function within the computer which may be used for communication and editing functions. Instead, one can connect the news-system to the typesetting system through an appropriate interface and protocol. Such a linkage helps eliminate effort and time in rekeying of news, which would occur otherwise, if the typesetting system is separately used for newspaper production. In such as integrated environment, the editors who primarily control the layout, font, size and title of the item can do so directly during the editing process. The typesetting becomes part of editor's tool in such a set-up.

Integrated Operations

The human operator in any system should be more important than the system itself and generally the system would be designed keeping in view the convenience of the operating staff. Nonetheless, the abilities and more critically the attitudes of various sections of system users play a crucial role in determining smooth functioning of the system and achieving the anticipated productivity improvement.

The teleprinter section, the editorial and reporter groups, the chief editors and reporters and the typesetter production chief editors and reporters and the typesetter production staff are all affected by the introduction of a computerised news system and each sub-group is likely to view the system with a different perspective. The teleprinter section stands to gain the maximum. Their working environment before computerisation is repetitive, laborious and noisy. The computerised news environment eliminates the tedium of reception and transmission. They can now control these functions, as well as key in new stories through a terminal using modern techniques such as the word processor. The system also provides them means of channel checking, channel monitoring, initiation of test transmission etc. The airconditioned environment of course enhances the pleasure of working.

Ironically, the same system may be viewed with disfavour by colleagues of transmission staff in other centres not equipped with computers. This is because computerisation also brings with it formalisation in the form of message format and communication protocols, whereas the pre-computer communication is virtually in free format. The computer system is less sympathetic to errors. The system does help these out-stating operators by acknowledging each message received (also indicating errors, if any) and by generating periodic charts of received and transmitted items.

Our experience is that while the transmission and reporting staff adapt quickly to modernisation, the editorial staff does face difficulties, some genuine and some not so genuine. Before computerisation editors principally worked with paper and pen and occasionally use typewriters. The corrected copy is actually keyed in by the transmission staff. The computerisation requires that the editors change their desk job for a terminal job, possibly sharing the same cluster with the transmission staff. On the composing side, the editorial staff also have to insert typesetting commands. To some extent, the workload of editorial staff may increase in the process. However, this workload is no different than the one shouldered by their professional colleagues in advanced countries.

Another major adjustment the editorial staff has to make is in the way the story moves electronically from one desk to another, a desk being represented by a directory in the computer. While the system permits browsing and scanning through a much larger amount of matter, the adaptation to new procedure can be slow. For example, instead of using the word processor, initially people continued to take large volumes of hard copy printout and then retyped the entire item after relatively light editing. This goes on till the use of the terminal becomes a second nature.

The priority of a message is an important means for allowing urgent matter to take precedence in transmission over accumulated lower priority items. Unfortunately, despite well-defined instructions, reporters and editors alike and likely to attach higher priority to their own items upsetting the very purpose of priorities.

Several steps are involved before a news organisation can catapult itself from the teleprinter technology to an organisation, which has successfully harnessed the power of computers for fulfilling its primary concern of news collection and dissemination. The management has to first decide on modernisation and allocate funds to size up the requirements. Then, it has to draw up specifications, interact with vendors and finally award and finalise the contract. The vendor has to design, develop, debug, install and commission the system.

This is followed by training and acceptance test. All these steps may need between one and a half to two years which is quite acceptable considering that computerisation is an important milestone in the history of a news organisation and caution and care are natural. It can take up to six months after the system is operational for the staff to adapt and acquire the expertise to exploit the system fully.

Conclusion

The educated population of India, whose numbers are ever on the increase are the prime audience for the news industry. These men and women are aware at least of the technological developments in the ever shrinking world. While local reporting will continue to hold major interests, the audience will also demand national and international coverage composed and printed in easy to read and easy to understand manner.

Customer and competitive demands apart, it is in the organisational and economical interest of news agency or a newspaper to usher in a modern news room. The process itself is a long-drawn one, because no standard solution exists. Technological and organisational complexities, some of them outlined in this paper, have to be well understood to successfully manage the transition.

News Agency Applications: National Networking

This section shall first give an idea of what PTI is attempting to do. And then, may be a few general observations about technology, and its impact on the media, its functioning especially the news agencies. At the outset, it may be stated that the Press Trust of India (PTI) is the foremost news agency in the country. Its efforts to upgrade its dissemination and news gathering systems, thus, are designed for its thousands of newspaper subscribers.

PTI undertook modernisation of its operations about five and half years ago. There were two aspects of this programme: One was computerisation of operations, *i.e.*, news collection and dissemination, the other aspect was upgradation of means of communication, modes of communication.

I will first explain the computerisation or automation aspect of it. Many news agencies in the world had already gone into automated systems when PTI attempted to enter the field. The obstacles were formidable. For instance, it was very highly capital-intensive and we were not such whether we could afford it.

Second, we did not have in the country any precedent of or any expertise in software package development that would be required for a news agency. We had the option of either importing a package wholesale, the same as Reuter or AFP or any other advanced news agency or try and develop something which will suit one specific requirements and in that process achieve two objectives: to keep the costs down, and to have a measure of flexibility in adapting the software to changing needs that an imported package will not give you. With these two objectives in view, we entered into a collaboration agreement with the National Centre for Software Techniques and with the Computer Maintenance Corporation. As a result of this triangular collaboration, we were able to complete in two years' time a package which we called IDEAS—Information, Dissemination, Editing and Archival System, which is used for information collection, processing and dissemination by PTI. IDEAS is an acronym evolved by us.

Phased Development

As a result of this development, PTI has an advantage which perhaps few news agencies in the world have of getting to know from the very start all the implications, potentialities and limitations of computerised operation. This enabled us to embark on automation in a phased manner, what is immediately possible, what could be achieved in the second round, and what should be the ultimate objective.

In the first round, what we have done is to install computers in the four metropolitan centres, Delhi, Bombay, Calcutta, and Madras. Delhi, being the major news centre, had the pride place in terms of capacity, number of terminals and other peripheral which are part and parcel of the operating system. This was done overnight and we were able to shift reception of news from various centres, editing storing and transmission, from manual to computer. Here there were no gradual phases, because that was not practicable. Initially, we did have lot of teething trouble but we found without interrupting the service even for a day we were able to handle the automated system. Inevitably the benefits that we got and we continue to get are marginal for the simple reason that the entire country is not yet automated, only the four metropolitan centres are automated, until the last subscriber also gets into the network of automatic news distribution system, the benefit of computerised news distribution system will not be fully available or reflected in the impact that the news agencies make on newspapers.

Information Links

These four metropolitan centres were taken up; they were linked to the other satellite centres. In the southern region, all the centres being linked to Madras, north eastern and eastern regions linked to Calcutta, the northern and central region linked to Delhi and the western and some parts of southern and central regions connected to Bombay. And the four computers were linked together to exchange information to deal with each other at high speed and to be able to stand in for each other. We do not have a hot standby for each computer machine that is installed, cost factor being the main constraint in providing hot standby. What we did was that each of the system was loaded with the same software that was common so that in the event of failure of one system the other machine automatically picks up the function and without interruption and is able to carry on the operation. We have not had any break-down so far and therefore the occasions we had to invoke the stand-by arrangements have been few and wherever we had to fall back on the stand-by arrangements we have had satisfactory results.

As a result of computerisation, we had achieved several tangible results: 1) We are able to improve the working environment. It used to be a noisy, dusty environment in which the sub-editors and other editorial staff had to work round the clock. That is now a thing of the past. Anyone visiting the premises can see that it has an entirely different look. You have a clean dust free environment. The whole building in Delhi is air conditioned and therefore air conditioning is not a new feature for Delhi, but it is for Bombay, Calcutta and Madras. There is no use of paper and pen in the editing operation, whatever news messages come into the system, a sub-editor is able to call up on the screen, select what he wants to use, edit, re-write, or eliminate, or whatever he wants to do and then at the push of a button, the message is on its way to the destination that the editor desires. So that is one tangible result.

Second, a number of repetitive, time consuming chores has been totally eliminated, so that all you have to do is to push a few buttons, pre-determined codes, and those operations are automatically performed by the computer and that is not only time saving but it saves drudgery for the sub-editor.

Third, the sub-editor is able to improve the quality of the copy, he can call back background material, add it to a story, or call back a number of stories which are connected to each other and evolve a common body or lead as we say in newspaper language.

Optimising Productivity

Then, one other result that we have been able to achieve is optimising productivity, that is, a person is able to handle more stories a day. With the employment of the automated system, the number is doubled or trebled. Initially, of course, the quality suffered because we were used to picking up a pen from a table or from wherever it is, and putting down ideas on paper, chopping, cutting, all that. But to achieve it through a different techniques of not physically coming into contact with the written matter, it took a little psychological adjustment. That took some time, and even now there are people on our staff who are not wholly at home with that sort of editing and re-writing.

I was in the office of the Associated Press of America in England. I spent some time there and at the Reuters too. Once when I went there I did see a few typewriters, here and there in addition to computerised terminals. So when I asked the manager of the bureau: What the typewriters were doing, (they had claimed that they had done away with typewriters), he said that they were there for the reporters to type out their expense accounts. The next time when I was there, seeing no typewriters around, I asked him what happened, don't you get any more expense accounts? Now it is all done on the computers, they have learnt to do it. There are no typewriters at all. Even whatever is normally performed on the typewriter or manually, they are all now performed on the computers. Most of our people, particularly the younger ones, the newer generation, have taken to use of computer terminals and use of automatic system with ease and they feel far more comfortable to use them than with pencils and typewriters that they had started with: A psychological change we have been able to bring about.

No Retrenchment

But at the same time, we have also been able to dispel through use of potentialities the fear created by computerisation, that while raising productivity, it inevitably leads to reduction of work force and retrenchment. Actually, this is one of the threats our telephone industry is facing. Although by going electronic, we find redundancy in work force, but what we did was to anticipate the kind of redundancy that could occur and started peripheral services which could immediately absorb the extra work force.

We ourselves, as we moved forward in automation, were needing more and more people. For instance, the central desk in Delhi had about 25 people five years ago, we have now about 70 people and we still need more people. Now that the output per head has come down, there are a variety of other functions that each sub-editor is expected to perform. For instance, we have started a service called News-scan which takes out automatically from the main stream of news flow important items and transmits them to a separate network for re-cycling and display on a screen. You must have been in hotels and public places and government offices and elsewhere these messages being recycled. It is a 24 hour service. Human effect is involved in selection of items, judging the importance, marking and all. So that is one area where we find more people are employed. Second is what we have linked up major stock markets in the country in a network for simultaneous display of changing prices. Within the stock market, whatever trading takes place, is immediately reflected on a huge display board. And then we also compile an inter-market price for the various stocks that also is displayed instantly in major stock markets. Here too, editing and journalistic effort, quite apart from other work of punching in information, operating key boards, operating systems, all these needed manpower. Our existing manpower could be used for it, and we have had to employ additional manpower too.

Then we have developed another system which will be called Com-scan, that is, commercial information and basic core news of national and international events which is available to subscribers on a retrieval basis. A key board is there and pre-determined sections are available which will respond to specific codes being punched on the key board. The subscriber can call up political information, economic information, bullion prices, stock prices, or commodity prices or foreign exchange information, or whatever he wants, all that is available. While the News-scan is one-way flow, one has to be content with the flow as it comes, you cannot choose what you want to see, you have got to see everything that comes. Here in Com-scan you can choose what you want to see; you don't have to look at everything that we normally recycle. So that is another service, another technology.

News Bank

The fourth one, that, we are in the process of developing is a news bank. PTI gets at least 5,00,000 words from outside the country every day of which only about 30,000 to 40,000 words are distributed, selected and provided to newspapers. Newspapers themselves use only about 20%, which means that what is available to the social researcher for political or any other kind of research is only a very small part of what we pay for and secure for the country just because of the constraints of space, constraints of communication, all that we have all is not available to the general public. So by creating the news bank, every bit of information that we get from anywhere in the world and that we generate within the country is stored away. Somebody goes over the information to eliminate duplication and any error and then it is all set systematically under various heads like in any library. Codes are available, subscribers can dial up, punch the code and get the information then they want. In about seven or eight months from now, this service will be available to anyone who want to avail of it. Software for it is being developed by us and we are half way through in the development process.

I am mentioning all these, because none of these developments would have possible had we not taken the first step of computerising our operations and, secondly, deciding that we would do so on the basis of software that we fabricate within the country and not accept a ready-made package.

Further, potentialities which computerisation offers is that we are now in the process of computerising our new Hindi service. It has been about two-year-old. We are providing the service at the moment on electro-mechanical printers which are highly unscientific so far as reproducing Devanagari script is concerned. The script is three-tiered and electro-mechanical printers produce only one tier of characters, which means, matras and other are set in a continuous time and you have got to put them in their proper place, before you could make sense out of the message. Use of electronic machine would for all times eliminate this cumbersome process. The electronic machines would have a huge capacity to receive and transmit at higher speed. If you were to use a computerised system, software and other facilities which exist in the country to process information and use high speed network and bring electronic printers into play. So for the first time at no formidable extra cost, we will be able to attempt a multi-lingual service, not limited only to Hindi but encompassing all other languages.

More Scope for Languages

In earlier years the typewriter producer, teleprinter manufacturers, had not attempted to product printers in numerous languages, because the market for it was very narrow and it did not pay sufficient return for them to justify the investment. Therefore, many languages had no facility of having even a typewriter. But that problem would no longer exist because software development is a one-time process and without repetitive costs as in producing a typewriter. With one-time investment, we would be able to produce copy in any language that we want to and I think that day is not far off when we would be able to offer multi-lingual services. A lot of work is now being attempted even for automatic translation of messages from one language to another, of terms and expressions which would lend themselves to systematisation on the basis of certain logic. Such expressions in areas and languages are numerous so that actual manual intervention could be limited to specific narrow areas. I wouldn't be surprised if a day very soon comes when you transmit in English and the messages come out in Hindi, Marathi, Tamil, Malayalam and in all different languages.

Now, to take up the second aspect, of upgrading communications following computerisation, we had already shifted from using teleprinter channel to use of data channel, the difference being wider spectrum, capacity of a very high speed; as against 50 bauds that a teleprinter channel or may be 75 bauds at the outside limit that it can handle, you can go 9600 bits per second on a data circuit at speeds which we have not been attempted yet. Because our communication lines are not unfortunately noise free, we have not been able to achieve results, when we go beyond 4800 BPS, that is the optimum the Department of Telecommunication is able to give us as of now. I am quite sure with the introduction of more modern means of communication by DOT, the performance should improve. Data channels we have already introduced.

We have linked up the four metropolitan centres by data channels. Beyond that we have a Madras/Cochin, Madras/Hyderabad, Madras/Bangalore, Bombay/Hyderabad, Bombay/Ahmedabad, Delhi/Chandigarh, Calcutta/Patna link. Stations like Lucknow are also linked by the data circuit. The price of course is very high. But we try to optimise utilization by committing this circuit also for distribution of pictures. Some of the extra costs that we incur, we are able to realise.

Satellite Links

Then we had finalised a project, when Mr. Gill was Secretary-Information, he was able to, with his dynamism, push through the projects for utilising a segment of INSAT for dissemination of all the news services including pictures to be picked up in any part of the country with the help of a dish antenna. Although the project was accepted and it has been in various stages of implementation for some time it has not got into full stride so far for the simple reason that has to be used in the project to be made indigenously, without having to import anything at all. So, the Space Applications Centre in Ahmedabad, Research and Development Wing in PTI, the

Department of Telecommunication all these agencies are involved and they have now been able to complete the proto-type which are undergoing tests in Bombay and by mid April, we will have one or two stations on trial run for transmission and reception of all these numerous services of PTI, over a single satellite channel to be received at any point. Before the end of the year from the four metropolitan centres, transmission on a dynamic time sharing basis will begin messages and pictures which can be picked up virtually in all parts of the country. You will have simultaneous reception at high speed of all the news services in English, Hindi and then photo service. All that will become possible. That is so far as the communication aspect is concerned.

Indigenous Production

Since we went into this area, and we found that at every stage cost is becoming a major factor and the electronic industry generally tends to take out their part of the investment in the returns it gets from the first few customers we are ending up as the guineapigs for most of them. Therefore we thought we should try and attempt to have a manufacturing enterprise of our own which would not merely help PTI get off the ground in areas of employment of high tech equipment, but help other organisations, media organisations with its products. So in collaboration on a 50%—50% basis with the Madhya Pradesh State Electronic Development Corporation the PTI have set up an enterprise in Bhopal called, NATIONAL INFORMATION TECHNOLOGIES LTD. (NITEL), which has already started producing micro-processors, and a number of other peripherals like multiplexors, relays and whole series of items. It has just concluded a collaboration agreement for total indigenous production of a heavy duty versatile electronic printer, which can be used as a teleprinter, also a computer printer. NITEL will go on and develop photo facsimile receiving equipment, transmission equipment and a number of other peripherals.

It is also developing a system which will have a split screen facility where on the screen you can translate on one side and you can call up messages in English or Hindi on the other side of the screen. Some such system exists abroad, and it is cumbersome. What is being attempted will be simple and cost effective. And after undertaking production here we found that we were able to economise. A microprocessor for which we have paid as much as Rs. 28,000/- we are able to get out of here for Rs. 8,000/-. So that has been the measure of economy that we have been able to achieve. Yesterday a distinguished friend was discussing this very theme. He asked me, alright the modern technology enables you to send more messages at a faster pace, so what? that kept me thinking. This capability imposes two obligations, one on the media itself, that I will come to subsequently, the other on the country. Technology has to be part of a total strategy, part of an integrated approach to development, socio-economic and political. Otherwise we will only create more confusion, more problems for ourselves. As part of this integrated approach we have got to ensure that this is going to liberate us from surviving areas of dependence on others. Except on the basis of self-reliance, not that we should attempt self-reliance in every field, attempt to reinvent the wheel as it were, but in critical areas, crucial areas, no matter what it costs, unless we are self-reliant we should not get into the race only to find that we cannot move without assistance from outside. We then become victims, willing or unwilling tools, of other people's designs, and eventually also dumping ground for other people's technologies, often totally unrelated to our own needs, ethos or genius. That is one part of it.

The second is, if we are able to carry more messages at a faster pace, then that message also must have social, political and economic relevance. The quality must improve. Unless we do that, we will only be providing more muck at double quick time to our unwitting consumers. So these two are also important facets of any technology development that information dealers, that is, the media should look at. In other words the technology should not be looked upon as an end in itself but as a means to some end and we should be clear about that end, adapt our instrument to enable us, equip us better to achieve those goals.

I think some point was made about ombudsman, PTI itself is thinking of an ombudsman not an internal ombudsman, that somebody from outside, to deal with complaints. As first step we are organising a workshop of editors in August when we would test out various ideas and I think we would move forward. We look up on it both as an assurance, as a guarantee as well as a protection for our independence.

Then Desk Top Publishing, we are already in publishing business. We publish Economic Services, Science Services, Corporate Services, we are undertaking work on behalf of other people also, typesetting on a very big scale using desk top publishing capability, of course. The PTI story that came out recently was not done by us because when the initial work started we didn't have the capability. We would be moving into that area, there is no doubt, we will be thinking in terms of in future years coming out with educational publications even if it involves, some cost adsorption by PTI. The major problem is dearth of talent. We do not have enough people who would be willing to work at the kind of salaries that we can offer.

I think I have not missed out any points excepting training journalists. I think along with whatever is being thought as good values in journalism, objectivity and what not, familiarisation with modern technology would be helpful, because that will enable the products of the Institute or any other training institution to be suitable for ready absorption by the media.

REFERENCES

1. *Handbook of Computer-aided Composition* by Arthur H. Phillips Marcel Dekker Inc., p. 434.
2. *The World of Digital Typesetting* by John W. Seybold Pub. Inc., 1984 Media, PA, USA, p. 428.

6

News and Journalist's Attitude

A CASE BOOK

THE extracts that follow, taken from news and editorial columns, from books and from propaganda of many kinds, are offered as further evidence, and as material on which the reader may test his own resistance. The sources are listed at the end of the book.

1. What motives accounted for the differences in these three reports of the same meeting?

I. "A.R.P. Shelter in Every Home"

> "Every building erected without due regard to structural precautions against air attack represents a wasted opportunity, and in many cases a downright neglect of public duty."
>
> This criticism was made at a conference on structural air raid precautions at the Royal Institute of British Architects last night by Mr. Thomas E. Scott, a member of the Structural Precautions Committee of the Institute.
>
> Mr. Scott said that they had studied the effects of aerial bombardment of towns in Spain and China.

Most modern buildings of steel and concrete construction, he said, would probably be safe against incendiary bombs. But buildings of a domestic type, particularly in built-up areas, might suffer considerable damage unless adequate fire-fighting services were available.

The best type of structure for resisting the effects of high explosive, he added, was the framed building of steel or reinforced concrete with light panel walls or large areas of glass.

II. A.R.P. Scheme Denounced

Scotland Yard Architect and 'Nonsense

Sir S. Hoare's Retort

There was a sensation at a London conference on structural air raid precautions at the Royal Institute of British Architects last night when the Home Secretary, Sir Samuel Hoare, heard one of his own subordinates attack the whole principle of the precautions and denounce Sir Thomas Inskip, Minister of Defence, as a hypocrite.

The speaker was Mr. F. D. Bush, Deputy Police Architect to New Scotland Yard. For thirty years Mr. Bush has been a member of the R.I.B.A., and this was the first time he had spoken in public.

"It causes me moral indignation," he said, "that we should be spending so much money and effort on something I believe to be useless. We are architects with ideals. Let us be frank and sincere and say that we will have nothing to do with this nonsense." He did not believe, he said, that air raid precautions could be effective to any extent. Recently he designed a building of which the cost for A.R.P. was 8 to 10 per cent, and he did not believe that it would be of any more use in an air raid than an umbrella.

The truth was that such precautions were merely intended to frighten the enemy. He suggested that they should call an international conference of architects, including those of Germany and France, to discuss A.R.P. together. Sir Thomas Inskip, Minister of Defence, had implied in a recent speech that a number of most eminent scientists had something most devilish up their sleeves. He was merely trying to frighten other nations.

"Sir Thomas Inskip is president of a Christian union which my children attend. I call this absolute hypocrisy on his part," and Mr. Bush. Sir Samuel Hoare was his chief, and he was still prepared to do everything he could for Sir Samuel, but also for other countries as well.

Sir Samuel Hoare, in reply, said that he did not doubt the sincerity of Mr. Bush, but he felt that, of all forms of defence, A.R.P. was the least provocative. The kind of precautions they had been discussing could not be regarded as an incentive to militarism or war. He was just as great a pacifist as anyone, and would be delighted to see the abolition of air forces the whole world over, but so long as the world was in its present state he was not prepared to see this great country the only one in the world to remain defenceless.

Sir Samuel's reply was loudly cheered. The conference will be followed by a number of regional conferences over the whole country, leading to the appointment of regional advisers to give expert advice to local builders of A.R.P. structures.

III. Structural A.R.P.

Official Advice

Sir S. Hoare's Talk to Architects

Sir Samuel Hoare, the Home Secretary, speaking last night at the inaugural meeting of a three days' conference on Structural Air Raid Precautions at the Royal Institute of British Architects, Portland Place, said that of all forms of defence air raid precautions were the least provocative. Such precautions could in no way be regarded as a stimulus to militarism or as an incentive to war.

The conference is the first of a series arranged by the R.I.B.A. at the request of the Air Raid Precautions Department, and other conferences in the provinces are to be arranged at a later date.

In opening the conference Sir Samuel Hoare said there were few fields in which architects had shown their genius more conspicuously than in that of defence. It was a sad commentary on the history of the world that now for the first time in England since the fifteenth century we were beginning to think once more of the fortification of private houses. They had to take steps which would help them to avoid panic on the one hand and unnecessary loss of life on the other.

During the next fortnight it was hoped to issue a detailed handbook on structural precautions which should assist architects and the general public in dealing with both new buildings and the more difficult problem of adapting existing ones. In a day or two that handbook would be supplemented by another dealing with the structural protection of hospitals. Police headquarters had already been dealth with. In the near future it was hoped to cover the whole of the field and enable every part of the country to know the kind of precautions that should and could reasonably be taken without prohibitive expenditure. Without the architects' help it would have been impossible to deal successfully or adequately with the many difficulties of the problem.

Mr. T. E. Scott, a fellow of the Institute, in a paper on "Air raid precautions as a problem for the architect," said that he was convinced that effective measures might be introduced as a new and permanent factor in design and construction of buildings without detriment to their artistic quality and efficiency. To devise protection in existing buildings was a more difficult problem involving the application of certain principles of structural precautions to the selection and adaptation of buildings suitable for the purpose—a duty which the architect was the man best qualified to undertake.

He deprecated the concentration of large numbers of people in any single shelter, and advocated rather the provision of accommodation within buildings in which people worked or lived.

Mr. Eric L. Bird read a paper on "Some general principles of structural A.R.P."

2. What are the motives and results of the kind of suppression exemplified in these two reports?

I. Members of the National Union of Journalists who refuse to undertake work which is not compatible with the dignity of their calling are to receive the Union's fullest support. This was decided at the final session of the union's annual delegate meeting at Torquay yesterday when the following resolution was passed unanimously:

"This conference views with alarm and august the increasing tendency of newspapers to require their staffs to pry into matters concerning private lives, the unwarranted intrusion at times of grief and bereavement, and the publication of details of domestic matters arising out of court proceedings.

"It regards the practice as one which, in its further development, will provoke legislative intervention and as such will be inimical to the interest of journalism and a menace to the freedom of the Press.

"It instructs the National Executive Council to give the fullest support, financial and otherwise, to members who refuse to undertake such commissions which are not compatible with the dignity of the profession or with the union code of conduct."

II. The National Union of Journalists, in conference at Torquay, passed an emergency resolution protesting against the "discriminating and arbitrary action of the Government" in refusing permission to Mr. Claude Cockburn, of the *Daily Worker* to return to his duties in Spain.

The resolution, copies of which were sent to the Prime Minister and Mr. C. R. Attlee, leader of the

Opposition, expressed the view that the Government's action was an "unjustifiable discrimination against the newspaper concerned, and a serious encroachment on the existing liberties of British newspapers and journalists."

Conference also sent a telegram to General Franco, demanding the immediate release from Spanish soil to neutral territory of Mr. Arthur Koestler, *News Chronicle* correspondent, who was captured by the rebels after the fall of Malaga.

Conference also decided at the final session yesterday that members of the Union who refuse to undertake work which is not compatible with the dignity of their calling are to receive the Union's fullest support.

A resolution was adopted vetting "with alarm and disgust" unwarranted newspaper intrusion at times of grief and bereavement, and the publication of details of domestic matters arising out of court proceedings.

3. Two analogies:

(*a*) The use of force, of the sword, by the State is the Ministry of God for the protection of the people.

(*b*) We have drifted into the position of the policeman who has to keep order in the world, but every policeman must have, in the last resort, a truncheon.

4. Which of these two writers has more to contribute towards solving the problems they discuss?

I. Before withdrawing much must be done to enable India to defend herself. Acute and complicated problems, of which the real magnitude will appear in the pages of the Simon Commission's Report, must be solved or brought within reach of solution before the country can be handed over to its proper and natural custodians. A period of transition is therefore to be provided for. Take only the question of the country's security. The Indianisation of the present army and the preparation of the citizens for the duty of self-sacrifice are processes which require not only time, but skill and delicacy of organisation. In spite of urgent and repeated entreaties they have received so far nothing but perfunctory treatment. It would be a gross betrayal, nothing short of infamy, if Britain were to leave India without liquidating this supreme obligation.

II. British India is ours. It was bequeathed as a trust to the present generation of Young British men and women by generations of splendid men and women who faced privations and perils to build for Britain the greatest over-sea Empire known to history. Before we went to India it was a land roughly with one-fourth of the population of to-day, decimated constantly by famine, plague and cholera. To-day India is a country of wonderful cities, splendid railways and roads, and with an irrigation system not equalled anywhere in the world. The India Office in London is gambling away British India. The energy and devotion of ten generations of British men and women are to be sacrificed to a policy of funk.

5. What are the respective aims and methods of these passages?

I. The French have broken—we could hardly believe their words. The story they told us we couldn't believe; put it down to their terror-stricken imagination. A greyish green cloud had swept down on them, turning yellow as it travelled over the country, blasting everything it touched, shrivelling up all vegetation. No human courage could face such a peril. Then there staggered into our midst hundreds of French soldiers, blinded, coughing, chests heaving, faces an ugly purple colour, lips speechless with agony. Behind them in the gas-choked trenches they had left hundreds of dead and dying comrades. The impossible was only too true. It was the most fiendish and wicked thing I have ever seen.

> II. Even a few grains of diphenylchlorarsine per cubic metre caused almost unbearable pain. The inhalation of this substance also led to serious resorptive effects on the nervous system, which revealed themselves in motor disturbance, unsteady gait, swaying and inability to walk. This was accompanied by severe pains in the limbs and joints. The inhalation of a very high concentration often induces numbness, fainting and unconsciousness, which may last several hours. Disturbances of the digestive organs have also been observed, accompanied, in the case of human beings, by a very marked loss of weight.

6. At what effects is the following extract aiming? How would you describe the way in which it is written?

> On this the ninth anniversary of the Armistice which ended the greatest and the most fateful of all wars, the heart of this world-wide Empire turns in a special manner to the memory of those whose lives were the price of our deliverance. As there has been no struggle in our annals so terrible and so exacting, no danger so prolonged and imminent, no cause so great, no sacrifices so cruel, and no victory on which larger or more lasting issues hung, so there is no day in our calendar like to this. For over four years we stood on the edge of the abyss, of ruin as an Empire, as a nation, perhaps of ruin as a race. The men we commemorate to-day saved us from that ruin by their death. The appeal is universal. Scarce a home in the land, from the most splendid of ancestral places to the humblest cottage or the poorest lodging in our towns, was unvisited in that dread time by the angel of death. He smote the best; a whole generation entering upon life in the flower of early manhood, and others already husbands and fathers, the stay and the guardians of the widows and the orphans they have left. To the bereaved, first of all, this is a day of days, dedicated to the memory of their dead, a memory ever living with

them, but by time and the everyday duties and occupations of life mercifully softened with the years. The annual testimony to the fallen, celebrated with such solemn and befitting rites as Church and State can give, bears recurrent witness to the full measure in which Empire and nation share the grief and the gratitude of the mourners. There is no day on which all sorts and conditions of our people are so widely and so deeply moved by thoughts and feelings common to them all.

7. The quotations that follow are from different speeches by Lord Baldwin. The reader is invited to notice the difference in style.

I. I hope that, if the sky has become overcast, you will find some encouragement in what I have said to work on through another year towards your noblest of ideals. You must look ahead in a spirit of realism. . . . Let your aim be resolute and your footsteps firm and certain. Do not fear or misunderstand when the Government say that they are looking to our defences. It does not mean that we look upon force as the judge and law-giver in the affairs of nations. We do not dedicate ourselves to such evil, and there is here no spirit whatever of aggression. But weakness or wavering, or uncertainty, or neglect of our obligations—obligations for peace—doubts of our own safety give no assurance of peace; believe me, quite the reverse. Do not fear that it is a step in the wrong direction. You need not remind me of the solemn task of the League to reduce armaments by agreement. I know and I shall not forget. But we have gone too far alone and must try to bring others along with us. I give you my word that there will be no great armaments.

At the annual meeting of the International Peace Society, 31 October, 1935.

II. The speed of an air attack, compared with the attack of an army, is as the speed of a motor car to that of a four-in-hand, and in the next war you will find that any town which is within reach of an aerodrome can be bombed within the first five minutes of war from the air, to an extent which was inconceivable in the last war, and the question will be whose morale will be shattered quickest by that preliminary bombing? I think it is well also for the man in the street to realise that there is no power on earth that can prevent him from being bombed. Whatever people may tell him, the bomber will always get through. . . . The only defence is in offence, which means that you have to kill more women and children more quickly than the enemy if you want to save yourselves.

House of Commons, 10 November, 1932.

8. How do these examples of propaganda strike you?

I. But do not force me to probe continually into this sickening wound. Atrocities, yes, both sides have committed them. Only we cannot forget that the real 'atrocity,' the greatest, the direct cause and the immediate occasion of the rest, is the war—for it is a war, not a *pronunciamento*, not a simple military *coup d'etat*—the civil war, fratricidal, frenzied. Who is responsible for the outbreak of war? They, the patriots. They, the conservatives. They, the innocent men. And, in addition, without cause or reason.

In face of these events, I, a Catholic, have chosen to stand with the supporters of the Government against the military and Fascist rebels. On all sides, with surprise and impatience, I have been asked the reasons for my choice. Only for those honest minds who really want to know the reasons, will I now attempt to explain them.

But I think that in my turn I have a perfect right to ask this question first: "What about the other side?" How do they, priests and Christians who have joined the revolt, justify themselves for choosing an insurrection against the legally established order, for choosing a fratricidal and murderous war, for choosing measures of violence which were bound, in this country and at this time, to lead to completely hysterical madness. . . .?

II. Like most of my countrymen I loathe injustice and cruelty, and unlike them I happen to have had some recent experience of Spain. And after reading the pages that follow it is hard to escape the conclusion that the people of this country have been misled into condoning cruelty and injustice of a particularly horrible kind. There doubtless have been many harsh acts committed by the Spanish Nationalists; men do not wage war with gloved hands. But they do not include the wholesale rape, murder and mutilation of non-combatant women and children, such as the Communist leaders in Spain will have to answer for—not to the Council of the League of Nations but at the Judgment Day.

Over here our intellectuals—our foolish wise—have misled us into thinking of such men as democrats, and of the Spanish Civil War as a fight between a properly constituted Liberal-cum-Socialist Government and a gang of Fascist saboteurs. But no university lecturer or anonymous B.B.C. commentator has told the just and compassionate people of England about the women of San Martin of Valdeiglesias. It was their fate that first impelled me to undertake the thankless task of writing this Preface (to *The Communist Atrocities*).

9. What differences do you see in the following quotations?

I. Until the senior University authorities realise that their duty in fitting the youth of England for the struggle of life does not only lie in the fostering of scholarship, and until they remove some of the handicaps which lie so heavily on the most serious sport at the University, I do not see how Oxford rowing can be lifted from the rut in which it now rests.

II. A serious problem confronts those who are concerned for the nation's soul. Recent exchanges of opinion between representatives of the Great Powers suggest the possibility of a certain cataclysmic situation

> for which no preparation has been made. There may never be another war. Now, the absence of the possibility of war will cause a gap in our social system. Without war, what will be the basis of national unity? What shall we put forward as the citizen's first duty if it is no longer necessary to defend one's country? I have carefully considered all forms of social activity with a view to their use as a National unifying principle. And I have come to the conclusion that there is only one thing that can take the place of war as a means of binding the nation in a common cause. And that is Cricket.

10. What do you notice about the use of words in the four extracts from advertisements that follow? *(i)* Tobaccos for cultured tastes. *(ii)* Balkan Sobranie is not a name which conveys much to the many. But to the few who smoke for the pleasure of smoking—and not because they have nothing better to do—Balkan Sobranie is more than a name, it is a philosophy of living. *(iii)* The Rhythm of Living. Human happiness revolves around simple themes . . . and its greatest pleasures are those shared. Thus do Player's fill their appointed place within the scheme of things. *(iv)* How many members of the public have a sufficiently educated taste in cigarettes to appreciate these refinements?

11. What do you think of the intention and methods of this extract?

> By this means our liberty becomes a noble freedom. It carries an imposing and majestic aspect. It has a pedigree and illustrious ancestors. It has its bearings and its ensigns armorial. It has its gallery of portraits; its monumental inscriptions; its records, evidences and titles. We procure reverence to our civil institutions on the principle upon which nature teaches us to revere individual men; on account of their age; and on account of those from whom they are descended. All your sophisters cannot produce anything better adapted to preserve a rational and mainly freedom than the course

we have pursued, who have chosen our nature rather than our speculations, our breasts rather than our inventions, for the great conservatories and magazines of our rights and privileges.

12. Which of these two passages do you find the more convincing?

I. Sir,—Now that we have a National Government, may we hope that its leaders will recognise and remove the real menace of the 'dole' and the bulk of our social services—that they are rapidly turning Britain into a degenerate and C_3 nation.

Through the dole, together with our colossal system of health insurance, relief, free hospitals asylums and charities, we are forcing the fit to keep the unfit alive. We give the unemployable, the weak, the shiftless and the mentally defective every encouragement to propagate their kind, while we tax the fit and energetic so heavily to provide the means of this encouragement that they cannot afford to have children.

Thus we are fostering the worst elements in the nation, while destroying the best. In the name of 'humanity' we are turning Britain into a land of physical, mental and moral degenerates.

Statesmanship should mean the fostering of the best and the extermination of the worst elements in the State—the extension, in short, of Nature's own law of the survival of the fittest. To-day we are reversing this law. Will our statesmen realise the danger before it is too late?

Yours truly . . . .

(*Letter to the Press.*)

II. Very few men and women really want to work in factories because that is their idea of the happiest way of spending their lives. . . . Therefore what we call unemployment is not really a curse. The curse is only the smallness of the dole.

There are remedies for this. The smallness of the dole, the smallness of wages, the shortage of money, could be remedied. But all the time we go on improving machinery (and machinery is being improved day by day, almost hour by hour) there is no remedy for unemployment. There is no remedy for unemployment unless we scrap machinery. Unemployment is the absolutely inevitable consequence of the introduction and improvement of labour displacing machinery.

If you introduce a machine which takes one man to make it and only needs one man to mind it and when made does the work of three men, then one man is bound to be unemployed. There is no escape at all unless you can get fresh markets. But we cannot get fresh markets. There is none left.

There are various schemes for the reform of the money system, the account keeping system, the wages system; schemes by which the power of people to buy things could be made equal to the power of machinery to make things. For everybody must agree that there is no shortage of things; there is only a shortage of money. The powers of production have increased a thousandfold but the powers of distribution have not increased correspondingly. The weakness is not in production but in distribution.

13. What state of mind is this passage trying to produce in the reader, and what are its methods?

Those who remember pre-war days have probably noticed how the England we knew is returning once again. The old friendly smile is re-appearing on the faces of passers-by. The newspaper-seller calls us 'sir' without effort. The shopkeeper takes our small order with cheerful courtesy.

This change in spirit has come, I believe, to stay. In my illogical way I point the nightmare of the last fourteen years to the fact that the money that was fired in Flanders' mud, or which went down to the sea in ships, had to be repaid. The debt said Nemesis, could be partly liquidated by four years of drastic depression.

We are getting back to the real England at long, long last.

England in those pre-war days, was a fine place to work and play in. There was income to be earned, true sociability, unforced laughter. Few save the rich ventured far on the creaking stairway of social ambition: only the inexperienced strove for that class equality that will finally come on Judgment Day. We were permitted to appreciate books and wine and music without being ballyhooed as intellectuals.

It is not very strange that false values fail to keep the sun from shining or turn the night before its hour to day. Strange it is, however, that all during this post-war period we have almost forgotten that at eventide the heavens fill with stars; and that one can still get lost in this countryside of ours to discover with amazement that materialism invited the Vandals to Rome and that Paradise still exists.

Some will think me in error in suggesting that in England the war turned into a memory is returning in reality. The financial stability of this country, they will tell me, depends on universal unity. I do not care. All I know is that the nations will follow as we decide. The world is calling "England, England" with its silent, foreign heart!

14. To what extent is the following a clarification of the writer's attitude?

The Archbishop of York, Dr. Temple, writing in the *York Diocesan Leaflet*, explains his recent statement that "extreme pacifism is heretical." "Friends have asked me to explain what was in my mind. Of course, I recognise that many who hold heretical opinions are personally devoted and even saintly Christians.

I should perhaps have qualified my expression by saying 'heretical in tendency' for I do not know of any formal condemnation by the Church of pacifism as such. But that in its extreme form it is "heretical in tendency" I cannot doubt.

This does not apply to those who say that modern warfare is such that to engage in it will almost certainly do more harm than good. That is a judgment concerning a balance of values, not a judgment of principle. The position with which I am concerned is that of pacifists who say that it is as a universal principle, un-Christian to use in support of law whatever degree of force is requisite, even to the taking of life, in restraint of lawless force or violence."

15. Analyse closely the way the following piece of writing works upon the person who is influenced by it:

Does your child suffer from "Clothes Repression?" (There follows a picture of a disgruntled child of about four years.) Does she get moody and irritable? Is she fidgety about her clothes? Garments that are too tight because they have shrunk; that have washed badly and gone out of shape; even garments that have faded or are the wrong colour may be the cause. These things conspire to produce what are commonly known as 'tantrums,' and to create a lasting sense of discontent. Frequently they may permanently warp a child's character.

What Child Specialists Advise.

Doctors and others who have specialised in child health and psychology advise that children's garments should be made of Merona. It is porous and lets the life-giving ultra-violet rays get to the body. . . . It is spun by a secret process. . . . A famous woman doctor said, "Research has proved conclusively that one of the most frequent causes of tantrums in children, little boys especially, is garments which are tight over the head. Tantrums, and that feeling of inferiority resulting from ill-fitting and faded garments, are definite, harmful, psychological disturbances. . . ."

16. There follow ten extracts, from five sources. Sort them into couples.

I. "Now you have cut, you must sew," said Catherine de Medici. The words were used at a more sinister moment than this, but not at a graver. They should be remembered at every hour by statesmen led into taking risks more venturesome and far-reaching than they had at first supposed. As the hazardous result of British initiative—usually and properly the most steadying of all influences—there is increasing disquiet, uncertainty, and apprehension throughout most of the world. The new Parliament at Westminster begins to assemble this week. Those whose ceaseless business it is to watch the map know beyond doubt that the statutory term of that Parliament will be full of crises and changes. The next few years—and probably the next two years—will be of incalculable import in world-affairs.

II. The quiet fields with the sky over them, the quiet remark passed by some unpretentious labourer or peasant: they are not picturesque—no; but some day, when one's temper is quiet, too, these things come home to the spirit, and one finds that they are what one loves. Or after a period of excitement—a hurried day in town, or the ruffling of one's peace by questions of the hour—then the peaceful landscape exerts tranquillising influence, the soft country air refreshes, the gentle platitude uttered in its old-world vernacular recalls one to what is permanently sane.

III. What he could say of the Conference was that every representative there, knowing his difficulties, was determined to come to no arrangement which meant that his difficulties were simply to be treated as though they did not exist, but was determined at the same time to come to an accommodation where accommodation was possible and to bend every ounce of resource that he could in order to get agreement. That was the temper and determination of the Conference.

IV. There is a peace in Sussex that no 'progress' can destroy—it is too deep, too old. Does a new bungalow raise an outcry—there was once an iron foundry where its garden grows. And how slight the sins of a rural council, to that evil administration which led Cade's desperate peasants to rebel. Does the city invade—what of sacking Norman and raping Dane? These things must come and go—the good in this England stays to ripen.

V. The essence of sea force was that the stronger power could take command of the sea; that material preponderance enabled that power (at least until the coming of the submarine) to repel attacks; to protect its bases and its nerve centres. And just because attacks could be repelled with fair certainty by the materially stronger, superiority of strength operated in large part 'silently,' without combat. Decisive material preponderance could not be offset for very long by suddenness of attack from the weaker side. Just as important as these aspects of sea power was the fact that its pressure was gradual, could operate through economic forces, could be begun and discontinued without irreparable damage to the general apparatus of civilised life; could give time for the adjustment of differences. And finally, special advantages attached to a state situated geographically as was Great Britain.

None of these charcteristics applies to the air.

VI. It was never contemplated that War Debts should come before the International Economic Congress. . . . No one ever suggested that. The debt negotiations will have to go on concurrently and on parallel lines. They have got to be dealt with by another body of men. I only throw this out as what I hope is a very commonsense reflection and not as an announcement. Far be it from an announcement, and I hope no one either here or elsewhere will take it as an announcement. I throw it out as a reflection.

VII. One fact, and among the gravest in history, is too well known to every competent authority at home and abroad. The Nation and the Empire have entered on a danger-zone. Mistakes and misfortune's during the last twelve months of Mr.----------'s third Administration have brought us to the weakest position in our annals, both in defence and diplomacy. The danger is that we shall be caught while far less prepared for emergency than even in 1914. Caught before the most vital part of our defences can be sufficiently restored and when our proper diplomatic supports have been wrecked by another experiment in sentimental delusion.

VIII. Now it is that a passionate urge goes on us to savour the "green life" again. An urge that sends us roving on bridlepaths and hillside, thankful with the birds that the drear dark days are safely overpast. And when in that lovely lassitude a day outdoors bestows, our food seems good above all victuals, let us remember that it too is part of Nature's rhythm.

IX. There is no general widespread recognition on the part of the public of the reasons which render the policies they impose upon their governments productive, inevitably, of war. The present risks of war arise largely from the peace policies imposed by the allied nations in 1919. But it is simply not true to say that the nations which made the Treaty of Versailles wanted war. They were weary of war. They would all have signed all the Kellogg Pacts renouncing or outlawing war that any statesman cared to suggest—and the result would have been exactly what it is, for the competition for national power as the only existing means of national defence would have gone on. . . . .

X. . . . Pagham, Bersted, Bognor, Selsea—the delightful south Saxon names call up pictures of a very ample sky spreading over miles of quiet cornfields; and when all is said, it was the wholesome strenuous work there, now in sight of the sea, now in secluded places no idle visitor ever approaches, that was the essential part of the life. Imagine the bracing air, the shade of the hedgerows, the corn steeped in sunlight, the idea of the sea near at hand, and you get the scene of this pastoral: the actors in it are strong men ripe with the harvest weather, whose speech sounds countrified as the fields.

17. Of the two passages that follow, one is a parody but not necessarily of the other, which is genuine. Which do you think is the parody?

> I. Another year has passed, and, once more, filled with the usual regrets that time so quickly slips by and the usual hopes and resolutions that the future may be better than the past, we provide ourselves with new calendars and enter upon a new year.
>
> The twelve-month to which we say good-bye has been one of hard work and struggle for all, and of hardship for too many. But I think we have been sustained in it by the thought that we were pressing along the right road, that we were making real progress, and that here and there glimpses of better things ahead could be discerned.
>
> It is my very earnest hope that in the year 19—— our country as a whole may receive some of the rewards which the efforts of the people deserve, and that all those who may read these lines may enjoy during the year both personal happiness and prosperity. Let us go on facing our tasks determined to finish them.
>
> II. In the course of a New Year's Eve Broadcast, the—, after dealing with the improvement in trade and drop in unemployment, went on to say that the international situation also gave ground for a reasoned optimism. . . . The world was becoming a wiser world. It was becoming a happier world. Above all, it was becoming a more honest world. The keynote of the age was a mistrust of phrases, an almost alarming sincerity in word and deed. Speedier communications, improved housing conditions, facilities for education and travel brought within the reach of the humblest the miracle of wireless which carried culture to the fireside—all were uniting to knit men together and make them one family. "In a long lifetime,"—said in conclusion, "which

has seen many changes, and most of them emphatically for the better, I have never looked forward to a New York with such a sense of opportunities for service opening out on every side, and hands and hearts eager, under Providence, to crisp them."

18. Witching hour—psychological moment—golden opportunity—crass ignorance—bated breath—yeoman service—prepossessing appearance—auspicious occasion—bitter end—sacred edifice—connubial bliss—unbridled luxury—immaculate evening dress—illgotten gains—beetling cliffs—speaking likeness—stony silence—burning topic—howling wilderness.

Have these phrases anything in common? Are there any that you would not use yourself—and why not?

19. How do these examples of propagandist writing respectively work?

I. An Englishman in India is different from an Englishman in England. Here in India, you belong to a system that is vile beyond description. It is possible, therefore, for me to condemn the system in the strongest terms, without considering you to be bad and without imputing bad motives to every Englishman. You are as much slaves of the system as we are. I want you, therefore, to reciprocate and not to impute to me motives which you cannot read in the written word. I give you the whole of my motive when I tell you, that I am impatient to end or mend a system, which has made India subservient to a handful of you, and which has made Englishmen feel secure only in the shadow of the forts and guns that obtrude themselves on one's notice in India. It is a degrading spectacle for you and for us. Our corporate life is based on mutual distrust and fear. . . . But I do ask you to help us in the boycott of foreign cloth. . . . The Lancashire cloth, as English historians have shown, was forced upon India, and her own world-famed manufacturers were deliberately and systematically ruined. India is, therefore, at the mercy not only of Lancashire, but also of Japan, France and America. Just see what this has meant to India. We send out of India every year 60 crores (more or less) of rupees for cloth. We grow enough cotton for our own cloth. Is it not madness to send cotton out of India, and have it manufactured into cloth there and shipped to us? Was it right to reduce India to such a helpless state? A hundred and fifty years ago, we manufactured all our cloth. Our women spun fine yarn in their own cottages, and supplemented the earnings of their husbands. The village weavers wove that yarn. It was an indispensable part of our national economy in a vast agricultural country like ours. It enables us in a most natural manner to utilise our leisure. To-day our women have lost the cunning of their hands, and the enforced idleness of millions has impoverished the land. Many weavers have become sweepers; some have taken to the profession of hired soldiers. Half the race of artistic weavers has died out, and the other half is importing foreign yarn for want of finer handspun yarn. This matter does not admit of any waiting. The interests of the foreign manufacturers and the Indian importers cannot be considered, when the whole nation is starving for want of a large productive occupation ancillary to agriculture.

II. We English are in many ways the most easygoing of people, and once we realised, after the war, that Communism in Russia was no passing phenomenon, our natural characteristic of fair play induced a feeling that we must to some extent keep the ring in order to give Russia an opportunity of trying out her big experiment and of showing the world how it works.

It was, perhaps, the right feeling to have, but it have meant that we have fallen an easy prey to the more obvious kinds of propaganda, and large numbers of our people have shown themselves prepared to take Bolshevist estimates of Russia and its progress at their face value. . . .

It is, after all, the most "infernal cheek" on Russia's part when she advertises her wares in Britain and the British Empire. The system she has devised for herself may be the best she can manage and possibly, in some respects, not ill-suited to a semi-Asiatic people, and if she would only keep to herself we should be quite satisfied to allow her to find her own salvation and her system to find the mellowness of age. Britain and her Dominions are, however, her betters judging by every world standard there is, and it is intolerable that we should for ever be having her unpleasant and vicious system shoved down our throats, covered, perhaps, by a thin coating of sugar. . . .

20. How would you describe the texture of the writing in each of these passages?

I. It is necessary to remind ourselves of this appalling past (the writer refers to foreign policy) because, in spite of criticism, a note of quite unwarranted complacency is to be found amongst members of all political parties in this country to-day. It is at least open to doubt whether any purely political organisation founded upon treaties as Versailles and Trianon can ever hope to succeed. And if it be true that the main causes of our present discontents are economic, then any effective form of international organisation ought surely to be primarily economic in character. I have always believed that the precipitate dissolution of the Supreme Economic Council was one of the most disastrous of the many mistakes made by the Allies after the war. The League ought to have concentrated its main activities upon the economic reconstruction of Europe.

II. Our common troubles should bring us intimately together in a determination to end the influences which, starting with the Great War, in the years of outward prosperity, as well as those of stark misfortune, have been undermining the economic fabric of our civilisation and producing a state of unemployment all over the world which threatens to involve the nations in bankruptcy and ruin.

These are the issues—and nothing less—which face America and ourselves and the other industrial nations as well. The British Government will enter upon these negotiations with a single-minded desire to restore confidence, to remove what barriers exist which do nothing but place obstacles in the way of the international exchange of products, and to establish peace which is an essential confidence of world prosperity and national co-operation.

In that work gladly will we meet America, hopefully will we face the problems, with no idea of dominating here and there, but with the sole idea of reaching an agreement.

21. What is the quality of the argument in each of these quotations?

I. Yet somehow this simple fallacy is little realised. (That the defence of national rights can be secured by preponderant armaments.) It has its roots in what has been named "the unilateral illusion"—the assumption that the other side in the case will not be moved by the same motives as ourselves. When the late Lord Fisher persuaded Great Britain to build an entirely new type of naval monster, the Dreadnought, he was quite sure that its power would represent a net gain to that of the British navy. As a matter of fact it started a competition which immensely weakened the British navy. So now, with the clamour for aeroplanes. There seems to be no realisation that it is a physical impossibility to get security by making aeroplanes a purely national arm, since then the 'defence' of one is secured by depriving the other of it. Still less is there realisation of the fact that in asking for a purely national power which will enable us to dominate another state, we are asking the other to accept a position which we refuse to accept: that we are asking for ourselves a right we refuse to accord to others. Out of that method cannot possibly come either defence or justice.

II. The air threat in the Mediterranean has increased the relative importance of successful diplomacy, for an attack could be so sudden and devastating that the goodwill of other nations towards us seriously matters; faulty policy and clumsy diplomacy might cause untold harm. The situation is the more serious because concerts of powers are to-day more evanescent than ever before. The importance of a friendly France and Italy has been stressed. If the friendship or active support of both France and Italy cannot be secured, there is more need than ever for our statesmen to act with wisdom and farsightedness.

7

English Language Journalism: Dilemma of a Foreign Tongue

A SPEAKER at a public meeting sometime ago, exulted, "The Congress (I) has decimated the Opposition parties." If the Opposition parties had been merely decimated, the Congress (I) victory in 1985 was not particularly spectacular because, according to the speaker, the Opposition parties' strength has been reduced *merely by a tenth.* However, that was not what the speaker meant. As all of us know, the Congress (I) had *routed* the Opposition. Some people think "decimate" means reduction to a tenth of the former figure, or by nine-tenths. That is a disputed interpretation according to *The Concise Oxford Dictionary*.

Sometime ago, a newspaper had the following sentence: "Denouncing President Zia's rule of repression, Mr. Pirzada said that at this moment 600 villages of Sind were under army siege and they were being "decimated" one by one." What did Mr. Pirzada mean? Were the villages of Sind being *reduced by a tenth?*

It is common to see sentences in newspapers and magazines like: "The 846-odd tolls that still exist come under a solitary insepctor, and even this inadequate post has been lying vacant for the last 12 years." Deplorable as this state of affairs may be, how can the writer be sure that the post has been "lying," and not sitting or standing?

When somebody says, "The governor *will be reaching* Guwahati tomorrow morning" all that he means is, "the Governor *will reach* Guwahati tomorrow morning."

Is "everyone" singular or plural? A newspaper had the following sentence in a recent issue: "Everyone wrung their hands."

Excessive use of archaism is as much of an oddity as the hoop and bustle would be for the modern woman. Nevertheless, it is common to see sentences in the popular Press like: "They could not score more than thrice;" "The president inaugurated the conference; thereafter, a number of resolutions were proposed."

"Thrice" is archaic or literary, and *Fowler's Modern English Usage* has the following comment on "thereafter." "Thereafter, thereat, therein, thereof, thereto, therewith are usual in legal documents, but elsewhere serve only to give a touch of formality or archaism to the sentence."

Another tendency is to join two separate words into one. Examples: "Display your product everyday;" "We shall smash this prison someday;" "alongwith;" "youngmen."

A common word commonly misspelt, according to British English is "pedlar." The American spelling, "peddler" is gaining wide currency outside North America. However, instead of the correct word, "pedaller," in a newspaper recently had, "All these players are from Chelsea Pedlars Bicycle Polo Club, London." Were they peddling pedals?

"Proven" is much beloved by the business community. However, *Fowler's Modern English Usage* says: "*Proved,* not *proven,* is the regular past or past participle, the latter being properly from the verb *prove* used in Scotland after it had given way to *prove* in England; compare weave-*woven,* cleave-*cloven.* Except in the phrase *not proven* as a quotation from Scots law, *proven* is better left alone."

Drinking water is often referred to as "potable" water. This is because some people prefer the uncommon to the common, the incomprehensible to the comprehensible. In Germany, it was believed that Lion Feuchtwanger was not a great writer because he was too easy to understand.

"Forego" is used when "forgo" is meant. The past tense of the latter is *forwent*.

A curious sentence I saw recently was: "According to reports from Chandigarh, security forces and terrorists exchanged fire in the vicinity of the Golden Temple this morning."

Did the security forces exchange fire with terriorists in the same way as people exchange gifts? Did they say: "You fire six shots at us and we'll fire an equal number at you?"

Mount Everest is frequently referred to as "the Everest." Here is no need for the definite article because the mount is named after a personality. Had it borne a name like Mount Grand—"grand" is a dictionary word and not a proper noun like "Everest"—it could have been referred to as "the Grand."

Famous foreign names are mispronounced. Pasteur (phonetic spelling: pastor) is pronounced "pastyor;" Buick (phonetic spelling: bewke) "bew-ick"; Renault (phonetic spelling: renno) "renawlt."

Even the common noun "connoisseur" (phonetic spelling: konnoser), is pronounced "konnosyor' or "konnoyser."

Language, written and spoken, is becoming increasingly slipshod, possibly because of the faster tempo of life. Moreover, the growing popularity of the electronic media (radio, television and video) is resulting in correspondingly less time for the printed media (newspapers, magazines, books).

A few days ago, I saw the following sentences in a newspaper: "All last week, evidence of the imminent Puja mounted. . . . Pujas do mean different things to different people and their impending arrival take many incarnations even in the same individual."

Durga Puja and the other Pujas are the happiest events in the Bengali calendar in particular, but the words "imminent" and "impending" in relation to these important festivals are misplaced, because both are associated with danger or unpleasant events. It would be correct to say, "A decision to increase taxes is impending" and "War is imminent."

A recent advertisement announced, "The Peerless opens a branch office at Andaman." But the Andaman and Nicobar Islands are a Union Territory with an area of 8,293 square kilometers, or almost the same size as Lebanon. From north to south, the Islands measure over 600 miles (1,000 km.), and so it is difficult to know at which particular point the Peerless office is situated. Or could it be that it is so large that it stretches across 600 miles (1,000 km.)?

Furthermore, when the complete name, Andaman and Nicobar Islands, is not used, the correct contraction would be "the Andamans."

Although it is not difficult to consult an atlas, the names of countries, cities and other geographical entities are commonly misspelt—specially by people who are expected to the accurate. For instance, the South American country, Colombia, is confused with its namesake in the USA —the university and the cities, Columbia. Another South American country, Ecuador, was spelt Equdor recently in a syndicated cartoon.

Bunting which is widely used in decorations, is often referred to as "buntings." Irrespective of the quantity used, bunting is bunting—singly or collectively. Another word of this category is "toffee." But recently, I saw a sentence, "He'd give us biscuits and toffees." Chocolates may be generously distributed, but only pieces of toffee. Yet another word of this type is "toast." I have three pieces of toast at breakfast—not three toasts. However, a number of toasts were drunk to Mr. Rajiv Gandhi, during his visit to the USA and other foreign countries.

Invitations were recently sent by the US Information Service to a number of people to attend a music concert. And cards, entitling holders to seats in the auditorium, were distributed on a first-come-first-served basis. Many people offer service erroneously on a 'first-come-first-serve" basis.

Even pharmaceutical concerns and medical personnel refer to tincture of iodine as "tincture iodine."

Japanese hostesses, or geisha, are often described by ignorant foreigners as "geishas." A man may be entertained by one geisha (not "geisha girl," which is another illiteracy) or two or more geisha. Another misapprehension is that "geisha" is a synonym for a Japanese prostitute.

We have to strive very hard to succeed in life, but last year we strove (not strived) to little purpose.

Daniel Defoe, father of the English novel and of British journalism, once marked: "If any man were to ask me what I would suppose to be a perfect style of language, I would answer that in which a man speaking to 500 people of all common and various capacities, idiots or lunatics excepted, should be understood by them all."

Nuance and Meaning

Newspapers carry a surfeit of reports such as: "The prime minister is understood to have written to all his ministerial colleagues in the government impressing on them that they ought to attend all important functions in Rashtrapati Bhavan to which they are invited."

One is led to interpret the words, "The prime minister is understood to have written" as: 'I'm not sure of the prime minister's exact action, but from what I can make of it, he has written. . . .' He could even have spoken "to all his ministerial colleagues. . . ." This vagueness results from the "Telegraphese" in the opening words of the quoted sentence. If it was written to convey the intended meaning, the sentence should have been: "It is understood that the prime minister has written. . . ." But if this had not been understood by the special representative in New Delhi of the newspaper concerned, he would not have reported this news. If the special representative was really in such a hurry that he had to resort to a kind of telegraphese, he need merely have written: "The prime minister has asked all his ministerial colleagues (or all members of his government) to make it a point to attend all important functions *at* (not in) Rashtrapati Bhavan to which they are invited."

Another report says: "*The* U.S., British, Italian and Turkish warships in the North Atlantic Treaty Organisation's Meditarranean emergency force will start 'routine' manoeuvres on Thursday, *the NATO Command here announced on Monday*, reports AFP."

"The exercises, which take place twice a year, will focus on naval combat, anti-submarine warfare, communications, navigation and refuelling at sea, *the communique issued by the Chief of Allied Forces Command, Southern Europe, said.*"

What was the necessity of the italicised words? Nobody would have sued the newspaper for failing to prove the authenticity of the news had they been omitted. It would also have been unlikely that anybody would have disbelieved the news.

Another example: "A pair of silver trinkets she wore around her ankles was *reported* missing. Police sources said it was suspected that a gang who snatched ornaments from children was involved in the incident".

There is excessive use of words like "reported" and "sources" in newspaper reports. Sometimes, "sources" is used too often in a report that the reader suspects that the reporter is colluding in concealing the identity of mysterious people.

Here is a typical newspaper report: "Finance has deployed batteries of . . . missiles . . . Defence Ministry sources said, reports AP.

"The missiles were deployed at the beginning of the week . . . , according to the authorised sources at the ministry, who spoke on condition they not be identifed."

"Five batteries of ground-to-air missiles have been deployed . . . . said the ministry sources. Reliable sources in the region said the batteries were deployed . . . ."

"In addition, radar has been reinforced . . . , the ministry sources said."

"The ministry said in a statement that the action was to conform . . . ."

There is no need whatever for burdening the reader with so many details of the source of the reporter's information. Most readers buy a newspaper they thrust and they are interested in straight news—not in the tangled skein of its origin. Moreover, what is the point in including the expression "reliable sources"? No reporter should waste time consulting unreliable sources.

In *Coups and Earthquakes* in which Mort Rosenblum describes how news of the world is reported for the USA, he says: "Readers should beware of unattributed stories with such easily overlooked terms as 'reportedly' and 'believed to be' . . . . The term 'sources', however qualified, is difficult to evaluate . . . Such weak versions as 'informed sources' and 'reliable sources' are banned on some (news) desks.

"In most cases, 'Western diplomats' translates to U.S. Embassy officials . . . . Phrases such as 'Observers said', 'It is generally accepted', and 'Most Indonesians believed' mean the correspondent is giving his own view but must defer to custom by adding some attribution. If a reporter feels obliged to include someone's viewpoint but thinks the speaker is lying, he may write, 'he claimed' instead of the standard, 'he said'. There is no fixed rule. Even the most waffling of code words 'generally reliable sources' - can refer to an ironclad statement by the person closest to the situation".

Reportage should not be transformed into an esoteric argot.

Rosenblum says: "The word 'allegedly' is a hedge designed to relieve the writer from having to make a questionable assertion on his own".

Perhaps for that reason, '*Punch* once featured a cartoon showing a policeman chasing a man escaping after burgling a shop. The policeman shouts: "Stop alleged thief".

Advertisers are going berserk. In a quick glance at this morning's issue of a national daily, I spotted a number of sins of omission and commission.

A three-column ad, 18 cm, deep, announces: "Now on stands!" But a news-stand is not a hat-stand on which headgear can be perched, but a stall at which newspapers are displayed for sale. Further, the adverisement has a line: "The Tantra hyponotism, and hypocricy (sic) at the 'abode' of the 'God'."

A six-column ad, 25 cm. deep, has the sentence: "Today the entity encompasses one of Bombay's largest soft drink manufacturing facility . . . " This is an extremely common error that stems from the misconception that because "one" in singular, "facility", too, should correspond. Actually, what is meant is: there are a number of soft-drink manufacturing facilities in Bombay, but the one advertised is among the largest.

Further, there are these words: " . . . . two hi-profile fruit juice-based beverages".

Presumably, "hi" - is meant to be 'high', in the same way that "hi-fi" is a contraction of "high-fidelity". However, there is hardly any justification for this orthographic liberty.

The Concise Oxford Dictionary defines "beverage" as a formal or jocular way of describing a drinkable liquid. *Fowler's Modern English Usage* includes "beverage" in the sections on Pedantic Humour, Working And Stylish Words.

A three-column ad, 30 cm. deep, has the words: "That no other newspaper quite meets up with *Malayala Manorama's* standards for sheer content and coverage".

"Meet up" is a colloquialism for "happen to meet (person)". What the ad intends to say is that no other newspaper measures up to the standards of *Malayala Manorama*.

A three-column ad, 20.5 cm. deep, asks in large type: Are you planning to buy air conditioner?" The rest of the copy, in the form of a letter from the partner of the concern to the customer, is full of grammatical errors and illiteracies.

A three-column ad, 19.5 cm. deep, on the front page of *The Statesman*, says: "The newspaper that reaches all Malayalee Elites. Incident and accident impartially reported. A name is everybody's eyes and ears. Advertise soon in *Kerala Kaumudi* to *reach* your message to people all over Kerala".

A four-column ad, 25 cm. deep, says: "Luxurious A/C and non A/C rooms and suites in cottages *layed* out in . . . .

". . . . declicacies served in an Airconditioned Restaurant and outdoor patio or in the *quite* of your room . . . . Centrally Air-conditioned and accoustically perfect conference room . . . For the nature lovers, camping facilities with hammock *is* provided . . . "

In a three-column ad, 19.5 cm. deep, "tranquility" is misspelt.

A three-column ad, 21.5 cm. deep, for an ice-cream, exclaims: "LOVE AT FIRST BITE!" However tempting the parody might be, do we take a bite at, or of, ice-cream?

Art and Craft of Book-Reviewing

Book-reviews are an integral part of the personality of a periodical. They endow importance and authority to a publication because they introduce books to their potential readers and buyers. It is through the reviews that readers learn about the publication, the price, the size and availability of books as well as about their subject-matter, style and an informed reader's assessment. The reviews have an educative value in addition to the informative one: Readers who are interested in a wide variety of subjects but do not have leisure to read books on all of them depend upon book-reviews for information about the latest trends, controversies and research in them. Reviews can be entertaining also. Different people prefer different forms of entertainment and there are some who read, for vicarious pleasure, reviews of books as well as those of films, plays, concerts of music and dance, and records. Thus reviews perform important functions such as information, education, and entertainment and help the readers in the selection of books.

Not all the book-reviews are of the same type. Some are brief while some others are quite lengthy; some are descriptive whereas others are evaluative. Book-reviews are usually classified on the following basis:—

(a) size and purpose of the review
(b) nature of the book
(c) nature of the journal

On the basis of the size and purpose of the review, we can recognise three types: *(i)* book notice *(ii)* small review *(iii)* critical review. A brief review which merely tells busy readers that a new book is out along with brief information about what it is like and what it is about, if often referred to as a "book notice." The facts which it reports are the name and identity of the author, the title, the publisher, the number of pages (including a reference to the size) the price, the physical appearance of the book (including a reference to the cover), the general subject and content of the book, and occasionally the author's aim in writing it. This information is usually collected from the title page, the preface (or foreword, introduction etc.) and the blurb on the jacket. It can be supplemented by referring to reference volumes like "who's who" or encyclopaedias. A hasty reading of various chapters will yield information about the writer's style and method of treatment. Outstanding features such as maps, charts, tables, footnotes, exercises and summaries are immediately evident. Thus, the man writing book notices does not necessarily read the book from cover to cover nor does he need to be a scholar in the field. He is basically a reporter who is reporting an event from the world of books. That is why a book notice is often described as a "reporting" or a "reportorial review."

A "small" review in the tripartite classification is longer than a book notice but not as long as a critical review. It consists of about five to eight paragraphs and besides the factual information, contains and reviewer's personal impression of the book. It is meant to guide readers in the selection of books. It can be normally divided into three parts; *(i)* factual information and classification of the book *(ii)* objective summary and *(iii)* the reviewer's personal impression and his assessment. The classification of the book is a preliminary means of telling the reader the content purpose of the book. A reader interested in books on stamp-collecting would thank a reviewer for informing him at the outset that a certain book is a novel and not a book for stamp collectors.

The objective summary forms the second important division of the review. In it the reviewer presents his reader with a clear idea not only of the content of the book, but also of the relative importance attached by the original author of each part of the book. A misplaced emphasis distorts the original picture and fails to preserve the relative values of the various incidents in the book.

Moreover, although this division of the review is termed "summary," it does not attempt to tell everything. It must adhere to the confines of time and space. In dealing with books which depend for their interest on the element of suspense, a reviewer should not give the plot away. Thus the summary contains matter which is important in itself or which symbolizes larger meanings in spite of appearing unimportant superficially.

Although the main purpose of a review is to inform and to report, most reviews contain, directly or indirectly, the reviewer's personal impression or assessment of the book. Quite often, the assessment is contained within the summary in a more or less subtle manner. The reviewer usually uses value-loaded objectives. For example:

> *This valuable sketch of a man, known for his foresight and courage. . . .*
> *The author deftly recreates the charm of the old world. . . .*
> *In one of the most engrossing passages of the book. . . .*

Evaluation of the book is often offered at the end of the review. It is, of course, certain that no reviewer should attempt to criticise or comment unless he has a broad knowledge of the subject matter of the book. We shall go into the details of evaluation while discussing the critical review. However, it is necessary to point out at this stage, that the reviewer should judge the book as a whole. It is unfair to attack parts without presenting a clear idea of their relation to the entire work. One more point needs to be emphasised; if the reviewer does not wish to criticise the book thoroughly and fairly, it is useless to dole out meaningless praise.

A critical review is longer than the two types of review discussed so far, the length depending on the importance of the book and the space available for the review in the publication. It differs from the other types in its purpose too. It aims not only at informing and guiding the reader but also educating him, at developing and nurturing his taste and at giving him perspective on the subject and the author. It is necessarily a judgment by one who knows the subject at very close quarters. It must supply the basic factual information but must stand by itself on the merits of the assessment made by a specialist or at least a knowledgeable critic. It analyses every aspect of the book carefully: the motivation of the author, his ability to expound a philosophy or an idea, and his style.

It is necessary to emphasise the importance of the word "critical" in our term "critical review." Criticism is a process of evaluation, of analysing a work in order to determine its worth. It is neither a catalogue of shortcomings nor an inventory of praise; it consists in weighing the "good" against the "bad," and from the result arriving at an estimate of worth. Personal likes and dislikes are of great importance to each one of us but they are of little interest or value to others unless we are experts or quite famous people. Therefore, we must set up, in order to evaluate effectively, some measuring standards or objective testing devices outside ourselves. Our first concern must be: does the book do what it is supposed to do? The characteristics essential to the general type will emerge from this fundamental question and form the bases of comparison by which the book should be judged.

The standards by which a reviewer evaluates a book, must themselves meet four tests:

1. The standards must belong to the same class or type as the book. Historical novels are often deprecated (by

historians mostly) as inacurate history; however, the authors were writing not history but literature.

2. The standards must be fair. A book intended to be used as a text book in schools should not be evaluated in relation to original research works on the subject.
3. The standards must be as specific and restricted as possible.
4. The standards must be relatively stable. In other words passing fads must not be mistaken for permanent qualities.

Heads and Headings

In the first week of May there was a front-page item in a national newspaper about a violent Naxalite intrusion into the house of the former Chief of Air Staff, Air Chief Marshal I.H. Latif, located in a village some 50 km from the Andhra Pradesh capital Hyderabad. It was a four-column item on the right side in the middle of the page and it gave in graphic detail how gun-toting Naxalites had entered the house and how they made away with the ex-Air Chief's pistol and binoculars. He was interviewed about the incident and was quoted at some length in the report. The next day, however, another national daily carried the same item, but identifying the affected ex-Air Chief as Antony de La Fontaine, and not as I. H. Latif. Which of the two versions was correct? It was the second that was correct, for that same day, the first paper which had front-paged the item had an eight-line item of regret, simply headed "Correction", in which it said that the ex-Air Chief whose house was intruded into was that of de La Fontaine and not of I.H. Latif.

How could that newspaper's correspondent have made that mistake about identity? One went back of the original news report to read it again and found that it did give the unequivocal impression that the correspondent had met Air Chief Marshal Latif and spoken to him: ". . . Air Marshal Latif told . . . . (this) reporter at his house situated about 100 yards from the Brahmanapally railway station near Toopran . . . ." Did the correspondent meet him at all? If he did, should he not have first made sure whom he was talking to?

When one starts as a reporter, the first thing that one is told is to clearly ascertain the identity of the person involved—where possible, by getting hold of his or her calling card. For, even after hearing a name right, one can sometimes go wrong while writing it: there was an instance in the early 1960s when every Delhi newspaper ran a "story" for two or three days consecutively about a man called Cochrane who had overstayed his visa and was, therefore, jailed: his name, it turned out, was Corcoran, not Cochrane.

Making absolutely sure about the What, Where, When, Why and How of a story is essential not just for the cub reporter but for every reporter, and throughout his career. And this is not really difficult. There, admittedly, is sometimes the risk of looking silly if one were to ask for supposedly elementary details like name and correct spelling, but is it not better to look temporarily silly than be permanently, and laughably, wrong in print?

Amazingly, in this particular case, even an Andhra Pradesh newspaper slipped up. Due amends were made the next day, but how many who read the prominently displayed first report would have also read the clearly less eye-catching correction? And that raises an important question: should not corrections be far more detailed and better displayed than they tend to be at present?

There have lately been some other notable slip-ups also.

In headings, for instance.

"House fails to discuss people's problems" is how one Andhra Pradesh daily headed its story on the budget session of the State Assembly. Should "House" actually not have been "Assembly", so as to avoid any confusion? Evidently, in the effort to fit the heading into the available space, the word that is shorter was preferred but this was done at the cost of clarity. These days "House" cannot necessarily be assumed as meaning Assembly.

In Delhi the word "House" is often used in reports about Parliament proceedings with no clue whatever to whether the Rajya Sabha or the Lok Sabha is referred to. It would not be a bad idea to mention the particular House specifically in the opening paragraph of the report, and also in the heading if a reference to the House is felt necessary.

In that same painfully vague category belongs this one: "Govt pursuing same policies: EMS". This is the heading given for a longish three-column spread in a national newspaper on the accusation by the CPI(M) General Secretary E.M.S. Namboodiripad that the National Front government is pursuing the "discredited" economic policies of the previous government, but does one get that meaning from the heading? Should it not have been longer for the sake of clarity? In any case, the word "same" is confusingly, even irritatingly, vague.

"Ryzkhov escapes" read a more recent heading in the same daily. A tantalising heading. Was he, by any chance, in custody and had he escaped from custody, one immediately wondered, not having followed Russian affairs closely. The actual fact, however, was something of a let-down; he had only escaped unhurt when his car was involved in a collision. Should not the heading have been clear, and certainly not misleading?

To that same category of headings written apparently in a hurry belongs this one from a Delhi daily in early May: "Visa rules for ethnic Indians relaxed". That adjective "ethnic" is obviously called for in view of the need to distinguish people of Indian origin from West Indies and such others—the item was one emanating from London—but must we in this country really use it for ourselves? Would not "Visa rules for Indians relaxed" have been sufficient? Actually, the word "ethnic" has turned into yet another mindless buzz word and it seems advisable to avoid it.

May was when the Shankaracharya of Dwaraka Peeth was arrested because of his threat to go ahead with the Shilanyas in the Ram Janma Bhoomi and practically every newspaper kept describing him as "seer" in headings for items relating to him: "RS furore over Dwarka seer arrest," "CM warns seer's followers", "Fallout of seer's arrest, "Arrest of seer to affect BJP-JD ties", and so on. The Acharya is probably a seer, but his position, which is what is sought to be referred to in the headings, is that of a head of a Hindu peeth or mutt. Can the word "seer" be used as a synonym for that position? A few newspapers, especially those from the south where they obviously know the precise position of a Shankaracharya, kept referring to him in their headings as Acharya or, for greater clarity, Dwaraka Acharya. This is, admittedly, a little long but it seems clearly preferable to a word that could be seen as grossly misleading.

One of the headings mentioned above—"Arrest of seer to affect BJP-JD ties"—merits attention from another perspective also: its use of "to". What is sought to be conveyed is that the arrest is likely to affect BJP-JD relations, but as it is worded, the heading could be taken by the uncharitable to mean that the arrest was intended to affect those relations, or, to read it less uncharitably, that such effect on the relations between the two parties will be the certain consequence. All because of the use of the word "to", which could easily have been replaced by "could".

"Cyclone to skip TN" read another heading in a Delhi daily in May. The irreverent could well ask whether that cyclone had, by any chance, handed its itinerary to the newspapers: for that is the impact the heading has. What is sought to be conveyed is, of course, that the cyclone is likely to bypass Tamil Nadu.

Not many years ago there used to be a similar irritating use of the preposition "for"—as in "Mr X for London", for instance. Mr X was merely proceeding to London, whereas the heading could mean anything from that he was being assigned to go there to that he was being dumped there. Mercifully, one does not see such usage any more.

Incidentally, how do you like abbreviations like TN (for Tamil Nadu) and RS (for Rajya Sabha) in headings? Should these not be spelt out for the benefit of the average reader?

There is, then, the use of words like "uproar" and "furore" to describe the almost daily noisy scenes in the two Houses of Parliament and in most State Assemblies: should there not be some care in the choice of words to describe such scenes, so as to reflect the precise nature and dimension of the scenes? Sometimes, the word used in the text of the report is sharply divergent from what is found in the heading: one report in a national newspaper, on the noisy scenes in a State Assembly, started off by describing them as "pandemonium" but the heading had the word "frore". Was what happened in the Assembly a mere furore, which denotes general commotion or uproar, or was it a more serious pandemonium, which is wild uproar or noise or chaos (and denotes also any place characterised by great confusion, uproar and noise)?

There is a host of words, each with its own particular shade of meaning, besides "furore" and "uproar", which have almost identical meaning, and "pandemonium", for describing the kind of scenes witnessed in our Parliament and State legislatures day after day; Bedlam, convulsion, disturbance, fracas, hell-broke-loose, hubbub, hullabaloo, melee, racket, rough weather, row, ructions, rumpus, squall, storm, tempest, trouble, tumult, turmoil, vociferation. The Thesaurus on your desk is certain to yield even more words to suit your precise purpose. Why not select the right word from these to put across the exact nature of the scenes witnessed in a House of Parliament or of a State Legislature?

A handy copy of Thesaurus is a must for every journalist, so as to be able to achieve the maximum possible precision, whether in writing headings or in preparing news reports.

So is a good dictionary, preferably the most recent one, a must. Elementary, did you say? Agreed, but, clearly, quite a few do not have a readily available dictionary, or are have a readily available dictionary, or are not in the habit of looking it up when in doubt; how else do you explain a heading like "Forgerer, cheat held in Sadar Bazar" in the Delhi edition of a national daily not long ago?

If such nonchallant use of words assumed to be correct is one extreme in this repect, the other extreme is the coining, by the fastidious, of ever newer words: such as, for instance, "oneuppersonship" (single word with no hyphen) in a recent article on Ms Benazir Bhutto in a national daily. A replacement for one-up-man-ship, this is obviously part of the continuing effort to rid the English language of words that even remotely smack of male chauvinism, but does it sound right?

While on the subject, one might refer to similar other replacements also: "Presspersons", for instance. What is wrong with "reporters" and "correspondents"? Can they be accused of being male chauvinist words? In any case, a replacement should not jar on the ear, as "Presspersons" and "one-up-personship" most certainly do. Euphony, or agreeable sound especially in the phonetic quality of words, is among the three criteria laid down by Somerset Maugham for good writing, and it is valid particularly today. The other two criteria are: simplicity, clarity.

Dictionary Use

What distinguishes humans from other living creatures is the faculty of speech. And what distinguishes more advanced people from their less advanced brothers is the wealth of vocabulary.

As long back as 2,500 years ago, Confucius was so highly conscious of the importance of correct speech that he wrote a long treatise, in which he warned his disciples tht if they were careless in their use of words, as also about spelling and punctuation, serious misunderstandings could arise, resulting in huge commercial losses and even wars.

But, regrettably, in this age of vaunted technological advancement, we pay scant attention to words—their spelling, precise meaning and pronunciation—and to articulation, intonation, accent and delivery. As a result, although we enjoy the gift of speech, we speak and write incomprehensibly. And if we fail to be comprehensible, the faculty of speech becomes meaningless.

To standardise and promote the development of a language, we have the facility of dictionaries. Happily, a distinctive characteristic of the English language is its seemingly unlimited flexibility and propensity for adaptability. Almost every word can be spelt and pronounced in different ways. Syntax and grammar, too, are free from rigidity, enabling almost every rule to have a number of exceptions. And as an instance of the adaptability of the English language, it might be mentioned that it was incorporated at least 4,000 words from Indian languages. In consequence, English is indeed "a language for all seasons" and means all things to all people. When Mahatma Gandhi was asked why he was so fanatically opposed to English, and thought it imperative to adopt Hindi as the national language, he replied with his characteristic guilelessness: "What makes English so dangerous is that it's so very seductive".

A further apparent disadvantage is that nobody can give a final ruling on disputed meanings, spelling and pronunciation of words on the lines of the Academie Francaise. In France, the Academie Francaise comprises 40 of the country's most distinguished scholars and constitutes a "tribunal on language" against whose rulings there can be no appeal. For that reason, the Academie's members are known as "the Forty Immortals".

But its seeming shortcomings merely serve to enhance the charms of the English language and to make it the piquant dish it is. Despite the absence of a counterpart of the Academie Francaise, it is possible to say who speaks well and who doesn't, merely from the accent and choice of words. In other words, the language has become the root of a "caste system", so much so that, some years ago, the Honourable Miss Nancy Mitford wrote a book, dividing words into "U" and "Non-U" categories. "U" words were those used by the "upper" classes, and "Non-U" words, those used by the commonalty. The ancient universities of Oxford and Cambridge are the traditional seats of English (spoken and written) at its best, but, in recent years, the astounding popularity of media such as the cinema and broadcasting have made a considerable contribution to the standardisation of the English language, beyond the confines of universities, and to the reduction of the extent of country dialects and accents.

In the light of this background, the importance of a dictionary is manifest.

Every enlightened household and every respectable office should possess a dictionary, and one that is up-to-date and authentic. But regrettably, in neither place is so indispensable a utility thought necessary.

When we hear or read a new word, we should obviously ascertain its exact meaning from a dictionary. If we fail to do so, we shall remain ignorant of its usage, or use it wrongly by associating it with the context in which we heard it, resulting in misinterpretation. Many people tend to take words for granted and tag on their own personal meanings to them. Indeed, some of us are brazen enough to seize upon a new word, which captures our fancy merely by its sound, or because it is in vogue, and use it in a sense diametrically opposite to what it actually means. Nothing could be more ludicrous and those guilty of this practice expose themselves to the scorn to which they should be deservedly subjected. We run a parallel risk if we ignore a new word, because as a result of that course, we limit our vocabulary.

A dictionary has a triple utility—it helps us to know the meaning of words new to us; it tells us how a particular word should be pronounced; and it is a faithful guide for spelling as well. Should we persist in going through life as blatant malapropists, and violators of pronunciation and spelling, we not only evoke the contempt of the *literati*, but are guilty of the far more pernicious offence of debasing language.

Another point that we commonly overlook is that language keeps changing in fashion in the same way as many other things, such as clothes and coiffures, keep doing so. For that reason, modern English is far removed from its Shakespearian variety, and Chaucer's language is totally foreign and incomprehensible to most of us. Being particularly vigorous and flexible, English perhaps keeps changing faster than most other languages. Words keep acquiring newer and wider connotation and alter in pronunciation and spelling too. Like debased coins and soiled currency notes, words too are withdrawn from circulation altogether when they outgrow their purpose and period. Therefore, we cannot claim to be modern and abreast of the English language if we sprinkle our vocabulary liberally with archaic, or obsolete, words.

For all these reasons, a good dictionary is a prime necessity. But astonishingly, many of the largest business houses and chambers of commerce in the country do not think it necessary to invest in one, and blithely continue in their vandalistic course of denuding and eroding the English language. Some otherwise impressively equipped offices do boast dictionaries, but usually the vintage, dog-eared, tattered relics of a bygone age. To consult an out-of-date dictionary is more futile than to go by an old edition of a telephone directory.

Still more lamentable is the arrogance of the opinionated scholar who considers it derogatory ever to consult a dictionary, in the belief that he knows all that is to be known and the dictionary cannot teach him anything new. Nothing could be more humiliating for him than to be caught looking at a dictionary. That would be like a judge caught stealing.

Unfortunately, many commercial and other executives, who dictate letters and notes to their stenographers, do not have the time or inclination to check the spelling of tricky words with the help of a dictionary, but prefer to leave the amanuensis to do so. In fact, some overworked tycoons, instead of consulting a dictionary when they are uncertain of spelling, find it easier to consult their secretaries, who are expected to be omniscient. As a result, wrong spelling is put into circulation and sometimes becomes entrenched.

When people are not accustomed to consulting a dictionary whenever they are in doubt over spelling, they are not aware of the occasional changes in it. In consequence, many obsolete or discareded forms are still used—to the amusement and dismay of purists.

In a free world of free enterprise, it is not astonishing that there should be various dictionaries, published under different names, by sundry publishers. Here is a further pitfall for the unwary: which dictionary is the most authentic and reliable that he or she should buy?

Lexicography, though a comparatively new science, is becoming increasingly developed and is a far cry from Dr. Johnson's days, when the first English dictionary was compiled and stirred a hornets' nest because of its acutely slanted definitions.

According to recognised authorities on the English language, the best dictionaries are those published by Oxford University Press, whose *Oxford English Dictionary,* or what is generally known by its abbreviated name of OED, is widely regarded as the Bible of the English language. Comprising 13 massive volumes with a total of about 16,600 pages, the OED costs about Rs. 7,600. A less exhaustive version, *The Shorter Oxford Dictionary,* which is in two volumes and illustrated, costs Rs. 600. But for the general public there are *The Concise Oxford Dictionary,* famous all over the world by its abbreviated name of COD, the seventh edition of which costs Rs. 62.50; *The Pocket Oxford Dictionary,* costing Rs. 37.50; and *The Little Oxford Dictionary,* costing Rs. 20, which is ideal for school children and office secretaries and stenographers. For the adult public, such as men and women in the professions executives, government officers, and others who wish to conform to standard usage of English, *The Concise Oxford Dictionary,* is unsurpassed as valuable guide and friend. Its rulings are accepted as pronouncements of a Supreme Court and it has established itself over the past 60-odd years as a standard work of reference.

One reason for the pre-eminence of the Oxford series of dictionaries is that their original editions were edited by the brothers H. W. Fowler and F. G. Fowler, both of whom were virtual Popes of the English language. *Fowler's Modern English Usage* is still regarded as an indispensable companion to the dictionary by the learned.

Of course, people in technical professions must consult their respective specialised dictionaries in addition. For engineers, lawyers and medical personnel in particular, there are elaborate, authentic, technical dictionaries.

Those who favour *Webster's Dictionary* may not be aware that it is an American publication, and therfore pertains to American usage of English in particular. And as is well known American idiom, orthography, pronunciation and accent are markedly different from their counterparts in the U.K. Moreover, modern American coinages and slang in particular, are almost incomprehensible in other parts of the world. Some of the more jingoistic Americans go so far as to declare proudly that they do not speak English but American.

Regional variations are understandable and merely contribute to the overall wealth of so widely spoken a language as English.

But in the interest of accuracy, and to safeguard against the danger of polluting language, let us strive to cultivate the habit of consulting a dictionary as often as we can.

Handling Crime

Reporting on terrorism, war, banditry and smuggling are challenging and exacting professional tasks, but in India this aspect of reporting is treated as a part of routine reporting on politics or crime by the generalist reporters. Reporting on terrorism in particular is not only amateurish or timid but erroneous. We have been blowing the wrong trumpets for we have not been able to treat terrorism as a class of saboteur war perpetuated by foreign trained, armed and controlled militants and ultras planted in sensitive areas, killing innocent or hitlisted people at the behest of political mentors across the border or operating in foreign lands to create a situation of destabilisation in India.

Modern reporting is becoming a specialist's job requiring a research based or investigative approach. But in our country, reporting or writing on terrorism is done by the second line of journalists. The reported stories, therefore, either smack of "the government says so" versions of the stray incidents or encounter scores or of subjective political coverage of incidents as some so-called liberal or progressive journalists or politicians see it is a part of the "Azadi" movement in a particular region or by a particular community. No wonder that the reporting is unconvincing and makes confusion worse confounded. No report in this category has won any media or professional award. These coverages lack the thrill or glamour of frontline war reporting. They are missing the sizzling exposures of investigative reporting. Such coverages are devoid of scintillating analyses of the trends or phenomena. There are no enlightening backgrounders or field-based or feedback surveys. Most of the big newspapers and current affairs magazines carry these reports as part of their sale promotion activities. Small and medium newspapers in the terrorist infested areas follow the game of survival by playing to the tune of the militants and ultras.

If some of the coverage of the liberal-minded or secularly oriented reporters was to be taken seriously, most of the territories of our border areas would have been packed off long ago by the secessionists. If their pleadings for direct talks with militants had been heeded continuously, the rule of the jungle would have engulfed a much larger area and elections would have been fought not on the basis of electioneering campaigns but at the point of gun. However, at times, influenced by these penpushers or their corresponding counterparts in politics, the government has loosened the noose round the militants and in that process lost the gains made by the security forces. And then, beguiled again, it had to resort to strong arm measures to ensure national security and save the lives and property of innocent people.

It is true that a purely law and order approach is not enough for tackling the problems of political extremists, ethnic autonomists or fundamentalists. That to promote popularly inspired mainstreaming, democratic processes have to be released in the economic, political, social and communication spheres. But the confusion in reporting as also in political tackling of the problem of terriorism arises on two grounds. First, we try to identify the enemy sponsored, aided and armed militants with the normal politically motivated extremists and, second, in mixing up the sphere of sovereignty with that of policies. The first type of confusion is now accepted by most journalists and politicians. The second type is not understood yet because we fail to distinguish the girdle of engulfing sovereignty from other spheres of encircled politics, economics, culture, religion, etc. in our polity.

The Constitution makes this distinction clear by identifying the area of national sovereignty, its emblems, its institutions and its sentinels, and provides for the legal and emotional aids and sanctions to sustain it, to maintain its aura, its capacity and power to strike back at the enemy inside and outside the country. The written Constitution, the National Flag, the National Song, the Parliament, the Union Cabinet, the Supreme Court and other national institutions are its visible symbols. The defence and security forces and the Supreme Court act as its enforcing agencies. The Fundamental Duties enjoin obligations on all citizens. In the sphere of soverignty, no government or agency can diffuse or barter it away. The national integrity, the national identity and the prestige and awe of the country depend on the viability of its sovereign power, on its might, on the support it commands from the defence forces, on the rallying emotional and communication aid that the media and the people offer as also on the potentiality of the state to punish or strike back at enemy agents, terrorists, and secessionists within and the extent to which it can protect the lives and property of the people from the attacks of the terrorists.

In this sphere, the polity is called the state. In other spheres of politics, economic, culture and religion, the polity is legally and politically known as the government which in its working is governed by a democratic or judicial process where flexibility, compromises, consensus, interaction, discussions or dialogues are accepted as the bases of taking decisions. In this category fall the issue of establishing normalcy with local people. But the sovereignty of the state is not negotiable or annullable, whether in foreign or demestic affairs. Any perceptible weakness in this respect will make the polity wither away. Surrender to terrorism is one such suicidal step.

This lack of clarity is one reason for utter confusion in our approach to the problem of foreign inspired terrorism in the current affairs, journalism as also in political dealing of the issue.

The second flaw is in the lack of will to resort to persuasive and blitz counter education through the media and the party and legislative forums. Timidity, callousness and absence of clear cut national policies or consensus decisions explain inaction in this respect. As a part of its national obligation the Indian media should give searching analyses of the dynamics, objectives and lure of terrorism confessions of some anarchists, the feedback of the people on the menace of terrorism, the success stories of how anarchism has been successfully combated in some other countries.

The Pakistani and militant propaganda is on. It is impactful and deeply penetrating at the grassroots level. Why can our media not rebut this? By exposing the inviability of the autonomy demand and the geo-political risks to which small units will be exposed, especially to the strangulating tentacles of Pakistan itself, the sinister design of the enemy propaganda can be exposed. Why can't the realities and myths of Pakistani propaganda be exploded? These are hundred eye opening reasons which can put sense into the minds of even fundamentalistically influenced people. Economically, it can be shown to the people what they are losing every day in terms of income and economic, educational and agricultural losses due to the foreign sponsored terrorists.

Enemy and fundamentalist propaganda may sway the people for sometime but their minds can be demagnetised through well planned counter publicity or education. We have permitted for long the enemy propaganda, infiltration of terrorists and given almost a free hand to them. Counter measures have to be taken on a war footing to stem the rot. Will our journalists, reporters, writers and politicians not rise to the occasion? Will our peace brigades not march into these terrorists and operate under the protective canopy of the security forces? Will our spiritual and religious leaders not lend their helping hands in this Kurukshetra war between the forces of evil and good? Mere sabre rattling or rhetoric will not do.

8

Respecting the Reader: Science Writer's Signposts

WHEN your co-authors and friends have read the second draft, think about their suggestions carefully and objectively. Read the draft critically yourself, and make any changes that you decide are needed. Before giving the article to a senior colleague or the head of your department for formal and detailed criticism, polish it into its near-final state. You will have to rewrite the title and abstract, list the index (or key) terms, check every part of the paper to ensure that it complies with the journal's Instructions to Authors, and construct the reference list in correct form.

REWRITING THE TITLE AND ABSTRACT

You wrote the *working* title and abstract for yourself, as guides defining and limiting what you were going to write about (p. 8)*. Now write a title and abstract for publication, bearing in mind that the purpose of the published title is to bring the paper to the attention of the people who ought to see it, and that the purpose of the published abstract is to tell them succinctly what it is about and why it will interest them.

---

* Page no. references in parentheses are to the publication *Authors and Editors Guide*, Gee Publications, London, 1982.

The Final Title

Make the title concise, accurate and informative. The object is to give the reader as much specific and intelligible information as you can in as few words as possible. 'Pollen morphology of *Saxifraga* hybrid *S. nathorstii* and its parents' has 67 characters (including spaces) and contains as much information as 'Notes on the pollen morphology of *Saxifraga* × *nathorstii* and its putative parents *S. aizoides* and *S. oppositifolia* (Saxifragaceae)', which has 130 characters. The journal's Instructions to Authors may specify a permitted or preferred length, although this will obviously vary with subject matter. If a title can be kept below 12 words and 100 characters (including spaces), so much the better. Readers find titles longer than this difficult to grasp when they are scanning a large number of them.

Many information-retrieval systems used by research workers now depend heavily on indexing by means of automated, computerized selection of words from the author's title. The trivial words ('of', 'the', 'on') are ignored; the non-trivial words in the title, and only these, are used for the indexing. In constructing your title, and only these, are used for the indexing. In constructing your title, try to choose the words you would think of if you were looking for the paper in a subject index. 'Pollen' and *Saxifraga*' are the two essential search words in the title quoted in the previous paragraph. A title must be neither too general nor too vague. 'Amino-acid composition' will not do, nor will 'Proteins in Plants'. A title such as 'Amino-acid composition of proteins of the geranium leaf: changes with age and browning' (13 words and 86 characters) tells the reader much more clearly what to expect. If possible, begin with a significant word or phrase, specify the experimental material, indicate what has been measured, and hint at the significance of the work.

In your efforts to be informative, do not inflate the title into a short abstract—if you keep it to less than 100 characters you will avoid that danger. Keep the title short neither by using abbreviations (which are highly undesirable in titles) nor by accumulating modifiers until all sense is obscured (pp.41-42), but by cutting out meaningless phrases such as 'Observations on. . . .', 'A study of. . . .' 'An approach to . . .', and similar expressions.

Give each paper you write a different title: that is, do not publish a series of numbered papers all with the same general title unless this is the only way to deal with a particular set of investigations. If it is important to link papers to previous papers in a series, you can do this by means of a footnote or by giving an appropriate reference in the first paragraph of the introduction.

Provide a short title—usually 45 to 60 characters—if the journal asks for one. This will usually be printed as a 'running head' at the top of the journal's right-hand pages.

The Final Abstract

Like the title, the abstract must convey as much information as possible when reprinted by an abstract journal or distributed by an information-retrieval service.

Abstracts may be classified as informative, indicative, or a mixture of informative and indicative (American National Standards Institute 1971). Write *informative abstracts* wherever possible: they are best for papers describing original research. They consist of succinct factual statements such as:

> A modified acetylene reduction technique was used for measuring microbial nitrogen fixation in four soil types in three areas of Europe. Maximum findings (µg/h in 1 g of soil) were: calcareous soil, Sweden 1.3-2.7; lime and loess, Germany, 0.07-1.6; mull. Andorra, 0. No fixation was registered in subsurface samples. Fixation in darkness, possibly bacterial, was 2-14% of values observed in the light.

Avoid the phrase 'X is discussed' in an informative abstract, for it is often a sign that the author is too lazy to sort out his conclusions (if any).

Indicative (descriptive) abstracts should be used only for reviews and similar papers. They contain general statements about the subjects dealt with in the article, *i.e.* its scope and coverage. Here is an example of an indicative abstract mistakenly written for a factual paper. Compare its information content with that 'of the abstract above:

> A method for determining the potential of microbial nitrogen fixation in soils under aerobic conditions is described. Four different soil types were studied: loess, lime, mull and calcareous. The soil samples were collected in three different areas of Europe.

Begin the abstract by stating the category (original article, case history, etc.) to which the paper belongs, if this is not obvious from the title. Describe the purpose of the investigation being reported but do not waste precious words by repeating or paraphrasing the title, since the abstract is always read in conjunction with the title. Indicate the methods used and summarize the results and conclusions. (Some journals prefer to have the most important result and conclusions first, then the supporting details, other findings, and finally methods.)

Keep to about 250 words for an article of 2000-5000 words and about 100 words for a short communication, according to the journal's requirements. Try to include all the basic information and to emphasize the different points in proportion to the emphasis they receive in the paper. Be brief, but state the purpose of the paper and the conclusions so that readers can immediately grasp the significance of your work. Write simply, as if you were describing the work for non-specialists. Do not add statements not made in the article itself. Do not keep rigidly to a recommended length if the subject matter demands a longer abstract for intelligible treatment.

The abstract should usually be compressed into a single paragraph, but split it into more if this is clearer for the reader. Some journals ask for numbered paragraphs or sentences in the abstract. Write complete, connected sentences and use the third person ('so-and-so was measured', not 'we measured so-and-so') unless this leads to clumsy or ambiguous constructions. This use of the third person, in contrast to the preferred use of the first person in the text, allows the abstract to be reproduced unchanged in secondary (abstract) journals. Avoid unfamiliar terms, acronyms and abbreviations—or, if you must use them, define them at first mention. Do not write footnotes to abstracts. Do not quote references to other work—or if you do, insert full bibliographical details in the abstract itself. Avoid tables, diagrams, equations and structural formulae if at all possible.

SELECTING INDEX TERMS

Many journals ask authors to supply about 10 index terms (key words or phrases; descriptors), suitable for use in the journal's subject indeed and in information-retrieval systems. In some journals, the index terms are *added* to the title in order to 'enrich' it and draw readers' attention to topics dealt with in the paper but not indicated in the title. In other journals, the index terms include words selected from the title. Find out which system is used by the target journal before you make your choice. Some journals specify that index terms are to be selected from a published thesaurus (for example, the Medical Subject Headings that are used in *Index Medicus*.)

ASSEMBLING THE COMPLETE MANUSCRIPT

When you have written the final title and abstract and listed the index terms, check that all the parts of the paper are in the form specified in the journal's Instructions to Authors. Unless otherwise stated, items (1) to (9) described below should each start on a new page, as should the legends for the illustrations.

(1) *Title Page*

On the title page put the title you have just written and the by-line—that is, the names of the authors (see p.7) and the name and address of the institution (or institutions) where the work was done. Ask your co-authors exactly how they like their names to be written. Some people always write out one given name; others may leave out some initials. Decide early in your publishing career how you will write your own name for by-lines, and write it that way consistently to avoid confusion.

In writing the by-line, copy the style in the journal. Indicate any changes of address that have taken place since the work was done. Do not anglicize addresses in the by-line if your department or institution usually prints its address in a language other than English. If several authors from several institutions contributed to the paper, list them in such a way that it is clear who works where.

Add the name and the postal address of the author to whom correspondence (including proofs and requests for reprints) should go, unless the by-line shows this unambiguously.

(2) *Abstract*

Place the abstract on a separate page, after the title page, unless the journal gives other instructions. Comply with the journal's instructions on the lay-out of the abstract, and provide bibliographic and other information (title of paper, authors' names and addresses, name of journal) in the form stipulated. Leave room for the volume number, page numbers and date of publication to be inserted later.

Index Terms

Put the index terms on the same page as either the title or the abstract, as specified by the journal.

(3) *Abbreviations*

List the abbreviations and their definitions on a separate page, after the abstract, if the journal asks for such a list. Keep this list short, and make sure that the abbreviations are acceptable (see p. 38 and Appendixes 2-4). List also any special symbols used, if the journal asks for these.

(4) *Text*

See that all the pages of text are present and correctly numbered in the top right-hand corner. Put the first author's name, or the short title of the paper if the journal requires this, at the top left of every page. Check the text again to ensure that spelling, symbols and abbreviations are consistent and correct throughout. If you numbered the paragraphs in the draft, remove the numbers now unless the journal uses them; check the headings and subheadings for usefulness and consistency. Make sure that you have referred to every figure and table at least once in the text, and indicated their approximate position by a circled note in the margin—'(Fig. 3 near here)'. Such notes are transferred to the margins of the galley proofs by the printer's reader; they enable the person who is making up the journal pages to lay them out most conveniently for the reader. Where you refer to other parts of the paper, write 'see Methods section' (for example) rather than 'see p. 10'.

In the text, use symbols for units of measure (*e.g.* A for ampere) whenever a number precedes them, but spell out the name of a unit if the number is spelt out, for example at the beginning of a sentence. The custom of writing out numbers at the beginning of a sentence often leads to cumbersome phrases ('Eight microlitres per square centimetre') and some publishers have now abandoned it; if your journal retains this tradition, try recasting the sentence so that the phrase '8 μl/cm^2' falls somewhere in the middle. Avoid the double solidus because of its ambiguity: not W/m/K but W/(m K) or W m^{-1} K^{-1}. Use the decimal system for concentrations (0.5 mol/1); do not use fractions such as M/2. You may use '%' for percentage with an arabic numeral in the text, but avoid '%o' for 'per thousand' because it is easily mistaken for %: give the unit of measure instead (5 μl/1) or write out 'per thousand' if there are no units. Never use '15 mg %': write '150 μg/g' or '150 mg/1', whichever is correct and in preference to '15 mg/100 g' or '15 mg/100 ml'). Mathematical expressions should whenever possible be written or transformed to allow typesetting on a single line.

(5) *Appendix*

If there is an appendix, place it either after the text and before the acknowledgements and references, or after the list of references, according to the practice of the journal.

(6) *Acknowledgements*

Place the acknowledgements on a separate page at the end of the paper, before the references, unless the journal prefers them as a footnote or elsewhere at the beginning of the paper. Keep them short. Ensure that names, initials, grant numbers and similar items are correct in every detail. When you thank individuals, make sure that they have agreed to the form in which you do this (see p. 25).

(7) *References*

Compile the references in the form required by the journal, as described below (pp. 54-57).

(8) *Footnotes*

Keep footnotes to a minimum, as mentioned earlier (p. 38), and place them according to the journal's instructions. Most journals ask for a separate page of footnotes, but some ask for footnotes to be typed on the appropriate page of text, either at the foot of the page or in the text immediately after the line in which the symbol calling attention to them appears, with lines ruled above and below to mark them off from the text.

(9) *Tables*

The tables will have been typed earlier (see p. 30). Now check once more that the observations noted in them are correct and consistent with the text, that totals and subtotals add up correctly, and that each table has its correct number and title. Identify each table in pencil with the name of the first author and (or) the title of the paper if the journal requires this.

(10) *Illustrations*

The illustrations that you drew or photographed, or sent to the technical artist or photographer (see p. 30), should be ready now. Check that they are all present and correct in every detail, complete with any necessary arrows, letters scales or overlays. Write the first author's name and the number of the illustration lightly in pencil on the back of each illustration, as well as indicating which is the top. Check that the numbers and the information in the legends match the illustrations to which they refer.

Permission to Reproduce Material

If you have not yet received written permission to reproduce previously published tables, figures, text or unpublished work by other authors, obtain it now (see pp. 15-17).

COMPILING THE REFERENCES IN FINAL FORM

Most journals use either a name-and-date system (sometimes known as the Harvard system) for citing references or a numbering system, in which the references are listed in the order they are first cited in the text. A third system is a hybrid numerical-alphabetical method, with the references arranged alphabetically by first author and then numbered. A fourth arrangement may be preferred in historical paper: references given in date order, the year being placed first. If you think this is appropriate, you should ask the editor whether he is prepared to accept it. Another method for references, rarely used in earth science or life science journals, is to place them as footnotes on the page on which the reference is given. This is expensive and unpopular with printers and it can also produce pages which consist mainly of footnotes, with just a few lines of text.

The first three systems all have their advocates, some of them fanatical, but you will have to use the system preferred by the journal for which your article is destined. The Harvard system seems to be gaining in popularity over the others, but each system has something to recommend it. For convenience and consistency most journals use only one of these systems.

References in the Text

If the journal uses the name-and-date system, its instructions about references in the text should tell you how to cite (1) several papers published by the same author (with or without co-authors) in the same year (usually as 1974*a*, 1974*b* and so on, and *not* as 1974, 1974*a* . . .), and (2) papers with several authors (some journals ask you to write 'Smith *et al.*' or 'Smith and others' when the paper has more than two *or* more than three authors; other journals ask you to write out all the names the first time the reference appears). The instructions may also say that if you refer to a specific page of a book or article you should give that page number in the text only: 'This was reported by Smith (1974, p. 15).

If the journal uses a numbering system for references, change the names and dates in your text to numbers at this stage (but first read the paragraph below about unpublished work). Write the numbers in the style used in the journal—usually either in parentheses or brackets on the same line as the rest of the text, thus (5), [5], or as small numbers above the line (superscript): ^{5},$^{5)}$, (^{5}). If you particularly wish to name an author, word the sentence accordingly: 'As Jones[5] has shown, this method . . . ' . Write authors' names in capital letters only if the journal you write for insists on this.

With any system of citation, if you wish to give credit to others by referring to 'unpublished work' or to a 'personal communication', give the author's name and initials in the text—for example as '(X.Y. Smith, unpublished work)' or '(Y.Z. Brown, personal communication)' and do *not* make this into a reference for the reference list. Do not use 'in preparation', which implies a promise that may never be fulfilled, or 'private communication', which implies that you are violating a confidence. One reason for putting such references in the text instead of listing them with the references to published papers is that readers are immediately aware that the work has not been exposed to the critical appraisal of editors and referees, and that it is not readily available for critical study. Obtain written permission to cite unpublished work (see p. 16); the editor of the journal may ask to see this permission.

List of References

Call the list of references 'Literature Cited', 'References Cited' or 'References', according to the journal's style. Do not include any references that are not in the text. (If you are writing a review article or a textbook and wish to draw attention to other publications useful for background or further reading, make a separate list entitled 'Additional reading'.)

Only material already published or *accepted* for publication should be placed in a reference list. If you cite a paper that has been submitted for publication, do not include it in the reference list unless you are sure that you will be able to change 'submitted for publication' to the name of the journal plus 'in press' by the time your own paper is likely to be in proof. If you are not sure that a cited paper will be accepted, refer instead to 'unpublished work' in the text. Before the references are typed, remove from your collection of reference cards any that refer to unpublished work, or to personal communications: cite such work only in the text, as recommended in the previous section.

If you cite documents of limited circulation—for example, technical reports or typewritten or mimeographed papers issued by institutions, government agencies, or commercial companies on special request—you must be able to give the reader (in the list of references) full details of how to obtain them. If documents of this kind are not available on request, refer to them only if you can include in your text all the information necessary to support your argument, giving the reference as 'unpublished work', with the author's (or institution's) name. If such documents are classified as secret and their contents cannot be described, you will have to do without both the reference and the information in it.

For references that you have to cite at second hand, without having seen them for yourself, include a name and date or a number for the secondary source in brackets at the end of the primary reference— '. . . [cited by Braun 1957]' or ' . . . [cited in ref. 3]'—and add the secondary reference in its appropriate place in the list. If you refer to an abstract, add this information in brackets too. If you refer to a paper in a language other than English, write '[in Russian]', or whatever language it is, at the end of the reference unless the bibliographic details make the language unmistakable. If you refer to reports of the kind that have copies deposited in many libraries, include reference numbers of other information needed for retrieving them. If you are in doubt about what bibliographic information to include, put in everything in full, as listed on p. 25: it is easier for an editor to delete details than to obtain them.

The different elements in references can be printed in an endless variety of ways, and before the reference list is typed you will need to arrange all the items on your reference cards in the order and with the punctuation favoured by the journal. You may underline—once—any items that will be printed in italics, but do not capitalize authors' names unless the journal asks for this to be done. Write the names of journals according to the system recommended by your journal.

There are two main systems for abbreviating the titles of journals for reference lists. One system—the 'International List' system, now the basis of a draft International Standard—is based on British Standard 4148:1970 and American National Standard Z 39.5-1969, which are in agreement. This is the system used by *Chemical Abstracts, Biological Abstracts* and *Index Medicus*. The correct abbreviations according to the International List system are most conveniently obtained from the *Bibliographic Guide for Editors and Authors* (BIOSIS *et al.* 1974), or from the most recent

January issue of *Index medicus*. Refer to the *International List of Periodical Title Word Abbreviations (1970)* for titles not named in these publications.

The other main system for abbreviating titles uses the abbreviations adopted by the *World List of Scientific Periodicals*, a three-volume publication last printed in full in 1963-1965 (covering journals published 1900-1960); this edition is supplemented regularly by the British Union Catalogue of Periodicals (BUCOP).

Some journals print the titles of all periodicals in full in reference lists. Check whether your target journal does this before you draw up your reference list. In any case, write out in full any journal title for which you cannot find an abbreviation. Do not abbreviate one-word titles or names of persons in a title.

Capitalize the elements of the title abbreviations according to the style of the journal. The International List system allows three styles:

Phys. Med. Biol.
PHYS. MED. BIOL.
Phys. med. biol.

The first style is used by most journals that abbreviate titles according to the International List system. Note that there is usually a full stop after *all* abbreviated words in a journal title, but no stop after complete words (such as *Acta*). You may omit accents and other similar marks in title abbreviations if the journal allows this, but do not change the spelling of any such words.

Examples of how to write out and type different kinds of references (using the name-and-date system of giving references and the International List system for abbreviating journal titles) follow.

(1) For journal articles:
Lourie, R. S., Layman, E. M., Jr and Millican, F. K. (1963) Why children eat things that are not food. Children 10, 143-146.
The next example gives the title of the article in the original language and in English translation:
Akoum, G., Beucler, A., Gayet, N., Gall, G. & Brocard, H. (1973) Un poumon de champignonniste [Mushroom grower's lung]. Nouv. Presse Med. 2, 1862-1863.

(2) For a single-author book:
Cantarow, A. (1970) The Lifespan of Bees. 3rd edn., vol. 2, Nordic Publishing Company, Oslo.
(If you need to give the total number of pages in a book, write this as 298 pp., not p. 298 or pp. 1-298.)

(3) For papers (titles omitted) in multi-author books with one or more editors:
Smith, P. D. (1969) in Biochemistry of Viruses (Brown, H. B., ed.), pp. 177-218, Associated Scienctific Publishers, Amsterdam.

(4) For whole documents such as books or technical reports (as for (3), but omitting page numbers):
Stubbs, A. (1965) Food Use and Nutritional Level of 1255 Texas Families (Bulletin No.H-B-1033), Agricultural Research Station, State College, Pennsylvania.

(5) For theses and dissertations:
Smith, A. B. (1962) Population Growth in Fishponds. M.Sc. thesis, Dept. of Biological Economy, University of Leeds, England.

Write out each reference in the correct form on a separate card. Then arrange the reference cards either in the order in which they are first referred to in the text (numerical system), or alphabetically (Harvard and numerical-alphabetical systems). Alphabetizing poses certain unexpected problems. Arrange double names and names containing connectives such as 'van', 'de', etc. according to the policy of the journal. If no policy is apparent, write the names according to the custom of the country in which those authors live, or according to a self-consistent system in which all names beginning with 'van', 'Van', 'von', etc. are listed under 'v' whether the first letter is capitalized or not.

The most important thing is to be consistent and write the names the same way in the text and in the reference list, so that the reader can find the references where he expects to find them.

Name an organization (for example, Ministry of Education) as the author of a report or similar publication when no individuals are named, and add the country's name to the bibliographical details if this is not obvious from the place of publication. List an unsigned article under 'anonymous' (abbreviate this to 'Anon.' in the text).

Even when the same authors' names or journal titles occur in successive references, write them out in full; do not use *ibid.* or similar shorthand tags like *idem, loc, cit.,* and so on. Too often these terms are ambiguous, and if a reference is later deleted they may become inaccurate.

Checking the Reference Cards

Now check the details on the reference cards or rough list against the original documents, or against reprints or photocopies of them. Except in the rare cases when a journal is paged separately for each issue rather than consecutively through the whole volume, delete the issue numbers on the reference cards before the list is typed.

Finally, before the paper is typed, check the reference cards or rough list against the text. With the Harvard system, check that the names in the text are spelt in the same way as on the reference cards, that they are in the same names in the same order, and that the dates are the same as those on the cards or rough list. With the numbering system, make sure that the numbers in the text refer to the publications to which you intended them to refer—listed or arranged on your reference cards with numbers matching those in the text. For a 'Reference list' (but not for a list of 'Additional reading') make sure that every reference is referred to in the text, and that every reference in the text has a corresponding reference card or appears in the rough list.

Although a skilled typist will be able to look after many of these details if you first explain the system used by the target journal, typing the references will be quicker and easier if you follow the above recommendations, writing every detail of punctuation, capitalization and italicization in exactly the form the journal wants, and arranging the cards or list yourself.

TYPING

Type the whole paper, or have it typed, according to the recommendations in chapter 6, but tell your typist to observe the journal's instructions in preference to ours if the two sets are in conflict.

CORRECTING TYPESCRIPT

Read and check the typescript word by word when it is ready: if possible, get someone to read the original aloud while you make any necessary corrections on the top copy and on all other copies. Do *not* use proofreaders' marks for correcting typescript. One reason for having everything typed double-spaced is precisely to allow words or characters to be inserted or substituted between the lines, where they are most easily seen by the compositor who sets the type at the printer's. The compositor can deal perfectly well with clear deletions, or insertions between the lines, but not with long insertions typed at the bottom of the page or with words or phrases marked to be moved to another page. If one or a few lines have to be corrected, type them on a slip of paper which can be pasted over (not pinned to) the original with a non-aqueous glue. Extensively corrected pages must be retyped. Of course, if the journal is printed by photo-offset direct from authors' typescripts (see p. 59), whole pages in the final version will have to be retyped even when the corrections are minor ones.

OBTAINING FINAL CRITICISM

Obtain a final critical review either from the head of your department or from an experienced colleague (possibly working elsewhere) who is doing similar work but who has not been involved in preparing the manuscript. Ask him or her to point out errors of detail as well as making larger-scale comments. While you wait for criticism put away the other copies of the typescript. Try to achieve a sense of detachment from the work you have described, so that when the critical comments arrive you can re-read the paper objectively with a fresh eye. Make any final changes neatly on the typescript, or have the relevant sections or the whole paper retyped, before you send anything to the journal. The mechanics of submitting the paper are discussed in chapter 7 of the publication referred earlier.

Finalising and Typing

Editors and referees get their first impression of a paper from its physical appearance. The way it is typed is therefore important, even though the intrinsic merits of the work described should in the end be the primary basis for its acceptance or rejection. A neat, clean and accurately typed article, on good paper, with a carefully laid-out title page attracting the eye, will make the editor's (or referee's) work much easier; he or she will be at least slightly biased in the author's favour at the outset. Later, these same qualities will greatly help the copy-editor and compositor, and there will be fewer mistakes in the printed version. If the journal is photographically reproduced directly from authors' typescripts a high standard of presentation is obviously essential; the journal may also ask for typing to be done on special paper. Corrections at proof stage are very expensive with this method.

The rest of this chapter is therefore addressed to the person—perhaps yourself—who is going to type the later drafts or the final version of your article. Even if you are *not* doing your own typing, you should read these recommendations. If our recommendations differ from the requirements of the journal, point out the differences and give the typist a recent copy of the journal and its instructions, as well as calling attention to this chapter. Alternatively, make your own list of instructions about how to type a paper for the journal. Find out how many copies of the paper should be made: *as a minimum*, you will probably need two for the journal, one for each author, and an extra one for your files. If you want the paper typed by a certain date, say so, but do not hurry the typist unnecessarily: a good-looking and accurate typescript take time to type. Remember to tell the typist when you have reached the final version—the one that will be submitted to the journal.

Annexure I

A NEWSPERSON'S CHECKLIST

Step

1. Assess your work: decide what, when, and where to publish. Refrain from duplicate publication, and define your purpose in publishing
2. Obtain and read the Instructions to Authors of the journal chosen
3. Decide who the authors will be

4. Draft a working title and abstract
5. Decide on the basic form of the paper
6. Collect the material under the major headings chosen
7. Design tables, including their titles and footnotes: design or select illustrations and write titles and legends for them
8. Write for permission to reproduce any previously published tables, illustrations or other material that will be used
9. Write a topic outline and perhaps a sentence outline
10. Write, type or dictate a preliminary draft of the text quickly, to give it unity
11. Check completeness of the references assembled
12. Put the manuscript or typescript away for a few days
13. Re-examine the structure of the paper
14. Check the illustrations and tables and make the final versions
15. Re-read the references you cite and check your own accuracy in citing them; check for consistency, and reduce the number of abbreviations and footnotes
16. (Re)type the paper (= first draft)
17. Correct the grammar and polish the style
18. Type several copies of the corrected paper (= second draft)
19. Ask for criticism from co-authors and friends
20. Make any necessary alterations
21. Compose a new title and abstract suitable for information retrieval, list the index terms and assemble the manuscript
22. Compile the reference list, cross-check references against the text, and ensure that all bibliographical details are correct
23. Retype (= penultimate version) and check typescript
24. Obtain a final critical review from a senior colleague
25. Make any final corrections (final version)
26. Write a covering letter to the editor, enclosing copies of letters giving you permission to reproduce any previously published material or to cite unpublished work
27. Check that all parts of the paper are present, and post as many copies as specified to the editor
28. If the editor returns the paper, revise it as necessary, send it elsewhere, or abandon it
29. Correct the proofs

Units of Measure and their Abbreviations

The Systeme International d'Unites (SI) is based on seven base units and two supplementary units. The base quantities, base units and their symbols are:

length	metre (m)
mass	kilogram (kg)
time	second (s)
current	ampere (A)
thermodynamic temperature	kelvin (K)
intensity	candela (cd)
amount of substance	mole (mol)

The two supplementary units are:

plane angle	radian (rad)
solid angle	steradian (sr)

Strictly speaking, volumes should be expressed in this system in cubic metres (m^3), but the litre—now redefined as 1 dm^3—is more convenient in medicine and biology. Again, although molar concentrations should properly be given in moles per litre (mol/l), in practice molar (M) is accepted by many journals (though not by all).

Certain *derived* SI units have approved names and symbols. Their definitions in terms of the base units are shown in Table 1.

Certain prefixes (Table 2) are recommended for use with the SI units. In general, these represent multiples or submultiples of the form 10^{3n} or 10^{-3n}. In addition, the convenient centi, deci, deka, and hecto are allowed when the standard prefixes would yield cumbersome or conceptually absurd units (*e.g.* 15 cm^3 rather than 15000 mm^3 or 0.000015 m^3).

Never use two prefixes, but 'melt' them into one: 6mμg = 6 ng; 4 μμl = 4 pl. When you raise the power of any unit that contains a prefix, there is no need to use parentheses: 2 km^2 is 2 $(km)^2$ or two square kilometres (2 × 16^6 m^2), *not* $k(m^2)$ or 2 × 10^3 m^2. Similarly, 1 mm^3 is a cubic millimetre and 1 cm^3 a cubic centimetre.

TABLE 1
Derived SI units

Physical quantity	*SI Unit*	*Symbol or definition for unit*
force	newton (N)	kg m s^{-2}
pressure	pascal (Pa) (N/m^2)	kg m^{-1} s^{-2}
energy	joule (J)	kg m^2 s^{-2}
power	watt (W)	kg m^2 s^{-3}
electric charge	coulomb (C)	A s
electric potential	volt (V)	kg m^2 A^{-1} m^{-2}
electric capacitance	farad (F)	A^2s^4 kg^{-1} m^{-2}
electric conductance	siemens (S)	A^2S^3 kg^{-1} m^{-2}
electric inductance	henry (H)	kg m^2 A^{-2} s^{-2}
electric resistance	ohm (Ω)	kg m^2 A^{-2} s^{-3}
magnetic flux	weber (Wb)	kg m^2 A^{-1} s^{-2}
magnetic flux density	tesla (T)	kg A^{-1} s^{-2}
luminous flux	lumen (lm)	cd sr
illumination	lux (lx)	cd sr m^{-2}
frequency	hertz (Hz)	s^{-1} (cycles per second)
temperature interval	kelvin (K)	
Celcius temperature*	degree Celsius (C)	(0°C = 273.15 K)
Celsius temperature interval*	degree Celsius	1 K

* Customary units that may continue to be used.

TABLE 2
Prefixes for SI units

10^{-18}	atto (a)	10^{-1}	deci (d)
10^{-13}	femto (f)	10	deka (da)
10^{-12}	pico (p)	10^2	hecto (h)
10^{-9}	nano (n)	10^3	kilo (k)
10^{-6}	micro (μ)	10^6	mega (M)
10^{-3}	milli (m)	10^9	giga (G)
10^{-2}	centi (c)	10^{12}	tera (T)

The 'micron' is no longer acceptable; replace it by micrometre (µm). Similarly replace 'lambda' by microlitre (µl) and 'gamma' by microgram (µg). In these cases, the number will remain the same, but when you convert other non-SI units into SI units, you may need to apply a conversion factor (for example, 1 angstrom = 10^{-1} nanometre; 1 dyne = 10^{-5} newton. For the necessary conversion factors see below (Table 3).

TABLE 3

Alphabetical list of abbreviations of units and prefixes

ampere: A	cubic centimetre: cm^3
angstrom: 10^{-1} nm	cubic decimetre (= litre): dm^3
atmosphere, standard: 101 325 Pa	curie: Ci ($3.7 \times 10^{10} s^{-1}$)
atomic mass unit (unified):	cycle per second: Hz
u (1.660×1^{-27} kg)	dalton: *see* atomic unit
atto : a (10^{-18})	day: d (if absolutely necessary)
bar: 10^4 Pa	decibel: dB
barn: 10^{-28} m^2	degree: ° (plane angle)
billion, if 10^9 (American usage): G	degree Celsius: °C
If 10^{12} (British usage): T	degree Kelvin: does not exist.
calorie: Use SI (cal_{IT} = 4.1868 J;	(use the Kelvin K)
cal (15°) = 4.1855 J;	disintegration per minute: dpm
cal (thermochemical) = 4.184 J)	disintegration per second: dps
Calorie (medical) kcal ≈ 4.2 kJ	dram: 1.117 g
candela: cd	dyne: 10^{-5} N
candela steradian: cd sr (= lumen)	electronvolt: eV (0.160 219 aJ)
centrifugation, speed and duration:	equivalents: eq or equiv (use moles
g-min	if possible)
coulomb: C	
count per minute: cpm or count/min	erg: 0.1 µJ
count per second: count/s	farad: F

(contd.)

foot: 0.305 m
foot-candle: 10.76 lux
gallon: Use metric: US, 3,785 litre; imperial, 4,546 litre
gamma: If microgram meant, use µg
gauss: 0.1 mT
giga: C
grain: 65 mg
gram, gramme: g
gram(me)–atom: g-atom
gram(me)-calorie: *see* calorie
gram(me)-centimetre: g.cm
gram(me)-molecule: mol
hecto: h
henry: H
hertz: Hz
horsepower: 745.7 W
hour: h
hundredweight: 51 kg
inch: 25.4 mm
joule: J (energy, including heat, work, nutrition)
katal: kat (proposed SI unit of enzyme activity)
kelvin: K
kilo: k
kilocalorie: 4.2 kJ
kilogram(me): kg
kilogram-force: 9.807 N
kilowatt hour: 3.6 MJ
knot: 1854 m/h
lambda: If microlitre meant, use µl
langley: 41.87 kJ m^{-2}
litre: 1
lumen: lm
lux: lx
maxwell: 10^{-8} Wb
mega: M
megacycles per second: MHz
metre: m
mho: use siemens, S
micro: µ
microlitre: µl (*not* λ)
micromicro: Substitute pico, p
micromilli: substitute nano, n
micron: Use µm
mile: 1.609 km
mile, nautical: 1.854 km
milli: m
milliequivalent: Convert to milliomolar, mM if possible
milligram percent; *see* p. 51
millimetre of mercury: mmHg; Give also SI equivalent (1 mmHg . 133.3 Pa)
millimicro: Substitute nano, n
millimicron: Substitute nanometre, nm
minute: min
minute (arc): (π/10 800) rad:
molal: Substitute mol/kg
molar (mole per litre): mol/l or M (note: M never means mole)
mole: mol
nano: n
nautical mile: 1.854 km
newton: N
normal (concentration): Use molar

ohm: Ω
ounce: 28.4 g
parts per million: parts/10^6
pascal: Pa
pico: p
poise: 10^{-1} Pa s
pound: 0.454 kg
pound per square inch: 6895 Pa
radian: rad
radiation absorbed dose: rad
(10 mJ/kg)
(do not abbreviate further)
radiation dose equivalent: rem
revolution per minute: rev/min
revolution per second: rev/s
roentgen: R (0.258 mCi/kg)
second: s
second (arc): ″
siemens: S
steradian: sr
stilb: cd/cm^2
stoke: 10^{-4} m^2 s^{-1}
Svedberg unit (10^{-12} s): S
Svedberg flotation unit: S_f
tera: T
tesla: T
ton: (2240 lb) 1016 kg: (2000 lb) 907 kg
tonne: Mg (10^3 kg)
torr: 133.3 Pa
unit: U or u
volt: V
watt: W
weber: Wb
week: wk
yard: 0.914 m
year: Avoid abbreviating, a (annus) is international symbol; use yr if abbreviation essential

9

Coping with Automation

SOME of those US papers which once prided themselves on technological leadership are now regretting it. Those who come second or third can benefit from the leader's mistakes. In New York, where the newspapers were late in the race and have only recent begun their plans for switching to photocomposition and associated systems, they have studied others, learnt the lessons, and adopted a cautious, pragmatic approach which may recommend itself to British newspaper publishers. This approach does not begin with the technology at all, but with the fundamental question, what *product,* that is, what quality of newspaper, do you want to produce? One moral is that it may be no disadvantage that the British newspaper industry, and Fleet Street in particular, is arriving late on the scene of new technology. The US has a fund of experience to draw on.

In earlier days, several US newspapers adopted the 'big bang' approach to the new technology. A good example was the *Daytona News,* at Daytona Beach, Florida, where the ruling Davidson family prided itself on technological leadership. As early as 1968, when the company moved to new premises, they took the opportunity to discard all their hot lead machines there and then, lock stock and barrel. A similar 'big bang' approach was seen at Richmond, Virginia.

But there are now few champions of that approach. Daytona says it would never do it again—the teething troubles of the new equipment were too great. Richmond was a special case, because of its strike. In Sacramento, California, there was a classic instance where one of two rival publishers went overboard for new technology with an expensive all-new plant, and then was amazed that he was still losing business to his rival. The answer was, according to the American Newspaper Publishers Association, that he spent all his money on the machinery, and none on developing the product *i.e.* improving his newspaper. The *Miami Herald*, for long the shining example of technological progress in the US, has now deliberately dropped back, to enable it to tackle the problems caused by its previous haste.

The moral of all this has not been lost upon the big metropolitan papers of New York and Washington in the plans they are now laying for modernisation. But one New York project (described later in this chapter) for an entirely new newspaper based on all new technology, seems to have ignored the moral.

The *New York Daily News*

With a daily circulation of over 2 million, and originally started in imitation of the London *Daily Mirror*, this newspaper of all US publications offers the best direct analogy with the Fleet Street newspapers. Its approach to the question of new technology also offers lessons for Fleet Street.

Since the new labour contract last year, it has shed about 100 printing staff with its special early retirement scheme (to bring the numbers of down to about 750 in the composing room area), and expects a slow attrition of numbers from now on, say, 50 a year. Even so, the paper expects to have twice as many printers as it will need in about 5 years time, with the implication that it may have to offer further special inducements at that time for early retirement. This approach is based on the high average age of its printers.

Since the new contract was signed, the paper has been laying its plans for new technology. These plans are essentially conservative, cautious, starting strictly at square one, both in a conceptual and in a technological sense.

1. The man who has been put in charge of planning the new system is not a technical expert at all, nor a printing manager. He is the design editor of the paper. This reflects the concern of the paper to establish what they want the paper to look like when the process is over (the paper is of course a tabloid, to which looks are important) and to avoid the new technology hampering or conditioning the paper and its activities or design. To help him, the design editor (Mr. Philip Ritzenberg) has an inter-department, inter-disciplinary team—a man for advertising, one from circulation, one from editorial, an engineer, a computer expert, an industrial relations man, a professional printer. This 'task force', as they call it, has been travelling round the US (not necessarily all at once) collecting others' experience, and its job is to report, to advise management, and to advise the team of consultants which the paper has employed.

2. The team of consultants has been employed to produce an analysis of what goes on in the *Daily News* office—what the copy flow is, who has to see what in order to reach which decisions, so that the *Daily News* will know what its operation actually is, before it sets about automating it. Anyone who is familiar with a newspaper office will realise the point of all this—it is often a baffling task trying to decide how things get done, since such system as there is, is usually highly informal and ad hominem. The idea was that the new equipment should not impose its own conditions on the operation, but vice versa. The object was to provide detailed specifications to potential manufacturers of what the equipment must do, and then award the contract to whoever could meet those prior specifications. Again, the point of this will be clear to anyone with experience of earlier generations of photocomposition and copy input devices, which, simply in order to get them to work, demanded changed routines and sacrifices of time and scope; that is, imposed *their* conditions on the newspaper.

3. A further illustration of this point is that the *Daily News* decided that none of the typefaces so far available on photocomposition machinery was suitable for its needs. Previously, users have tended to have to take the typeface the manufacturer offered, which is not a good thing for any self-respecting paper to have to do: the manufacturers tend to be

electronics companies, not printing companies with real knowledge of type, and anyway, are interested in selling a standard typeface to as many customers as possible. So the *Daily News* is having new typefaces designed to its requirements.

4. As to equipment, here again the *Daily News* has been starting very much at square one, with tape-driven hot lead linecasters. This sounds and is an elementary beginning: tape-driven linecasters would seem terribly old fashioned to the more advanced US papers, and are of course common-place in British provincial newspaper works. But they are not commonplace either in New York or in Fleet Street. They work two to three times faster than a manually operated linecaster, and need fewer men to supervise them—hence resistance to them in the big printing centres—but they are another classic instance of how substantial savings in manpower could in principle be made with the traditional technology. However, the point of this for the *Daily News* (as it could be for others) is that it introduces *tape* into the system, in a gradual one-step-at-a-time manner: and tape is also the medium of photocomposition. Once the paper's staff have got used to producing tape on special keyboards, which is then hyphenated and justified and used to operate a tape-driven linecaster, the next stage—harnessing a photocomposition machine to the tape operation—will be that much easier. The cost of 20 second-hand tape-driven linecasters is well worth the benefits of a 'softly softly' approach, the paper reckons.

The approach of the *New York Daily*, typified by putting the design editor in charge, puts the new technology firmly in its place. But the paper is also going to great pains to establish the final objective—that is, what the final system will, on present knowledge, look like—before embarking very far on its plans and purchases. The present schedule calls for conversion of advertising sections from hot to cold this year, with the introduction of VDUs for proofing of copy, and for interrogating the AP and UPI news agency computer storage.

The *New York Times*

With a daily circulation of over 850,000 and perhaps 70 pages per issue, with a huge Sunday edition, the *New York Times* is a large operation. Since the new labour contract was signed, jointly with the *Daily News*, it too has shed (as of end January 1975) over 100 printers, at nearly $300 a week each in wages, through special inducements to retire (basically 6 months pay plus a bonus of $2,500 per man). Average age of printers was 58. The staff seems to have settled down since the dispute last year, and there is a lot of enthusiasm about the new equipment and about retraining for it. The *NYT* had been doing photocomposition of display ads before the new contract was signed, and with the transfer of stock prices to photocomposition the number of hot lead linecasters in use at the *NYT* had by early 1975 already dropped from a one-time peak of 137 to 64, of which 27 were tape-driven.

Because of its different starting point, and with 4 years of planning and thinking already behind it, the *NYT* adopted a different approach to the *Daily News* in making its plans for the future, although one important feature is the same—it has done a complete analysis of the flow of copy, and how it is handled and what needs to be done to it, as preparation for ordering a large scale video screen system for its editorial department. This analysis has been carried out by an editorial person—in fact, the deputy foreign editor. It expects to begin ordering the video screen system—perhaps 70 or more screens—before this year (1975) is out. A similar impression of greater urgency and speed, compared to the *Daily News*, is given by the *NYT*'s approach to classified ads, and it is here that the different *NYT* approach to the new technology shows up most clearly.

With a huge volume of classified ads (unlike the *Daily News*, which has relatively few—hence the difference in approach) the great push at the *NYT* at the moment is to apply new technology to the setting and billing of classified ads. All classified ads are now being put on to special forms suitable for OCR scanners (some come from specialised agencies already typed on these forms, which the *NYT* provides for them along with the typewriters; some are typed in the building from phoned-in or sent-in ads). The OCR forms are then checked for style and content (no call-girls, no rude works, no libel etc.), and are then put through the OCR scanner (an ECRM model). This produces a tape which is justified and hyphenated in the normal way by a computer, except that the computer also at the same time checks the credit-worthiness of the advertiser and issues the billing for the ad—that is, handles the accounting side (see the Wolverhampton *Express and Star* in the UK for a similar dual role). At the outset, this tape has been used to drive tape-operated linecasters, but it will eventually be used to drive tape-operated linecasters, but it will eventually be used to drive photocomposing equipment. In time, the *NYT* expects to use perhaps 130 video terminals for its own classified ad taking, while retaining OCR for outside agency ads.

In some areas, therefore, the *NYT* has been pushing ahead fast-display ads before the new labour contract (this was possible because they were and are still being keyboarded by ITU members); classified ads now; an editorial screen system soon; next year, parts of the mammoth Sunday edition will, it is hoped, go over to photocomposition. That is a relatively fast but phased programme, but there is an important qualification to this, again showing that the *NYT* is basically in the gradualist school and not the 'big bang' school. That qualification is that *news* is expected to remain a hot lead operation, done by traditional methods, for many years to come. This is because, in the view of the *NYT*, it takes too long to process news through photocomposition and the associated plate-making process. That loss of time cannot be afforded, especially in view of the competitive situation between the *NYT* and the suburban papers round New York (which, incidentally, are often non-union). This supports the view taken by many others, that hot lead is still the fastest way yet known to handle late news, and the decision on whether to put news onto photocomposition depends entirely on a judgment about the final product—the newspaper. Does it need the latest possible news, or not? That is a fruitful field of argument.

The concern for quality at the *NYT* shows up in another way—the editorial screen system. The *NYT* considered using OCR for editorial copy also. But it concluded that OCR did not permit the depth of editing that the *NYT* required (which it certainly does not) and that it was wrong to require its writers to type with the accuracy (of characters and spacing and correcting) that OCR demands. Their job was to create, not be professional typists. So OCR was ruled out by that criterion alone, even though the alternative, a large screen system, is considerably more expensive.

This groundswell of technological change at the *NYT* is strengthened by its recent decision to build a new printing plant, away from Manhattan and its high taxes, in New Jersey, where the *NYT* has a lot of readers, and where operating expenses are expected to be lower. It is to be a web offset plant, and by the end of 1978 all of the advance Sunday sections, and about a third of the daily paper copies and of other parts of the Sunday paper, will be printed there. This is a $35 million project, and page images will be transmitted by facsimile from Manhattan to the new plant.

In terms of organisation, the *NYT* has also made innovations. It now has a new division of managerial responsibilities. A director of pre-press operation is in charge of data processing, composing, photo-engraving, and communications—that is, everything up to the plate making. A director of printing and distribution is in charge of the rest of the process, from moulding of plates for stereo, through printing to delivery.

There have been a number of snags. For example the paper never expected so many people to leave all at once under its special retirement scheme, and was seriously embarrassed, at least temporarily, by a shortage of labour to produce its mammoth Sunday editions. This shows the need to plan such rundowns in manpower, as far as one can.

Again, the hyphenation and justification programme on the computer is a poor one, which has to be extensively checked and corrected by human eye and judgment. There is a high proportion of errors on the OCR and on the tape-driven linecasters. All the plans for change should not disguise the fact that the *NYT* at this present moment is still a highly traditional and typically chaotic big newspaper works, but there is a theme of pragmatic realism in the planning at both the *NYT* and the *Daily News* that should commend itself to British and other papers taking this road.

The *Miami Herald*

The most striking feature of the *Miami Herald* is that it is still using hot lead machines to set its late news, even though it was in its day a technological trailblazer, which began planning for photocomposition in 1963, that is, 12 years ago, and had its first installations in 1965, 10 years ago. This emphasises the long time span of the change-over from one technology to the other. Almost equally striking is the readiness with which executives admit the faults and snags which the new technology has given rise to, and which they are now actively striving to correct, having deliberately surrendered their claims to technological leadership. As one says: 'We told people the process would get quicker and cleaner; instead it has got slower and dirtier'. Here are some of the snags encountered:

1. Because the management broke the power of the unions during the strikes in the late 1940s, pasting-up of pages has been done by girls—that is, cheap non-unionised labour. But they are often slap-dash, not fully understanding the importance of getting it right, and bad work gets done at this stage. The management on the other hand will not brother to give them full training, because they tend not to stay long, they do not acquire the 'feel' of a newspaper and its requirements. Clearly, much depends on the standards required—at Richmond, Virginia; the management appears to be happy with its untrained girls doing paste-up: in Miami, they are not happy.

2. In the OCR typing pool, the girls should in theory get the typing right. But in practice they do not understand what all the various symbols (setting instructions, etc.) actually mean, and so make mistakes or leave them out, so throwing out the OCR machines.

3. The *Miami Herald* also grew dissatisfied with the typefaces on offer (see *New York Daily News* for similar view) particularly the headline faces. So it is getting its suppliers to design stronger and clearer faces.

4. The newspaper has become very hostile to OCR when used as a 'stand alone' device. Editing usually means retyping before insertion into the OCR, and this slows down the operation, introduces a new stage where errors can be made, and is expensive on labour.

5. The newspaper is also sceptical about plastic plates, for the same reason as many other people—poor reproduction of half-tones.

A great deal of the *Miami Herald's* present planning is therefore aimed simply at retrieving the mistakes of the past, at curing the faults engendered by the previous rush into new technology.

1. The classified ad pages will soon be printed out on an APS4 photocomposition machine in full page form, with spaces left for the display ads. This is already being done at Richmond, Virginia. It will cut out a lot of page paste-up work.

2. It is installing an editorial VDU system, modelled on that at the *Detroit News*, but with the difference that it will complement the existing OCR installation, that is, the raw editorial copy will be inserted into the system via the OCR, and then edited on the display screens, in a linked OCR-VDU system which should get round many of the snags of the present OCR system. The screens will also be used to edit agency copy that comes direct into computer storage.

The *Miami Herald* already has a very extensive OCR classified ad system, using VDU screens to check, update or cancel the ads, and a bank of 30 VDU screens in the circulation department, which is converting to direct ordering by subscribers rather than through agents and therefore needs the screens for checking on complaints, temporary cancellations, changes in orders, bill queries and all the rest of the day-to-day detail.

The *New York Press*

New York has been full of rumours and counter-rumours for a year or two now about the intended new afternoon newspaper to be launched in the city by oil millionaire Mr. John Shaheen, from a highly automated brand new newspaper office, full of the very latest equipment. The origin seems to be that Mr. Shaheen was a supporter of Richard Nixon, and thought there should be a paper that supported his brand of politics. Shaheen believed he saw a market gap in the afternoon in New York: as an oil man, he was also a fervent believer in technology. Since the idea was launched, and especially since Nixon resigned, there has been much speculation about whether the new paper will in fact appear.

Mr. John Olson, an experienced newspaper manager appointed by Shaheen last year as publisher of the *New York Press*, insists that it will appear, with a circulation of 300,000 or more, in broadsheet form. He admits that the project is 100 per cent over budget, with a latest estimated cost of $20m. plus $5m. launch costs, and that Shaheen will have to borrow money to complete it, instead of paying for it all from his own pocket, as originally intended: but he maintains that Shaheen will in fact see it through. Rival papers, perhaps not totally disinterested, are not so sure, and at the date of writing there is still no firm date for launching.

However, on the technical side, it is clear that things are not as they might be. On a recent visit in March 1975, the building (an existing one being renovated) proved to have little or no activity going on inside. Several floors had been gutted and new walls, air-conditioning, electricals etc. put in, but no fitting out work had been done, and no workers were in evidence. About two years ago now Shaheen went out and bought off the shelf the most modern presses and photocomposition systems he could then find (a complete Harris system for example), but since then there has been nowhere to put much of the stuff. The $8 million web offset presses are installed in the basement, but standing idle: the photocomposition equipment, computers, screens etc. have either been sitting under wraps in the shell of the new premises, or are still scattered around warehouses in Manhattan. It is doubtful whether this does the equipment any good, and what was modern two years ago may not be so modern by the end of this year.

No doubt all this can be put right with enough effort and money. But even assembling and debugging the new equipment will take time, and Mr. Olson is also treading a delicate path in trying simply to ignore the existence of the printing unions. Overall, this latest example of the 'big bang' approach to new technology cannot, on present evidence, be regarded as a successful model for others.

Cooperation among Publishers

US publishers share experience, information, and costs of development with each other to a greater extent than British publishers. While this is made easier by the fact that most US publishers are not in competition with each other, being often local monopolies based one in each major city, nevertheless it points to one serious weakness in the UK situation. US publishers have also learnt by bitter experience to cooperate in negotiations with the unions over the introduction of new technology—pointing to another weakness in the UK situation.

Cooperation between US publishers, the pooling of experience, the exchange of information, and the sharing of R and D costs, takes place at several different levels: 1 The trade association, with its own research institute; 2 Formally constituted joint ventures between ad hoc groups of publishers, for specific technical projects; 3 Looser ad hoc groupings for specific technical ventures, usually based on particular company executives who agree among recruitment methods, but spreading experience and knowledge from the more advanced companies to the less advanced; 5 Joint negotiations with the unions.

The Trade Association

The American Newspaper Publishers Association maintains its own research institute at Easton, Pennsylvania. In my opinion this plays a far larger and more positive role, certainly in the field of automation, than its UK counterpart, the Printing Industry Research Association (PIRA). The ANPA institute has a staff of 35 experts in various fields, plus secretaries etc, and an annual budget of $\$1\frac{1}{4}$ million, which is not huge, but apparently well spent. Its functions related to new technology are:

1. To do tests and reports on new equipment in real operational situations on newspapers.

2. To do confidential 'consultancy' reports for particular newspapers, for a fee, recommending what to do and how to do it in the field of automation.

3. To make suggestions to manufacturers about possible markets for new equipment. The institute sometimes does limited development work itself before passing the idea on to a manufacturer. The ANPA also sometimes joins with one or more newspaper companies in signing specific development contracts with a manufacturer for some piece of equipment. An

example is the Telegram, a portable video screen that can be plugged into a telephone line, for use by roving reporters; this is a joint ANPA—*New York Times* research and development contract that recently yielded its first prototype working models.

4. To carry on a dialogue with manufacturers, who frequently bring to the institute new equipment they have developed for criticism and comment.

5. To act as an informal grapevine and information clearing house for the industry, mostly on the telephone.

6. To issue regular research bulletins and statistical information on the industry and its progress.

7. To sponsor research, for example, at the Massachusetts Institute of Technology with which the ANPA has a close relationship.

The main limitation of the institute is that it has little contact with the big metropolitan newspapers who are rich enough to do their own development work: its direct activities are confined to the mass of medium and small daily papers in the US. But those are the papers that have been setting the pace on new technology. Also, the institute has on occasion influenced the policies of the big organisations. For example, it was instrumental in getting the two big news agencies, AP and UPI, to agree to a common coding structure for their wire services, so that a newspaper's computer could receive them both into its central information storage without unnecessary complications.

Formal Joint Ventures between Publishers

Easily the best known—perhaps also the most criticised—of these is the Newspaper Systems Development Group, the NSDG project which is more fully described in this chapter. The main points about it are that it is a joint development between IBM and (originally) eight newspaper companies, all done under signed contracts, with formulae covering allocation of the (substantial) costs between the partners and the sharing of the patents, licences and royalties that arise or may arise from the project. There is a formal committee of the partners to oversee the project, and (now) a full time project director.

Another example is the joint Mead Corporation-Media General (Richmond, Virginia) project for a full-page composition system. This represents cooperation between a paper company, Mead, which has the financial resources and is anxious to break into a related field, and a newspaper company which has specific experience to contribute; which will act as a test bed for the system when it arrives; and which is anxious, given its current state of development, to have such a 'total system' as its next big jump forward. Again there is a formal contractual relationship, with Mead supplying most of the money and Richmond getting a royalty on eventual sales.

A third example is the BUNPAPS venture, between Brown University and 5 newspapers, including the *New York Times*, *Detroit News*, *Chicago Tribune* and a Stockholm paper. It is a low-cost venture, has a committee to oversee it, and is aimed again at progress towards a full-page composition system.

It will be noted that all three examples are related to a similar type of development, and this shows the determination, again described more fully elsewhere, among US publishers to push ahead, by one route or another and with pooled resources, towards the goal that many have set for themselves—a single comprehensive newspaper composition system. Also, US publishers have at least one successful precedent for joint technological ventures—the OCR scanner as now used was a joint development of a more primitive machine between a group of publishers and, again the Massachusetts Institute of Technology.

Looser Groupings

An example of this type of cooperation is the loose collaborative arrangement between the *Houston Chronicle*, the *Washington Star* and the Gannett chain of papers to develop an automated mail room (dispatch room). This developed on the basis of Mr. X knowing Mr. Y, and indeed the grouping changed, with the *Miami Herald* dropping out and Gannett coming in, when one such Mr. X moved from Miami to Gannett. Houston was the first in the field with a computerised mail room; Gannett is putting up a new newspaper plant in Camden, New Jersey, with a more advanced version; and so on.

Movement of People

The electronics and computer business has long been known for rapid movement of people between companies, and between manufacturers and users. As newspapers have adopted electronics, this phenomenon has appeared in newspapers too. The result is the swift dissemination of knowledge, experience and expertise by this means alone—some may add, the dissemination of bad habits as well. Examples are: the publisher who was brought in to sort out the troubles of the *Washington Post*, John Prescott came from the *Miami Herald*, as did the man brought in to direct the NSDG project: the *Washington Post* technical systems manager came from the Richmond, Virginia, newspaper group: the man from the Hendrix manufacturing company who installed the trend-setting video screens at the *Detroit News* is now employed by the *Baltimore Sun* to design and install its planned video screen system: the *Houston Chronicle* computer systems expert came from the *St. Petersburg Times:* and so on. People also visit each other and discuss each other's project with great freedom.

Joint Negotiation with Unions

Until recently, each separate newspaper company in the US negotiated its own labour contract, and this was, from the employers' point of view, a source of weakness, especially when, as in Washington and New York, there were competing newspapers but only one union. This weakness is also endemic in Fleet Street, and for the same reason—that the union can act as a united body, whereas the companies are inhibited by fears of handing over circulation and market share to a rival, in the event of a strike or other industrial action. In Washington and New York this lesson was learnt, and in the last round of negotiations, the *Washington Post* and the *Washington Star*, on the one hand, and the *New York Times* and the *New York Daily News* on the other, negotiated jointly with the ITU and the other print unions. Not only did this enable them to adopt a stronger stance, especially in respect of new technology, but it also enabled them to adopt a more positive and constructive stance.

As a result, although the negotiations were often acrimonious in both cities, and although the companies were undoubtedly seeking to coerce the unions (for example, by training non-union staffs to operate new equipment and get the paper out if it came to a strike), nevertheless the fact remains that settlements were reached, that the vital if belated breakthrough towards peaceful introduction of new technology was achieved, and that the terms offered to union members were not un-generous considering the problems posed by the new technology. Indeed, some other US employers regard them as over-generous.

To complete the picture there must be added three other ways, not perhaps in themselves remarkable, in which the work is spread.

1. A manufacturer using one newspaper office as a test-bed and pilot site for new equipment, with special financial terms for that newspaper. The *Today* paper on Cocoa Beach, Florida, testing out Harris screens on behalf of the whole Gannett chain to which it belongs, is an example.

2. One big newspaper chain, like Gannett, using different newspapers that it owns for different pilot and test-bed projects—Cocoa Beach for screens, Elmira (New York state) for laser-produced printing plates, Camden (New Jersey) for mail room automation.

3. Simple trend setting. The *Detroit News* put in a big video screen system, and showed that it could work; others are now scrambling to follow the example. Houston with its pioneering mail room, St. Petersburg with its then novel APS 4 photosetters, are other examples.

From all this, it is clear that the *velocity of information* in the US newspaper industry is, on the analogy of the velocity of money in the banking system, very high. The British newspaper industry, which is more secretive despite the willingness of some individual companies and executives to receive visitors and show them round, should take note. The advantage of a joint approach to the unions on technology and manning also stands out.

New Technology and Editorial

New technology has become too important to leave to the technologists. Faced with, for example, poor and limited typefaces on photosetting equipment, bad correction and proofing systems, the limitations of OCR, and poor picture quality on some new equipment, journalists and design staff have in the US been moving into positions of control over planning for technological change, because they are in the end the best judges of what the new technology ought to do. Also, the new technology—most visibly expressed in the arrival of large numbers of video-screens—is giving to the editorial department a firmer, even eventually a total, grip on the final product, by transforming the composing room from a managerially separate department into an ancillary technical arm of the editorial department. All this means more power, and more responsibility, for the journalists (and by analogy their advertising colleagues) in the total newspaper organisation.

Video screens are the current fashion in American newspaper offices. The *Detroit News* was the pioneer, with a system of over 70 screens (or VDUs, for Video Display Units) operating in its news room. But now dozens of US newspaper publishers are ordering screens, in configurations ranging from a dozen or so up to the 76 ordered by the *Baltimore Sun* (cost $2 million) and huge and expensive systems of over 200, as at the Long Island publication *Newsday*. Within a year or two, these video screens will become an almost commonplace sight on many American journalists' desks, replacing the traditional typewriter and altering their working style. They will have become the most visible evidence of the impact of automation on editorial departments, and on advertising departments as well.

In this country, as in the US, until quite recently this aspect of automation has been largely ignored, and little understood. Automation has been thought of as something that happens 'down there' in the printing works (if, that is, it happens at all). But the new technology has advanced far enough in America now for it to be clear that it affects *all* departments of a newspaper—advertising, circulation, as well as editorial and production—and that the most of profound long-term consequences may be for the journalists, even though the immediate impact is clearly on the printing staffs and unions.

The crux of the matter is that the more the printing works is automated and moves nearer to the final aim of being just a collection of 'little black boxes' with a few skilled maintenance men, the more it becomes simply an adjunct to and arm of the editorial department. Of course, there is a sense in which this has always been true. But in practice editorial and printing works tend to be separate departments, separately managed, with a separate ethos and separate rules, and indeed different types of people with different backgrounds. That distinction is being eroded and in time abolished by the new technology.

Conversely, editorial departments in the US had been finding that the push to replace traditional hot lead by electronics 'down there' was suddenly affecting the look and style of the paper, in ways which they had not previously been warned about (limited type-faces, poor picture quality, etc.).

The result has been a general move, deriving from the logic of the technology as much as from any collective decision, by the journalists and editorial departments to take charge of both the planning for new technology, and the actual use of the new equipment once installed. The arrival of video screens on a large scale, as the main technical link between editorial and composing areas, dramatises this trend.

The trend shows up in two ways. One is the number of US newspaper offices in which the man in charge of technical planning, procurement, and development is not a technical man at all, neither a printer nor a computer man: he is a journalist, chosen essentially because he is a good judge of *what the new equipment will do to the product.* At the *Miami Herald,* that man is the former News Editor; at the *Daytona News,* it is the ex-City Editor; at the *New York Daily News,* it is the design editor of the paper; and so on.

The second and in a way more fundamental aspect is the abolition of the composing room as a managerially separate department. This has happened at a few US newspapers already, and, despite reservations, is expected to happen in many more. At Richmond, Virginia, for example, they have split the composing room roughly down the middle, and simply given half of it to the advertising director as his direct responsibility, and half of it to the Editor, as his responsibility. In other words, the direct and unqualified responsibility of the Editor and the editorial department now runs right up to the stage of making a printing plate, and may in due course extend right up to the printing press itself, as new automatic plate making systems are integrated backwards into the composing system.

Here then we arrive at the nub of the matter for the journalists: that the new technology enables them to take a much firmer grip than hitherto on the product, indeed eventually a total grip, by controlling it right through to the final production stage. They will soon be able, personally and probably without moving from their desks, to control the pages they have designed right up to and even including the plate making stage, making last minute changes and personally being responsible for authorising the completed page.

The videoscreen is the linchpin piece of equipment for all this, and that is why the large-scale move to screen systems in US editorial departments is so significant. A screen is, or can be, both a story *composing device*, like a typewriter; an *editing* device for subs and editors; and *input* device, which drives the phototypesetting machines; and a *lay-out* device for making up the pages. (They can also of course be used for classified and display ads in analogous ways.)

These changes are not necessarily easy or without headaches, either literal or metaphorical. Talking to journalists at the *Detroit News* is instructive. They were more or less obliged to convert to using screens (about 70 of them in editorial) because a new printing works was built 25 miles away, and an electronic link was the only way to get the news stories fast enough from the editorial offices to the works. Some say that they compose stories and/or edit them as fast on a screen as on paper: others say that there is no way in which you can work as fast on a screen as on paper. Some say the screen turns them from a creative person into a technical person, more concerned with operating the screen correctly than with the words. Many complain of headaches and eye strain after a day peering at a small screen with slightly indistinct and perhaps flickering characters on it. Others say that this is fundamentally conservatism: the paper gets out, after all, and if there are ergonomic design faults (which there certainly are) those will be ironed out with experience.

Far more tangible problems for journalists have been created by the OCR machine. These machines have a great charm—at least for newspaper accountants. One (or two, if you need a fail-safe back-up) OCR machines costing perhaps $30,000 to $50,000 a time will gobble up copy almost as fast as you can feed it in, and all the journalists need are special typewriters (mostly IBM ones) with the typeface which the OCR machine 'recognises'. Even with a set of new typewriters to pay for, this is still far cheaper than a big set of screens costing perhaps $8,000 a time. It is also apparently a far smaller intrusion on a journalist's normal working habits (because he still sits in front of a typewriter and types) while also yielding the saving in composing room labour costs which has been the main motivation of US newspaper managements.

However, there were snags, and the bigger US newspapers now planning automation are using OCR strictly as an ancillary device for mass input of repetitive data like classified ads. The main snag is that the typing of the copy for OCR has to be very exact, usually on expensive special paper, with exact line spacing, and most importantly, with only very limited possibilities of making changes and editing, without having to have the whole thing re-typed.

This might be acceptable for a small and/or lightly edited local paper, but certainly not for a heavily edited national or metropolitan paper. The constraints imposed by OCR were therefore yet another reason why journalists moved in to take greater control of automation planning, for it threatened to limit them in yet another direction. OCR has its place in the new technology, but the general view in the US now is that it is a limited place.

Another but more acceptable area of impact on journalists is through the wire services—the agency news. Along with much higher speeds of transmission from the agencies themselves, there is a big move to have the agency services fed directly into computer storage at the newspaper. The sub-editor then calls up a story he needs on his video screen, edits it as he wants, and then handles it as he would any 'in house' story. Here again the screen is the linchpin of the system.

These changes are still going on in the US, and it will be some years before they are complete. The process is often messy and expensive, takes longer than expected, causes unforeseen snags, and even now one cannot see quite where they are taking the business of being a journalist—or indeed the business of newspapers. But the gradual elimination of paper as the internal medium of a newspaper in America: the recently drawing together of the journalists' union and the typographical union in a closer working relationship: the scramble by numerous electronics companies, large and small, to get in on the act of automation of printing, especially in the area of screen (VDU) systems: and the breaking down of old lines of responsibility, job demarcation and definition of skills inside a newspaper building—these are all symptoms of the change now impending in the working context of journalists and editors. While the basic creative function is obviously separate from the means of its expression, it is important that new technology should if possible endorse, and certainly not limit or put constraints on, the writers' and editors' creativity. This lesson has sunk in, at least in some parts of America. Apart from the case of Mr. Peter Preston, the new Editor of the *Guardian* and formerly its production editor, who has himself written authoritatively on the subject of new technology, I know of little evidence that it has sunk in on this side of the Atlantic.

Mapping Future Newsmaking

Some of the more publicised development projects in the US, like the IBM-based Newspaper Systems Development Group, need to be treated with considerable caution: some of the less publicised developments, such as in news agency services, may provide at least as good evidence of the direction in which new technology is taking the newspaper business. But what is, or was until very recently, probably the most advanced electronic full-page newspaper composing system in the world is a British one, which has now been sold to the Americans because no one in Britain is prepared to take it on. Some may see this as typical of so much advanced British technology in the last decade.

The dream of many US publishers, which they expect to see as a reality within five to seven years, is of a 'total system', an all-electronic fully automated newspaper composing system, in place of the labour-intensive hot lead system of the past, and in place of the often messy hybrid systems, part electronic and part traditional, of the present. They are in many instances backing this dream with hard cash and the concept of the 'total system' lies at the back of much planning of new technology, as the ultimate goal towards which they are striving, and to which all present investment and equipment must be compatible. The argument centres on how this 'total system' will be constructed—brick by brick, as it were, in an evolutionary or modular manner; or by the 'mother earth' principle, building the whole thing into one giant computer. But there is a high degree of unanimity that *present* planning, investment, and technological development only makes sense in terms of this ultimate system.

Apart from doing away with huge numbers of people this ultimate system ought to have other potential advantages—greater control over the product; lower costs; speed; space saving; and above all else the simple attribute of being all-electronic, so that it becomes merely fortuitous that the information being processed is distributed on paper, it could as easily, as quickly and as naturally be distributed by an electronic means, by television cable for example. Much of the urgency for US publishers derives, as already mentioned, from their belief or hunch that paper may not be a viable means of distribution for much longer. In the US, the news agencies have been exerting a strong influence on the means and direction of the electronic dissemination of information, which may hold both morals and threats for the traditional newspaper operation.

The NSDG Project and other 'Total Systems'

This is by far the most expensive, most ambitious and most contentious development project in the US newspaper industry. It began with work which IBM did in Japan in computerising Japanese newspapers. IBM decided that the expertise so gained could be transferred to the US, and in 1973 gathered a group of newspaper publishers into a joint project, the Newspaper Systems Development Group. Centred on Gaithersburg, Maryland, not far from Washington, the project took in as partners the *Dallas Morning News*, the *Miami Herald*, Norfolk (Virginia) newspapers, the Atlanta newspapers, the *Minneapolis Star and Tribune*, the Scripps-Howard group, the *Toronto Star*, and the *Washington Post*—a powerful group. Since then a few partners have dropped out, some have come in. The aim was to create the newspaper industry's first totally integrated computer system for performing full page composition, with editing and typesetting. It was meant to be a three year project, and the aim was a system that would produce *either* a printing plate or transmit via future non-paper communications facilities. The system would take in news, classified and display ads. In short it would be a people-less composing room.

The project has had wide publicity, and recent seminars about it in the UK (held by PIRA) seem to have had maximum attendance. The NSDG has glamour. But it would be wrong to place undue reliance on it at this stage (as some UK newspaper planners may be in danger of doing); the original Japanese experience has had to be almost totally jettisoned; the project is heavily over-budget, and well behind the original schedule; it has a number of prominent heavyweight critics among US newspapers; and the system will certainly be very expensive to buy, if and when it is designed.

The original schedule called for completion of programming of the computer by late 1975, but in February and March of 1975 the various partners were still wrangling about the technical specifications of the system. What is already clear is that instead of the 1976/77 deadline originally spoken about, something like 1980 may be more realistic, even if, as is still hoped, a test system is under way by 1976. Both IBM and the various partners are coy about costs, except for admitting that it is very expensive, but one estimate is that the partners have committed between them $11 million to the project so far; that they may have to commit as much again; and that IBM's contribution equals that of the partners. An informed guess about the cost of buying a final system is about $5 million to $8 million, which is very expensive.

It is undeniable that the NSDG project has as its aim the sort of system that someone, some day soon, is bound to evolve—a system in which all the elements of a newspaper are stored in a computer, or computers, with corrections and changes transmitted to the computer via terminals, so that at the desired time the computer will assemble the page elements and print out a whole page on a high speed photocomposing machine. Such a system is almost bound to employ video terminals (for entry and editing of copy, and for lay-out of pages and ads), OCR scanners, graphics scanners for the introduction of pictures, proof printers for checking and reference, and a big storage capacity for data. It is quite possible that the NSDG project will produce such a system, and certainly the planning of the *Dallas Morning News* and the *Washington Post*, for example is predicated on the eventual arrival of this 'total system'.

But critics attack it on two fronts. One is cost. The Richmond, Virginia, newspaper group has deliberately entered into a different development project, in partnership with the Mead Corporation, a big paper company, for an automated composition system which will, like the NSDG design, be for general sale if and when it is ready. A Richmond executive says that 'the benefits of such a system will be the virtual elimination of all typesetting and paste-up operations in a newspaper; this means, in effect, that there will be no need for a composing room in the future'. The difference between the Richmond project and the NSDG project lies mainly in the computers used. The NSDG project centres around one or two large IBM 370 computers (the *New York Times*, which was invited to participate in the NSDG and refused, rather unkindly calls it 'the mother earth concept'), whereas the Richmond project will centre around a series of much cheaper mini-computers. Richmond executives also see an eventual connection between their project and the plateless printing systems in which Mead is also interested (these are based on ink-jets, and are generally agreed to be 15 years or more away, and are therefore not yet within the timescale of practical newspaper planning).

Critics of the Richmond-Mead project question whether a paper company like Mead really has the expertise to design a proper composition system. Critics of the NSDG cannot question the expertise of the partners, which is overwhelming, but question the excessive scale of the project, and say that they do not want to be tied to 'an IBM solution'. One partner in NSDG, the Norfolk (Virginia) papers, now says that it will take up an NSDG system much later than originally anticipated, and probably last among the partners. There is a general agreement that the NSDG system will be for big newspapers, rather than for smaller newspapers, when and if it comes.

While therefore it would probably be rash to rely on the arrival of the NSDG system, certainly rash to rely on its arrival by a particular time, nevertheless the concept of a totally automated composing room is sound, and inherent in the whole technological movement we are now witnessing.

The IPC Full-Page System

Because of the circumstances surrounding this project, there are differing versions of the story. But about 7 years ago the International Publishing Corporation decided to develop its own electronic composing room, or full-page composition system. A design team set to work. Over two years ago a final system was completed—a bit Heath Robinson to look at, being a room in an IPC building with a lot of machinery and wires. But as a pilot system, it worked. Printing executives who have seen it agree on this point, although at least one potential manufacturer was critical of its design.

Last summer (July 1974) almost the entire design team was declared redundant, and it was made clear that IPC was no longer interested in the system, on the development of which it had spent large sums. The *Mirror* has now announced plans for technological change on a different basis.

In the end, after the *New York Times* had come near to buying the full-page system, it was sold by IPC to Dow Jones of the US (whose best known publication is the *Wall Street Journal*). In the late summer of 1975 it was physically dismantled and sent off across the Atlantic. It would be ironic if at some future date some British companies were to pay out precious foreign currency to buy a system which was created here. The story of British industry not being able or willing to take up and exploit the inventions of its best brains, is by now a familiar one. It is hard to resist the conclusion that here we have yet another example of that depressing phenomenon.

The News Agencies

Technological change in the news agencies is almost a study in itself, but here the importance is the influence the agencies have had on technological developments in newspapers through their pioneering of the use of video screens for editing, and the influence they may have through their developments of very high speed news transmission systems and the recent harnessing of news agency services to cable television distribution.

AP in New York has over 200 video screens already in use, and will get over 200 more in the next 3 years. The financial justification lies in getting rid of the 300 keyboard operators who used to shuttle the news stories round the US within the AP network, and send them out to newspapers. In New York these earn about $14,000 a year and the cost of one screen is down from about $14,000 two years ago to about $7,000 now: the pay-off is therefore clear.

A news agency is really a system for the multiple handling of news—re-writes for different areas, and for different customers, plus internal and external distribution—and they have found that screens bring not only economies but also greater facility in this handling process, because the location, status, origin, and other information about a given story can be checked so quickly.

UPI is installing a similar screen system, to replace the 235 teletype operators which it had: this number is expected to be down to nearly 40 by the end of this year. UPI cites as additional benefits the much lower noise level, and the elimination of the errors that the human keyboard operators make. This becomes very important as and when the wire service punch tape is used as a direct input to the photocomposing equipment of a customer newspaper, as is now happening with stock market prices and may presumably extend to other news.

AP and UPI are also developing a new high speed news distribution system. Present speeds of transmission are under 100 words a minute but the new services operate at 1,200 words a minute, and could operate much faster, except for the high cost of the print-cut device that would be needed at the receiver's end. Whereas at present speeds a big backlog of unsent stories is apt to build up (it can take a story up to 3 hours to get transmitted), at the high speed the whole lot gets sent out in about a quarter of an hour in each hour. The main aim of the new high speed services is however for direct input to the home computer of the receiving newspaper, when and as newspapers develop such a facility.

But the development does open the intriguing possibility that in future, newspapers will not simply be passive recipients of whatever the news agency chooses to send out, when it chooses to send it, but will instead take an active, interrogatory role. The *New York Daily News* is already experimenting on these lines. If an editor *inside* the news agency can call up stories or indices of stories from his computer, there is no reason why an *outside* editor on the customer paper should not do exactly the same, and simply ask for the stories he wants to be sent over. The news agency-newspaper relationship may alter quite significantly.

But a more staggering development is the new Reuters service in New York, operated in conjunction with one of the local cable TV companies. The Reuters central computer sends out its entire store of information in one great rush down the coaxial cable, at the rate of 70,000 words a second, or over 4 million words a minute, re-transmitting the whole thing every three seconds. At the receiver's end, the subscriber has a special device that is instructed to pick out and display on a screen what the subscriber wants from this huge rush of data as it goes by; that is, stock prices, racing results, commodity market results, or whatever. At the moment this service is for big company subscribers, at the quite high price of $600 to $1,000 a month: but Reuters expect to sell, say, a racing service to bars for under $200 a month, and in due course a service to the home for perhaps $10 to $20 a month, taking in much more general news, weather reports, local news, TV listings—anything the subscribers want. The fact that this is a *one-way* system, and does not require two-way dialogue between subscriber and Reuters, makes it cheaper.

Although the New York newspapers believe that they will themselves become in due course subscribers to this service, it is clear that the service—or services like it—will in time present a threat to newspapers themselves, perhaps by taking over a lot of the pure information service at present provided by newspapers. Much the same possibilities arise from the new British services Ceefax and Oracle, run by the BBC and IBA respectively, as yet on a very limited basis, but essentially distributing information in word and number form via the air waves to TV screens.

Satellites

Among the other technological projects that may indicate the trends of the future (like plate-less printing by ink jet, or the laser method of making printing plates which Gannett Newspapers has pioneered but which is still too expensive for general use), it may be worth singling out the recent satellite experiment that the *Wall Street Journal* carried out with COMSAT, the communications satellite corporation. This consisted of sending facsimile pages of the *Journal* from one printing centre to another (the *Journal* uses 9 different plants over the US) using direct signals up to and down from a satellite. Special transmission and reception equipment were set up next to the printing plants, and transmission time average 6 minutes; the result was a full page negative from which a web offset printing plate was made. So successful was the experiment that the company (Dow Jones) is now building transmitting stations so as to go over entirely to satellite transmission of all domestic US news and editions in the near future. While expensive at the moment, such a method could one day be of use to any newspaper using two or more separate printing plants. It has the great advantage of being more or less error free, as well as fast, and could be a more advanced version of, for example, the still unusual system whereby the *Herald Tribune* now sends over facsimile pages from Paris to London via land wire and radio link, for printing of the UK and Scandinavian edition at a printing plant at Slough. The *Guardian's* plans for its link between its London and Manchester offices, and the proposed *Mirror* facsimile link from London to Plymouth for its West Country edition, are other examples in the same area. Apart from other considerations, a lot of jobs are eliminated by such methods of automatic and electronic transmission, which do away with the need for rekeyboarding and resetting of material sent over long distances, and it shows that the attack on composing room labour costs is not and will not be bounded by the four walls of any one printing works.

10

Approaches to Journalism Education

JOSEPH Pulitzer thought that "unprepared journalists who learn by experience, learn at the cost of their readers." When he first suggested that journalists should be trained, he was laughed at. Journalism schools and department in the United States went through a hard time in the 1920's convincing newspaper editors and proprietors of the utility of training. Now the newspapers and other media are heavily dependent on these schools for the supply of not only trained people but research data of all kinds. As against the United States which took to institutional training, the British believed in training on the job. India, which has emulated Britain in so many spheres, somehow followed the American system in respect of training in journalism. It is American to the extent that it is institutional training at the university level. But unlike the American schools and colleges where students study journalism as a "major" for the B.A or B.S. degree, India chose one-year post-graduate course leading to a diploma, now increasingly a Bachelor's degree. In the recent years, however, not only other types of courses have developed at the university level but pre-service training programmes have been initiated also in a large number of private colleges and under the auspices of the government.

THE UNITED STATES

Journalism training in the USA can be said to have completed its eight decades in 1984 because the first four-year curriculum was organized by the University of Illinois in 1904. The University of Missouri was the first to set up a full-fledged School of Journalism in 1908 and Columbia University's Pulitzer School of Journalism came on the scene four years later.

At present about 200 colleges and universities offer the four-year curriculum leading to the degree of Bachelor of Arts or Science with a major in Journalism. More than 400 other four-year institutions offer some courses in journalism but these do not comprise a full major; a major consists of 30 credit hours or one-fourth of a four-year Bachelor's degree course. Besides, many junior colleges provide a few courses in journalism and almost all high schools give instruction in production of school and magazines.

Of the 200 colleges and universities offering full-fledged professional courses in journalism, about 70 have the facilities for post-graduate studies leading to the Master's degree in Journalism or Communication and 21 of them have the doctoral programme of one or the other kind. The total enrolment of journalism/communication students today is estimated to be around 75,000.

Nature of Courses

Most of the schools of journalism are on par with the schools of law, medicine and engineering. The first degree in journalism (Bachelor of Arts or Science) comes on the completion of four years of under-graduate studies. Only one-fourth to one-third of the course work is in journalism or communication. This includes the various skill-oriented courses like news reporting, editing and writing advertisement copy and others such as history, principles and ethics of journalism and laws of the press. The rest of the course work is in the areas of social sciences, humanities and natural sciences. This results in a good blend of theory and practice of journalism besides a well-balanced general education.

Post-graduate studies (called "graduate" studies in the US) developed fast after the Second World War. These lead to the degrees of Master of Arts or Science and Doctor of Philosophy (Ph. D.) in Journalism, Mass Communication or Communication. The Master's course usually takes one to two years and the doctoral programme three to four years. While there is no uniformity in the course offered by different universities at the under-graduate level, the variations are much more marked in respect of their post-graduate programmes. The Pulitzer School of Journalism of Columbia University, for instance, lays heavy stress on technique-oriented courses for the Master's degree whereas so many other universities emphasize communication theory and research. The subjects of study are such as international news communication, public opinion, propaganda, freedom of the press, economics of mass media, social effects of the media, theories of mass communication. There are several "seminar" courses which require writing and discussing of research papers. These "graduate seminars" are on design and process of survey research,, media research methods, communication research design, research in history of journalism and advertising problems. Most universities also require a thesis for the Master's degree, some accept one or more research papers in lieu of the thesis. For the Ph.D. degree, the social science component, specially of psychology and sociology, is large. The Ph.D. programme is designed to provide advanced study of mass communication theories and experience in use of research techniques. A student has to go through a large number of courses offered by different departments of the university and these are related to his specific research interests. On the completion of the course work which usually takes two years, the student has to clear a comprehensive examination before undertaking research for his dissertation. In these universities, one may also take a "minor" in journalism or communication while doing the major doctoral work in another area like sociology, psychology, political science, economics or English literature.

Besides teaching and research, the third important area of journalism schools' activity is service to the mass media and the general public. They maintain a close liaison with the professional groups of journalists, publishers, advertisers and broadcasters and organise a variety of short-term courses, clinics and symposia for mediamen.

Infrastructure

The schools and departments of journalism in most universities are well-equipped in respect of faculties, laboratories and libraries. The percentage of those holding Ph.D. degree on the faculty is high. Almost always they also have media experience of one or more types.

It is usual for the schools to be self-contained units with classrooms, faculty offices, libraries and reading rooms, research and seminar rooms and laboratories of different kinds for practical training. For students involved in newspaper and magazine work, there are enough typewriters, editing desks, all the leading wire services and photo and type laboratories. There are several student publications but the most valuable is the daily produced by students of journalism. The student publications have their own editorial, advertising and processing sections.

Several of the universities own radio and television stations which are used also as laboratories for students of radio and television journalism. In the alternative, the schools of journalism have their radio and television laboratories and they make arrangements with the broadcast and telecast of the student produced programmes. There are enough cameras for both still and motion photography besides other processing equipment.

Apart from the journalism school's well-stocked library, the students have access to the libraries of other schools on the campus and the university's main library. Duplicating facilities of different kinds, either free or at a nominal cost, are of great help in studies and research. A few schools have their own computers whereas in others the students have an easy access to the university's computer centre for processing their research data.

Any discussion on the nature of courses in American colleges and universities will remain incomplete without reference to the sea-change which the course pattern has undergone in the last few decades. In the beginning, the courses were largely vocational in nature, all technique-oriented and tailored to the needs of the print media. In course of time subjects like the history of journalism, press laws, newspaper management, advertising and photography figured in the curriculum. Radio then broke the monopoly of the print medium and later television invaded the field. The mass media scene changed drastically. Apart from the fact that the technique courses now covered all the print and electronic media, the need was realised for a better understanding of the role of mass media and of the relationship between the media and the society. So newer courses developed and in the last three decades a great deal of stress has been laid on communication theory and research. As a result, the schools of journalism have built up a substantial body of literature in these areas and this has been a major factor in the development of communication as an academic discipline.

Professional Organisations

The two most important professional organisations concerned with the improvement of education in journalism are the Association of Education in Journalism and the American Council on Education for Journalism. Two others with specialised interests are the American Academy of Advertising and the Association for Professional Broadcasting Education.

The Association for Education in Journalism (AEJ) was founded in 1912 as the American Association of Teachers of Journalism. It took the new name of AEJ in 1949 and a year later took within its fold the American Association of Schools and Departments of Journalism (AASDJ, organised in 1917) and the American Society of Journalism School Administration (ASJSA, organised in 1944) as "co-founding affiliates."

One can get some idea of AEJ's activities from the list of its 15 Divisions: Advertising, Graphics, History, International Communication, Law, Magazine, Mass Communication and Society, Minorities and Communication, Newspaper, Photo-journalism, Public Relations, Qualitative Division, Radio-Television, Journalism, Secondary Education, Theory and Methodology. AEJ's largely attended annual conventions are stimulating and very helpful to teachers in the exchange of information on the latest developments in studies and research in different parts of the country. AEJ also provides facilities of the "Placement Service."

The American Council on Education for Journalism, formed in 1945, is an outgrowth of an earlier less representative National Council of Professional Education for Journalism. The present ACEJ consists of "professional", "education" and "public" members and has an "accrediting committee." It undertakes evaluation of the teaching programmes in colleges and universities throughout the United States. Its purpose is to improve standards of journalism training, to develop mutual understanding among teachers and other professional groups, and to set up policies whereby various instructional programmes can be assessed and accredited.

Together with the AEJ and ACEJ, other professional bodies such as the American Society of Newspaper Editors, the American Press Managing Editors Association and the American Newspaper Publishers Association are playing a vital role in strengthening professionalism among journalists. A notable feature of journalism scene in the United States today is the existence of a great many trade, professional and research journals of high standard. And their impact on the practitioners and would-be journalists is all too evident. Most prominent among these journals are *Editor and Publisher, Columbia Journalism Review* and *Journalism Quarterly.*

The industry support to journalism schools has been steadily improving and there is an ever-growing collaboration between the media and the training institutions in their common endeavour to upgrade the media. More and more schools are receiving endowments from newspaper groups and graduates majoring in journalism and finding ready acceptance in newspaper, magazine and news agency offices and of course in other media organisations.

The absorption rate of journalism graduates in the media has been variously estimated between 60 per cent and 70 per cent. If a good number of these trained men and women do not get into the profession, it is not so much because they are not acceptable to the media or because there are not enough openings for them. What has happened is that so many young men and women now take courses in Journalism merely to understand the role of mass media and the relationship between the media and the society, they do not aim at a journalistic career.

The salaries for new entrants to newspapers and news agencies have been almost continuously improving ever since *The Wall Street Journal* set the trend in the mid fifties with a view to attracting the trained graduates who were drifting away into more lucrative, radio, television public relations and advertising jobs. Even today the order of preference of journalism majors is said to be: Radio-TV, P. R.—Advertising, Magazines, Newspaper-News Agency. Their actual absorption rate, however, is the highest in daily and weekly newspapers, followed by advertising and public relations, magazines, radio and television, news agencies. Many of course take to teaching of journalism in high schools. Some go to journalism schools again for higher studies and eventually take teaching positions in colleges or universities or do research in industry.

A constant evaluation of the teaching programmes and improvement in the accreditation process is now a well established feature of journalism in the United States. Surveys of different kinds are periodically conducted by a variety of agencies to assess the value of training. Further, co-operation between the mediamen and educators to make training more effective is evident in many forms and at different levels. Here is one example to illustrate the seriousness which the business of training is approached:

The American Newspaper Publishers Association Foundation, in collaboration with the Association for Education in Journalism, had sponsored a three-day conference at Reston in 1972 to resolve "wide differences in perceptions and expectations that dramatised a long-existing gulf between many professional newspapermen and journalism educators." One hundred educators and journalists participated in the conference. What is noteworthy is that this dialogue was arranged after two years of meticulous planning. Sixteen working papers, specially commissioned for this conference, were prepared by experts after months of research. They cover all aspects of training and are of a uniformly high standard. No wonder the discussion at the Reston meet was most meaningful and mutually beneficial to educators and practitioners. The resultant publication called *Proceedings: Education for Journalists in the Seventies and Beyond* is a valuable document and a worthy example of effective collaboration between educators and journalists.

INDIA

Though training for journalists started late in India, the last two decades have brought about a phenomenal increase in the number of institutions offering courses of one kind or the other. We have now pre-service training and in-service training. We have institutional training and on-the-job training. Institutional training itself is being imparted in university departments, private colleges and government institutes. The focus here is on pre-service training for the print media at the university level.

The first successful effort to provide journalism training at the university level was that of Professor P. P. Singh who set up a department of auspices of Punjab University at Lahore in 1941. After the country's partition in 1947, the department functioned in Delhi for 15 years before shifting to the new campus of Punjab University at Chandigarh in 1962. Presenting a paper at the Communication/Journalism Teachers Seminars at Honolulu in 1971, Professor Singh recalled that in the forties "journalism education met with strong opposition from working journalists. Few thought that journalists needed training or that they could be trained."

From 1947 to 1954, five more university courses in journalism (Madras, Calcutta, Mysore, Nagpur and Osmania) came into existence. Ten years passed before the next addition was made and from 1964 to 1985, 23 more universities launched journalism courses. These are the Universities of Poona, Gauhati, Shivaji (Kolhapur), Jabalpur, Punjab Agricultural (Ludhiana), Ravi-Shankar (Raipur), Marathwada (Aurangabad), Banaras Hindu (Varanasi), Saurashtra (Rajkot), Bangalore, Berhampur, Punjabi (Patiala), Madurai Kamaraj, Garhwal (Srinagar, Garhwal), Rajasthan (Jaipur), Aligarh Muslim, Calicut, Kerala (Trivandrum), Maharshi Dayanand (Rohtak), Dharwar, Sagar, Allahabad and Indore.

Simultaneously, a large number of private colleges, offering part-time courses in journalism, have sprung up all over the country. The first was the American College of Journalism which B. G. Horniman established in 1936, it is now known as the Horniman College of Journalism, in Bombay. The largest chain is that of Bhartiya Vidya Bhavan whose main centre at Bombay, set up in 1961 is called the Rajendra Prasad Institute of Communication and Management. The Institute now has in all 30 constituent and affiliated colleges in India. It offers a series of diploma courses in communication and management sequences. There are very many other private institutions imparting instruction in journalism on part-time basis in Delhi, Bombay and other cities. Quite different from all these is the whole-time diploma course of one year in mass communication techniques and TV production being offered by the St. Xavier Institute of Communication, Bombay.

Correspondence courses in Journalism are available from Rajasthan University (Jaipur) and Mysore University besides from agencies like the British Institute of Commerce and the International Correspondence School, both in Bombay. The Andhra Pradesh Open University, Hyderabad, has recently started a diploma course in public relations.

Among the governmental training efforts, the Indian Institute of Mass Communication, set up in New Delhi in 1965, is most relevant for the print media. It came into existence in pursuance of the recommendations of the Mass Communication Study Team sponsored by the Ford Foundation in 1963 at the request of the Ministry of Information and Broadcasting. The basic recommendation of the team, headed by Wilbur Schramm, was for the setting up of a Centre of Advanced Study in Mass Communication "with responsibilities for consultation, training, and research and development, particularly in the use of mass communication in support of national economic and social development." The Institute offers three whole-time courses of one academic year: Post-graduate Diploma in Journalism for Developing Countries; Post-graduate Diploma in Advertising and Public Relations; Diploma in News Agency Journalism. Besides, short-term orientation/refresher courses are arranged from time to time, tailored to the needs of specific groups.

The Press Institute of India (1963) is interested in promoting better standards of journalism. It organises seminars, workshops and conferences for journalists and other media personnel. Besides publishing a mass media bimonthly *Vidura*, it brings out *Data India*, a weekly record of development and economics-related events, serving as a cumulative reference system. The Institute has published several books and monographs on different aspects of journalism.

On-the-job training has been attempted by many Indian newspapers of which the most well known is that of *The Times of India* group of publications, started in 1963. Among the Indian language dailies, *Eenadu*, a Telugu daily published from Hyderabad, periodically organised a three-month course in the late seventies for its new entrants along systematic lines. The enterprise was notable for the attempt to combine theory and practice in a methodical way.

It is evident that the training efforts have expanded a great deal in the last two decades and have taken varied forms. The need for training is no more in doubt or dispute. What is being debated at present is the type of training that we need and the manner in which it should be organised to serve the media needs. Nearly every form of training mentioned here probably fills a need of some kind and will survive. However, the bulk of the need for trained personnel for the print and other media and for communication/journalism teachers and researchers will have to be met through institutional training at the university level.

University Courses

The courses being offered at the university level differ widely from one another in respect of duration, syllabi, admission and examination procedures, faculty standards and facilities for practical training.

The first courses in journalism led to the award of a diploma. Osmania University in Hyderabad was the first to upgrade the diploma course to the Bachelor of Journalism degree course in 1962. Many other universities followed suit. The dominant pattern of training today is that of one-year post-graduate course leading to Diploma in Journalism of Bachelor's degree variously called as Bachelor of Journalism, Bachelor of Mass Communication, Bachelor of Journalism and Mass Communication, Bachelor of Science in Communication, and Bachelor of Communication and Journalism.

There are of course exceptions. Mysore University has journalism as one of the subjects (major) for the three-year B.A. degree course. Lately, a couple of other universitites have also introduced journalism as one of the elective subjects at the B.A. level. Besides, there are some shorter term certificate courses for undergraduates.

As in the USA, the course content has changed significantly in India too over the years. From the strictly technique-oriented courses confined to the print media in the forties, the present-day courses cover a host of allied areas such as advertising, public relations and radio, television and film journalism. Some also include small doses of communication theory and research. Then there are requirements of laboratory newspaper, internship and study paper. This is as it should be but unfortunately one academic year of eight to nine months is hardly enough to do full justice to all the subjects. Often, in the process of trying to cover too wide an area in too short a time, practical training becomes a casualty. Here lies an important difference between the training programmes in the U.S. and in India. Here lies also a major reason for the failure of many an Indian training institution to win the confidence of newspaper editors and proprietors.

With regard to course contents, yet another issue is often raised and that relates to the need for background courses in humanities, social sciences and natural sciences. A provision for these can be made either in a post-graduate course of two years or in a post-matriculation course of three or four years. Any such course would allow enough time for a proper mix of liberal education with the theory and practice of journalism and the allied areas. In this connection, the three-year Bachelor's programme after the 10+2 recommended by the USEFI sponsored All India Workshop on Journalism and Communication Education, held in Bangalore in June-July 1984, seems to be appropriate and deserves serious consideration.

There are at present eight Master's degree courses in the country. In three cases, the Master's degree course of one year follows the Bachelor's degree of one year (Osmania's Master of Communication and Journalism after B.C.J., Bangalore's M.S. in Communnication, Panjabi University in Patiala's Master of Journalism and Mass Communication after a similar Bachelor's degree). The other five courses are of two years after any graduation leading straight to the Master's degree (M.A. in Journalism of Mysore and Calcutta; M.A. in Communication of Madras; Master of Journalism of Kerala, M.Sc. in Agricultural Journalism of Punjab Agricultural University, Ludhiana). Except for three, all these programmes are pathetically poor suffering from nearly every conceivable weakness.

Admission Procedures

It may sound like stressing the obvious to say that admission to journalism courses should be on the basis of a thorough screening of the candidates. But there are universities which admit students indiscriminately. Some departments, because of either poor reputation or unfavourable location, have the problem of attracting enough students and they can hardly afford to be choosy. In either case, the quality of the finished product is low. Where the number of students admitted is large they don't receive individual attention of the faculty and the department finds it difficult even to arrange their internship.

The pressure for admission is heavy at most places and the good departments (relatively speaking) insist on an entrance test to verify the candidates' flair for writing and aptitude for journalism. They admit a restricted number of students. By and large the system works well except where the faculty members themselves choose to be dishonest or cannot resist pressures for admissions out of turn.

Practical Training

Practical training is imparted through classroom exercise, laboratory journals and internship in newspaper or news agency offices or in other media organisations. All of these are complementary.

Most of the departments do have internship, though of different forms and durations. Some arrange it for 6 to 12 weeks after the course—before or after the final examination. Some have it in the course. Unless the department is located at a place with a sufficient number of newspapers, the students have to be sent elsewhere. This raises the question of supervision and control, only two or three departments provide for supervised training in such situations.

That internship should be an integral part of the training programme is beyond doubt. In the existing pattern of one-year post-graduate course, perhaps the best thing to do would be to send the students to work on newspapers for, say, three afternoons in a week. This will have the advantage of theoretical instruction and practical work going hand in hand and the faculty will be able to keep an eye on the trainees. This system, of course, will work only where the department takes a small number of students and the place has some well produced newspapers. Students can be divided into two batches—one to work on the laboratory newspaper and the other to go on internship in the first half on the academic year; the two batches can switch their positions in the second half. At a place where the required number of newspapers are not published, the students must necessarily go out for 6 to 12 weeks. The period of internship can certainly be much longer in a course of two or more years.

The laboratory journal is an important vehicle of practical training for it is here that the students learn their first practical lessons in reporting and editing. Not all departments produce the laboratory newspaper. Where they do, its frequency and quality are low for want of budgetary support, printing facilities and adequate staff. A fortnightly tabloid of 4 to 8 pages is the minimum to be insisted upon.

Practical training in the three forms mentioned here can be effective only it is accompanied by a system of internal evaluation. Unless the students get credit for their performance (which will count towards their degree requirements), there is no incentive to work and the assignments are ignored. Internal assessment is necessary, in fact, also for other course work like seminar discussion and dissertation. Unfortunately there are some courses with no provision for internal evaluation.

Other prerequisites to effective practical training are restricted admissions through rigorous screening, whole-time faculty of adequate size and calibre, facilities for practical training in the department, newspapers' cooperation in the internship programme. When these conditions are not met, journalism courses invite the criticism that they are too theoretical.

Faculty, Books and Equipment

It is an incontrovertible fact that most of the departments are far from well provided for in respect of faculties, libraries and laboratories. The most pressing problem is that of faculty standards. A national survey which this writer had conducted in 1980 for the UGC revealed that the total sanctioned staff strength of Professors (9), Readers (22) and Lecturers (50) for 23 university departments was 81 giving an average of 3.5 whole-time posts per department. Further, only 51 of these posts were filled. No wonder there were departments without even one whole-time teacher. There were others with just one lecturer. Even more distressing is the fact that many whole-time teachers lack academical and professional credentials to teach journalism.

Besides weak faculties, the training programmes have been handicapped by the lack of indigenous text-books and essential equipment. There are departments with no more than one typewriter. Only a few departments have teleprinter news service of any news agency. For the lack of printing and other laboratory facilities, the responsibility rests squarely on the university authorities who often enough are unaware of the requirements of journalism training and journalism in any case is low in their list of priorities. So much so that even the UGC directives in the middle of the Sixth Plan to ensure a minimum staff pattern of 1 Professor, 2 Readers and 4 Lecturers and secure the prescribed essential equipment for journalism departments have been ignored with impunity.

We have noted the many specific shortcomings of the training programmes within the university framework. It is heartening to record that in the last few years some earnest efforts have been made to take stock of the situation and suggest remedial measures. The one-day seminar organised by the Indian Institute of Mass Communication in Delhi on 2 July, 1977 was about the first occasion when almost all heads of journalism departments assembled to exchange views and highlight the needs and problems of training. The seminar was significant inasmuch as both the Union Minister of Information and

Broadcasting and the UGC Chairman were present at the closing session and took note of the seminar's recommendations. This led to the UGC constituting for the first time a Panel on Mass Communication in 1978. The UGC also appointed an Advisory Committee on Modernisation of Journalism/Communication Syllabi and shortly afterwards, in 1979, sponsored a national workshop in Hyderabad where the journalism heads examined in depth all issues relating to training. Finally, the UGC appointed a three man committee to prepare the first-ever Report on Status of Journalism & Communication Education in India; this was published in 1981.

If journalism training in India has not progressed as much or as fast as in the U.S.A., it is because our educational as well as mass media structures are in some ways different from their counterparts in the United States. Radio and television being completely under government control has the effect of drastically curtailing the role of university level training for these media. The bulk of the resources are diverted to government institutes which alone are relied upon to meet the electronic media's need for trained men. Also, the universities here and so tightly bound by rigid rules and procedures that they cannot respond promptly and adequately to the changing requirements, of the print and other media. So far as the professional organisations—whether of newspaper proprietors, editors or other categories of journalists—are concerned, training interests them least. The lack of standard professional and research journals which play a very important role in creating an environment of professionalism is another serious lacuna. In the ultimate analysis it would be seen that there is a strong link between good quality training and development of professionalism in the media. Good training promotes professionalism in journalism. Also, where there is a truly professional press, the quality of training cannot but be good. It is in the mutual interest of the training institutes and media organizations to cooperate with each other in order to accomplish the objective of better media performance for the larger good of the society. In this context, the importance of Reston type conference periodically to ensure an effective dialogue between educators and mediamen cannot be overstressed.

The Future

In any effort to streamline the system of training, the very first need is to set up a national body—somewhat like the American Council on Education for Journalism—which would work as a liaison group representing journalism educators and all wings of the mass media industry. All journalism education programmes should be required to be accredited with this body. For accredition, a programme would have to fulfil the requirements laid down by this body in respect of admission and evaluation procedures, course pattern, student, and staff strength, minimum qualifications and experience for teachers of different ranks, duration and pattern of internship and library and laboratory facilities. The system of accreditation will effectively check the proliferation of ill-conceived and ill-equipped courses and ensure a certain minimum standard of training all over the country.

It deserves to be noted that the Second Press Commission did recommend the establishment of a National Council for Journalism Training and Communication Research—to supervise and certify journalism training. It is rather unfortunate that the UGC has opposed the acceptance of this recommendation by the government. One hopes the UGC opinion does not prove decisive.

Any plan for reorganisation of mass communication in India must take into account some hard realities. The most important of these is the acute shortage of trained teachers. Further, we do not have enough resources to support too many programmes of high standard. Consequently, not only must the number of university departments involved in training remain small for the time being but we must evolve a kind of tier system.

We should identify four to six university departments in different parts of the country to serve as regional or zonal centres. They should be staffed and equipped for high level training in all areas of communication. In the area served by each centre there may be four or five departments providing mainly skill-oriented basic courses in journalism and the allied areas, leading to the Bachelor's degree. Those wanting to specialise in any of the professional areas or to pursue higher studies of communication theory and research (leading to the

Master's degree or even the Ph.D.) should go to the regional centre. The two-tier system will ensure the optimum utilisation of our limited resources and the products of the regional centres, in course of time, will meet the growing demand for communication teachers and researchers and thus pave way for the expansion of training facilities along systematic lines.

Training in Educational Journalism

The concept of educational journalism is amorphous; its domain covers various areas where education and journalism converge. The term is applied to school and college magazines, bulletins and house journals of educational institutions of educators, scholarly journals focusing on particular disciplines, journals devoted to policies, problems, and practices in the field of education and newspaper coverage of education in general. The domain of educational journalism is being further expanded now by the decision of the U.G.C. and the N.C.E.R.T. to harness electronic media such as radio and TV in the service of both formal and non-formal education. We may justly describe this area as 'educational electronic journalism' as distinct from the more familiar area of 'educational print journalism'. It would, therefore, be misleading to assume that the problems, issues and training needs in the field of educational journalism are likely to be the same in all its manifestations. I propose to discuss, in this paper, the nature of the various varieties of educational journalism and the training facilities required to be made available for the practitioners in them.

Let us begin with school and college magazines. Usually only one issue of the magazine is published every year. It aims at presenting brief reports of the activities conducted during the year, felicitating top-notchers in a co-curricular activities and providing a vehicle for the students who are inclined to express themselves through poems, stories, essays etc. It is normally edited by language teachers and the layout is designed in consultation with an artist in the institution with an artist in the institution or the printer. It may be helpful to organise short-term workshops for the teacher-editors so as to make them aware of the basics of reporting, sub-editing, layout designing etc. The teacher editors could also be encouraged to choose student-oriented material for the magazine and to collect feedback on a regular basis. However, I believe, that we have not reached a stage where regular courses in school and college journalism would be justified. It may be enough, at this stage, if basics of journalism are included in the teacher-training programmes.

The bulletins and house journals of educational institutions and professional organisations of educators are rarely handled by professional editors. Only a few institutes such as CIEFL, Hyderabad and NCERT have posts of editors. Usually these publications are looked after by public relations officers or editorial boards consisting of teachers. As a result, they are conventional and imitative and aim at being only informative. Quite often, they are irregular in their periodicity and are subject to constraints of budgets. The quality of these journals may be significantly improved if their editors get some professional training in news-gathering, news-writing, layout-designing and photo-journalism besides orientation in public relations. The NCERT could prepare a blue-print of such workshops, spread over one or two weeks, meant for editors, public relations officers and editorial assistants working on these journals. It may not be difficult to organise the workshops on a regional basis with the help of journalism departments of the universities and professional journalists.

What has been said above about the bulletins and house journals, is more or less true about the scholarly journals devoted to particular disciplines and journals devoted to policies, problems and practices in education, the only difference being in their target audience. Scholarly journals are normally edited by subject-specialists who are not necessarily well-versed in skills of logical and terse writing and uniform practices in referencing.

11

Journalists and National Sensibility: A European Casebook

A FOREIGN observer is sure to notice that the Danish Press more than those of most other countries interests itself in the more or less important affairs of everyday life, and he will not be far off the mark in considering this a national trait. The small area of the country is not a sufficient explanation, as other countries of the same size have a Press with wider horizons than those which, at least until 1940, circumscribed the vision of most Danish newspapers. We print more "gossip" not only compared with great dailies in Switzerland (which occupies a central situation as regards international politics) or with the daily Press of Holland (with its colonial empire), but also in comparison with Sweden and Norway. With regard to information about current events the Danish Press, even including the *chronique,* lags behind the English, the Swedish, and the German (prior to 1933) Presses, and as to *esprit* and urbanity behind the French. I. V. Christensen, the historian of our Press, said that our newspapers are not quite so scientific as in some countries, not quite so *spirituels* as in some and again less thorough than in others. The foreign observer will surely be surprised at the lack of thoroughness, or rather the lack of concentration, with which even important events of the day are often treated. The motto Danish newspapers seems to be: A little of everything. Both the English and the German Presses, in their classical forms, dealt far more thoroughly with current problems than has been customary in this country. The former's main interest being home—and foreign policy, while the latter specialized in literature, art, and economics. The old-fashioned German newspaper, bearing the stamp of solid respectability, and devoid of pictures, forms a striking contrast to the Danish daily, presenting with journalistic skill and numerous illustrations a manifold picture of everyday life, not forgetting that the public must be educated, yet rather superficial in dealing with details.

The weaknesses of our Press—whose average standards are high, became we have not got a real "yellow press"—are surely partly due to its having the vices of its virtues. Its chief virtue is its close contact with the people. In that respect it is "second to none" in the world. This is partly due to the way in which the Danish Press is organized: many dailies are owned by the local population, each district having one or more papers. Partly it is due to the fact that journalists are recruited from the common people. We have already dwelt upon the very great advantages which, according to Danish opinion, derive from the close alliance between Press and People. Nevertheless, it is obvious that this alliance may easily result in the newspapers devoting too much space to the portrayal of life in Denmark, and too little to the world outside Verona, or Rudkobing. An examination of Danish newspapers would presumably reveal that home news took up 75 per cent of the space.

It is a well-known fact that the "*Times*" keeps up strict annonymity, no articles being signed. This is a matter of principle: it is the newspaper's views which are printed, not those of the individual journalist. In France, on the contrary, newspaper articles are very often signed, either by name or by *nomde-plume*. And this is quite natural because of the personal and literary form of French journalism. Especially since 1905, Danish dailies follow the French custom. However, the leading article is rarely signed, but is alone supported by the authority which the newspaper in question may have been able to create for itself among its readers. The Danish view is that the journalistic signatures make for a livelier paper, and stress the individual responsibility of journalists. The fact that the signature betrays the identity of the writer to the public, or at least to an inner circle, has not in Denmark led to the scurrility and demoralization complained of in certain other countries.

Pre-1914 Tendencies in Journalism

The evolution of the Press which dates from about 1905 is marked by a shift from literature to popular information. The "journal" becomes a "newspaper." Up till then it had been a political medium, now it becomes an end in itself. At the same time there is a change from contemplation to action. In the years immediately preceding World War I the Press, and especially the Copenhagen Press, is possessed by a new spirit of enterprise. The Press is no longer content to be the mere passive link between current ideas and the public. From a conviction of their own power newspapers wish to utilize their contact with the public without the constant interference of others, and they have ideas of their own. This brings us to the "journalism of action," which has given up being a mere reporter in order to become itself a creator of events. This tendency in the Press to follow English and American examples by setting its own tasks became all the more marked, because the years leading up to World War I were relatively uneventful, a lull. So newspapers took the initiative in performances of historical dramas and firework displays, imported international celebrities of stage and sports. They arranged exhibitions, cheap foreign tours, bicycle-racing, competitions for "balcony-gardeners" (*i.e.* people ornamenting the balconies so numerous in Copenhagen block of flats by growing flowers in green wooden boxes along the balustrades)—all of them events chosen to interest the public. This diversity of enterprise was, as we have said, partly the result of a greater consciousness of its own power in the Press: a great newspaper comes to feel that it dominates a certain section of the public, while, on the other hand, readers expect to get something more than mere news-service for subscriptions paid. When the paper has launched a smart idea, gathering a large audience and occasioning lengthy newspaper reports, members of the editorial staff will say with a smile, "In olden times we sat waiting for the news to 'drop into our turbans', later on we made up our minds to sally forth and fetch it, and nowadays we go so far as to manufacture our own news!". Later on the Dailies become less active as leaders of the dance. This, no doubt, had a salutary influence on what was properly the work of the Press. Nevertheless, there remained an acuter sense of the efficacy of Press initiative in certain aspects of public life. One feature of the journalism of action then adopted by certain dailies was a great work of charity which has been kept up ever since: providing summer-holidays in the country for slum children, Christmas dinners, and many similar activities. Henrik Cavling considered it the duty of a newspaper to put certain elementary principles of justice into practice.

The Press Act of April 13th, 1938

For more than three quarters of a century Danish newspapers lived under the Press Act of 1851. Then, on April 13th, 1938 it was superseded by a new Press Act, re-affirming the Freedom of the Press. With very few exceptions, only one person, the editor, is responsible for the anonymous contents of a newspaper. While the word "editor" was not expressly defined in the 1851 Act, the new Act defines as editor: the person who decides the contents of the daily. Further, the real editor is bound, under penalty, to state his name on the paper. This did away with the so-called "dummy editors." From now on the printer and owner disappeared from the list of person who could be held legally responsible. This meant a greater concentration of responsibility than under the old Act. As, now-a-days, editorial work is usually divided among a number of specialists, each independent as to the contents of his columns, there had been thoughts of making each of these departmental heads legally responsible for his department. The thought was opposed by the Press, desirous above all of avoiding interference in internal editorial policy.

It will be seen that the editor-in-chief retains sole responsibility for the entire contents of the paper. This responsibility is exactly as it would have been, had his signature been appended to every anonymous article. The anonymous writer or correspondent is still immune, provided, when the action is commenced, the chief editor is within Danish jurisdiction. From this immunity of staff-members and correspondent the new Press Act makes only one exception. If, in and by the article in question, certain crimes are committed against the independence and security of the country (Treason), or against the Constitution and Government (High Treason) the ordinary legal rules for personal responsibility are applied. In such cases the Judicature preserves the right of attempting to track down the person or persons responsible, who in such cases are not covered by editorial responsibility. In other words: The 1938 Act places treasonable acts outside the Press Law.

Under the new Act, the editor is still exempt from responsibility for signed articles, the legislature recognizing that, under an arrangement making him responsible for these, he must of necessity hesitate to accept contributions even from expert sources. By hindering salutary informed criticism this might endanger the healthy management of public affairs. However, the new Act established certain exceptions to the fundamental principle of editorial irresponsibility for signed articles. The editor is not immune 1) in case he has incurred part responsibility for an article, either by himself soliciting it, or when it has been written with his own or staff assistance, so that the contributor is in reality a mere cat's paw, and 2) if the editor is aware that the contents of the article are punishable by law. In such cases the editor is now held partly responsible, and so, after serious consideration, the principle was laid down that the author, as originator of the article in question, must bear the main responsibility for its contents, but the editor must be held responsible for its distribution, *i.e.* for its increased injurious effect on the victim. This tends to make him rather critical and chary of accepting such contributions. Of course editorial censorship had been the rule also prior to 1938.—The staff journalist who writes signed articles is in exactly the same position as the outside contributor. The 1938 Act offers him better protection than he used to have, seeing that, under the new regulations, his chief shares responsibility for the criminal article, at least when it was commissioned by him, or produced with his collaboration, or if he knew its contents to be criminal. In the past, the journalist would have full responsibility in such cases. Now, if an editor orders a journalist to sign f.inst. the opening article of a series, it means that this journalist will have to accept his share of responsibility before the law, but under the 1851 Act he alone would have been held responsible.

It was recognized that unfavourable mention of a person or his conduct, spread by a mass-produced newspaper, may cause considerable injury to the economy or reputation of such a person (or association, or public authority), if he is not secured the right to reply. So the Act lays down that, in such cases, an editor must print, unchanged and free of charge, a factual correction from the person concerned. This correction must be printed in the same type as the rest of the text and given such prominence of place as the circumstances of the case make it reasonable to demand. The attacked person's right to reply is unconditional, independent of any examination of the truth or falsity of the statement he wishes to correct, or of the correction itself. The underlying principle is that, in no case, should a person be condemned by public opinion without a hearing. In order that the newspaper should gain the least possible distance, the correction must be printed not later than the second issue after it has been requested. The Press thought it essential that the right of correction be limited to a statement of facts (so that no person dissatisfied by a mere opinion or criticism voiced in the newspaper can request correction), and that no third person should have the right of requesting a correction. In case the editor wishes to comment on the reply in the same issue in which it is printed, he, too, must limit himself to facts, *i.e.*, he is not allowed to append to the correction the well-known tag which so often gave the sender a feeling of having fallen from the frying pan into the fire. Thus the public's right to retort is safeguarded. If the editor finds that the contents of the protest are such as to free him from the obligation of printing them, the complainant can appeal to a commission whose chairman is a Supreme Court Justice. Independent of appeal to this commission, and regardless of its result, the complainant can, in case he wishes to go to law, request the acceptance free of charge of an item stating that such an action has been commenced.

Another innovation is the rule that hand-bills and posters must not contain statements which by their form and contents cause undue injury to persons or firms. They are to be considered part and parcel of the newspaper to which they refer, and so the editor is held responsible for their contents. Injurious statements on a poster are treated as a police case, *i.e.* the action is brought by the authorities and dealt with summarily, an offender, if found guilty, being liable to imprisonment—irrespective of whether the contents of the newspaper itself occasion a private criminal action.

The Press Act of 1938, institutes a series of new rules concerning *Compensation*. This liability is still limited in the same way as the liability before the criminal law, *i.e.* as a rule compensation for injury suffered can only be claimed from editor and authors of signed articles, not from the anonymous journalist, contributor, or informant. A right to sue for damages from the latter would, even if in another way, lead to a revelation of internal editorial arrangements, which might prove detrimental to the functioning of the Press. An innovation is the principle that the publisher of the newspaper (the person at whose expense the paper is published) is liable for the amounts of damages, fines, and costs to which the editor is sentenced, so that amounts due can be recovered by seizure from the publisher. This accords with the unusual juridical principle that he in whose interest a business is carried on, *i.e.* who pockets the economic profits, is liable for compensation for injury caused by persons employed by the business. The rule also holds, if the newspaper is run by a joint-stock company.

The contents of an advertisement may be criminal. An advertiser may, f.inst., make an untrue statement to the effect that he is the sole vendor of certain goods; or the advertisement may contain a veiled invitation to prostitution. For the advertisements of a daily paper there is no question of protecting anonymity, so he who inserts a criminal or illegal advertisement is liable to punishment under the usual regulations whether his name or that of his firm are stated in the advertisement or not. Thus, if the identity of the advertiser is known, the editor has no responsibility, unless he, or one of his assistants, has taken part in its formulation, or unless he was aware that its contents were false and criminal. As, therefore, the editor can be made responsible also for advertisements, the Press Act permits, in certain cases, the transfer of this responsibility to the person who independently decides on the acceptance of advertisements, provided his responsibility for this part of the contents is expressly stated in the paper. This method was frequently used during the German occupation, 1940-45, when the Germans' directions for advertising made vigilance advisable.

When the Act had been passed by the Rigsdag, opposed only by the Communists, it was clearly seen that it meant no breach with, but only an adaptation of the traditional distribution of responsibility. With regard to editorial responsibility a middle course had been steered so as not to hinder the ordinary citizen's access to the columns of the Press. In fact, the new Press Act was a renewed guarantee of the Freedoms of Thought, Speech, and Press, granted by our first Free Constitution. And so, in its final form, the Act came into being with the support of all Press Organizations.

The Press: Proprietors and Capital

In our days no description of the legal position of the Press dealing with its responsibilities under Criminal and Press Laws could be accepted as complete. When newspapers were small and owned by one individual, or a small company with a capital of only kr. 30 or 40 thousand, interest naturally centered on the Freedom of the Press considered as a fundamental principle. To-day, when the estimated cost of starting a great Copenhagen daily capable of competing with the veterans, is at least kr. 5 mill. (as compared with 50 mill. in London), attention is just as naturally focused on the already existing dailies' virtual monopoly of this same Freedom. It is not only the purchase of machinery and office equipment which makes the start so costly under normal conditions, but also the unavoidable temporary deficit of several thousands of kroner per day. The international newspaper world, like business in general, is characterized by increasing concentration: the great dailies are gaining ground at the expense of the smaller newspapers. This concentration offers obvious economical and technical, and also some journalistic advantages. However, with the decreasing number of newspapers the readers' choice is restricted, which constitutes a real, though indirect, danger to the Freedom of the Press. In these circumstances the suspicion that corrupt practices are being resorted to in order to influence public opinion is easily aroused. So the public will turn to the few surviving newspapers with the demand that they make known what capital is invested in them, and the names of their proprietors. There is a feeling that in a democracy every citizen has a right to know who is responsible for propagating a political ideology. It would not be fair, if that control of the Press which, in the name of Democracy, is denied the Government fell into the hands of a dozen financiers.

In Denmark the Daily Press is so organized that control of its management is not so urgently needed as, f.inst., in Britain or France. We have no real "Newspaper Kings," holding absolute sway over their newspapers and adopting a changeable and hysterical policy.—"Caesarism" is an unknown phenomenon in our Press. Sales of newspapers are extremely rare, and it would hardly be possible to find a single case of a hard-fisted businessman having bought up an important newspaper in order, through it, to pursue private ends. In a small country like ours such a transaction, had it taken place, would not have escaped notice. Most Danish Dailies have not changed hands for générations, the great majority of them, representing a very considerable proportion of the total circulations, being the property of wide sections of the local population (The Four Paper System) it must, of course, be next to impossible to suppress news and opinions, seeing that the best news-item is often the one which the colleague was unwilling to print.

In Denmark, as in other countries, the number of dailies has been decreasing in recent years: in 1925 the Capital had 18 newspapers, in 1949 only 13. In the same years the provinces had 144 and 101 respectively, running their own printing plants.

In Denmark privately owned newspapers, and newspapers owned by political or cooperative groups enter into useful competition. It would hardly be advisable to give preference to one of these forms of ownership, to the exclusion of the other. For no existing system of management can give a newspaper, or any other human enterprise, absolute economic independence. It has rightly been thought salutary that very great numbers of our newspapers are the property of numerous small shareholders among the local population, because this system of ownership prevents individual owners from making the newspaper subservient to their own economic and political purposes. It would, on the other hand, hardly be advisable by legislation to forbid all other systems of Press ownership than those of the limited liabilities company and the cooperative society. Such legislation already exists in this country concerning insurance companies, but for different reasons. It has rightly been maintained, that such a system would abolish our traditional form of the Freedom of the Press, *i.e.* the right of every citizen to put his thoughts into print, be it as writer or publisher. Yet it would hardly be a good thing, if the entire Press should pass into the hands of more or less influential organizations. The history of our Press abounds in examples of responsible individuals having made excellent use of this right.

The demand that the public be kept informed of the identity of the economic supporters of a newspaper (if such there be) need not in Denmark cause the Press overmuch anxiety. For that matter the demand has already been partly complied with. Newspapers belonging to companies, or organized as cooperative societies, are under the obligation of informing the Public Joint-Stock Companies' Register (Aktieselskabsregistret) of the amount of the share capital, how (but not by whom) it has been paid up, the activities of the company, the board of directors, etc. This information is open to anyone enquiring at the Register. Further, if the company has more than 10 shareholders, its statement of accounts must be made public. Anyone can order a copy showing whether the company is making a profit or being left with a deficit. Similarly information can be obtained about contingent mortgage debt and the amount due to creditors (but not the names of mortgagor or creditor).

One Danish newspaper, the "Information," with a circulation (in 1949) of 28,000, gets its capital in a unique manner. It has "anonymous backers," but they number at least 1000, and accepting the newspaper' own explanation, there seems to be nothing odious about this arrangement. The "Information," after an underground existence during the German Occupation, was established as a legal daily after the Liberation. According to its own explanation it inherited a large sum of money from an underground organisation known as "Ringen." This sum was afterwards increased by the business committee of the "Ringen." But that was not enough to pay for the start, and the "Information" could not pay its way until the summer of 1948. There was a monthly deficit, decreasing gradually from kr.

40,000 per month in 1945 to kr. 38,000 for the whole of 1947. A friend of the paper was then entrusted with the task of raising a round sum from persons suggested by its local committees in all towns, a local initiative with which the editors and management had nothing to do. No shares were distributed in return for sums received. The "Information" has stated that the money was given subject to no obligations; if they can repay the money well and good, but they are under no obligation to do so. Neither the board of directors, of which the two editors are members, nor the representative committee are elected by persons having donated money; nay, according to the written statement of the editors, no member of the board is allowed to invest money in the newspaper. So nobody can be said to own its capital. On these grounds the "Information" claims to be an economically independent foundation.

Abolition of Newspaper Privileges

From time immemorial Denmark had had special arrangements for making Government decrees, proclamations, and announcements known to the people. Throughout most of the 19th century The provincial "Stiftstidender" (Diocesan Times) and the Copenhagen "Berlingske Tidende" held the privilege of printing official announcements, such as legal notices, notices about bankruptcies, public auctions, annulments, meetings of heirs and creditors, etc. Every announcement of this kind must be inserted both in the local "Stiftstidende" and in the "Berlingske Tidende," which besides being the "Stiftstidende" of the island of Sealand, was also a sort of "State Gazette." The privilege was subject to an impost payable to the Exchequer. Thus the "Berlingske Tidende" paid kr. 20,000 annually. The newspaper privileges, which proved particularly lucrative to the Conservative "Berlingske Tidende," were abolished at the introduction of Parliamentary Government, in 1901, when the Liberals came into Power. In 1904 the last vestiges of the announcement privilege had disappeared, which was a hard blow to the "Berlingske Tidende," but there were compensations. Now there was no impost to pay, while for many years readers went on regarding the "Berlingske" as an official gazette. Even to-day, we find in its columns relatively large numbers of notices about estates, announcements of sales, and especially numerous "Funds Available" advertisements. And the "Berlingske Tidende" did its utmost to keep alive the belief in its special position within the Press. It kept the words "By Royal Privilege" and the Coat of Arms of the Realm in its title, and it was still preferred medium for announcements from the Court Steward. For years still its Conservative readers liked to regard their newspaper as a public institution. This wish was easily fulfilled by editors and managers who could not themselves in the first decade give up the conception of the "Berlingske Tidende" as an official announcement gazette. *Captain Chr. Blangstrup,* chief editor 1902-12, lacked the open mind and interest in contemporary thought and events, essential to the leading newspaperman. At this time *Svend Poulsen,* who was "of the family," modernized the "Berlingske" somewhat. He was a good travelling journalist with valuable connections in the business world, too. Nevertheless, he was unable to alter the impression that the "Berlingske" was in a period of stagnation. And there was economic stagnation as well. True, there were often 3 or 4 big advertising supplements per week. Profits were still great, but they were decreasing. At the turn of the century the morning edition sold 15,000 copies, in 1914 14,000; the evening edition 7,800 and 8,000, respectively. This meant for one paper an absolute, for the other a relative decline.

We have seen that after the political changes of 1901 the "Berlingske Tidende" was left with a past which had become history, and a future which was yet to be conquered. And in 1912 the offensive had not yet begun.

While the "Berlingske Tidende" was going through "lean years," the Ferslew Newspapers, partly thanks to excellent business management, were climbing towards the climax of their success. As yet the "Berlingske's" total mass of advertisements far exceeded that of the Ferslew Press but while both subscribers and economy were slowly oozing from the "Berlingske Tidende," the Ferslew Company was progressing steadily. C. Ferslew had, too, in time understood that the traditional Conservative policy based on "privileged classes" was doomed. After the Folketing Election of 1906 the Danish farmers surrendered their privileged position in the parish coucils. This made Ferslew realize that manhood suffrage was bound to come in national politics, too. So his newspapers accepted a political programme worked out by Asger Karstensen, their political correspondent, and whose first clause was that the Conservatives give up all privileges with regard to the Landsting-franchise derived from the possession of money and land. In 1909 the Ferslew morning-papers' circulation was estimated at about 75,000 copies. If it is true that in his heart of hearts the Titular Councillor of State cherished the hope of some day taking over the "Berlingske Tidende," it will be seen that this hope was not unfounded. Nor would he, presumably, have found its proprietors unwilling. However, in 1910 he was overtaken by death.

About that time the proprietors of the "Berlingske Tidende" were beginning to read and understand the signs of the times. The fact that, since the abolition of Newspaper Privileges, incomes were not as stable as formerly, forced the proprietors to keep an eye on economy. Further, the younger generation of the family realized that the future of their newspaper could only be secured by the investment of fresh capital. It would no longer do simply to pocket the profits, because they might be needed to meet future demands. On Jan. 1st, 1913, *Chr. Gulmann* (1869-1934) was appointed chief editor. Gulmann was neither a Ph.D. nor a Captain, but he *was* a journalist. He had profound respect for journalism as a fine art, having cultivated it from early youth, his real field being literature and theatre. He had literary culture, and in spite of his exclusive nervous temperament, which made public appearances physically painful to him, he possessed an all-round journalistic *flair*. It seemed as if a strange set of antennae made it possible for him to live in isolation and yet keep closely in touch with everything which appealed to the public. He combined a fine sense of tradition, with a realization of the necessity of speed. So Gulmann was the right chief for the old daily, now that it was to attempt the conquest of the future, in spite of the lead gained by its rivals, and at a time when Conservation was no asset to a popular newspaper.

Gulmann's plan was to undertake thorough reforms, but to go slow so as not to frighten the old *clientele* whose grandfathers, way back in the days of good King Frederik VI, had been Berlingske subscribers. From April, 1913, the Berlingske

Tidende" published a Sunday Edition with the added charm of a fine Supplement. The first journalistic interview, the first picture were put on. A modern printing press was ordered. Till then the evening edition had been the main thing, while the morning edition, its front page covered with shipping advertisements, still smacked of its early start as an advertising Supplement. Now the morning edition, while preserving its character of a commercial gazette, was to be transformed into a great universal *newspaper*, relying on numerous telegrams, whereas the evening edition was to furnish reading matter for the family circle. Preparations were made for a large-scale extension of the Berlingske's news-service with permanent special correspondents in London, Paris, Berlin, Stockholm, and Oslo. The staff was enlarged, too. A born journalist, Gulmann did not distinguish between good and poor "stuff", but between good and poor journalism. Poets and authors joined the staff, for he strove to make the contents of his paper no less valuable than vivid. What the new chief wished for was a newspaper combining the reliability of the "Times" with the literary quality of "Le Journal" and the *grand reportage* of the "Daily Express"—and the Berlingske must be made to appeal to the ladies.

Gulmann, who in his reconstruction of the newspaper had the full support of the board of directors, had finished his preparations just before the outbreak of the War. This was most fortunate for his newspaper; if at that juncture it had possessed only its old, dilapidated printing-house, it would have been unable to compete, and might have sunk to the level of a mere "advertiser". As it was, the Berlingske was well armed to join in the big fray, and the "news-hunger" which possessed even the "old regulars" among its readers made possible a much quicker switch-over to modern editorial methods, than Gulmann had dared to hope for.

Of the evolution of the "Berlingske Tidende" since 1913 it has been said that it has been an unbroken chain of journalistic and technical records. At least, the figures speak for themselves. In 1913, as mentioned above, the Morning Edition printed 14,000 copies; in 1920, on weekdays 35,000, and on Sundays 47,000. In the same period the evening edition had climbed from 8,000 to 28,000 copies. From the beginning of World War I, the

"Berlingske Tidende" grew faster than any other newspaper in Denmark. For, if only the "Berlingske" became as readable as other Copenhagen newspapers, the number of subscribers was bound to increase very considerably because of the large mass of advertisers, pushing the carriage forward from behind. The effect of the 1913-14 reforms was doubled, because it created a reserve which could again be used to increase circulation.

At Gulmann's death, in 1934, the "Berlingske Tidende" had developed into a many-sided Press Company, still Conservative in outlook, but independent of the Conservative Party. The production of the Berlingske Press had become industrialized, but Gulmann always stressed, that industrial methods must never invade the editorial work, or its spirit would be killed. He believed in continuity as a sort of Guardian Angel, who would, irrespective of changing technical equipment, guide journalistic pens.

Revolt of the Types

The rise of the "Politiken" has been smoother than that of the "Berlingske Tidende". Only in 1920 there was a slight hitch. When, on March 29th, during the political crisis (The "Easter Crisis"), the Zahle Government was dismissed by the King for its attitude to the Slesvig Frontier question, and the workers threatened to establish a General Strike, the "Politiken" lost favour with large sections of the Copenhagen middle classes who felt that they had been betrayed by the paper which was supposed to be Radical-Liberal, but not Labour.

In March 1920, the "Politiken"s weekday edition printed 83,826; in July, 68,139; in November, 65,240. Only then the figures began slowly to rise again.

When, in 1927, Henrik Cavling resigned, *Ove Rode* gave up his seat in the Folketing (Lower House of Parliament) to become for six years—until his death—chief editor of the "Politiken". However, Rode was prematurely old, worn out in the service of the country as war-time Home Secretary. So in the following decade the course of the "Politiken" was mostly set by his co-editor, *Valdemar Koppel.* The latter had an unfailing eye for details, and a steady hand for carving the face of the newspaper. As a journalist he may have been a miniature artist, but as an editor he combined a liberal mind with a considerable business acumen.

In 1924, Frejlif Olsen's nephew, *Ole Cavling* (b. 1898), became associate editor of the "Ekstrabladet". In co-operation with *Erik Arboe-Rasmussen,* the new sub-editor, Cavling reorganized the paper with such thoroughness and speed, that his terrified uncle dubbed the newcomers "The Madcaps". In early youth, Ole Cavling had gone to U.S.A. to study the American Press, and had served as London correspondent to Scandinavian newspapers. The British Press had greatly influenced his attitude to newspaper work. What mattered after the War was *facts,* nothing but *facts*! So the "Ekstrabladet" banned "literary journalism, and instead took to sober, matter-of-fact reporting. Nevertheless, the young reformers gave proof of a certain idealism in their common motto: "For the weak again the strong!" They never betrayed Frejlif Olsen's spirit, only they were far less interested in craftsmanship than in news and in useful day-to-day criticism of social abuses. This work was not carried out on a political basis, but by taking each case as it arose, irrespective of whose corns they happened to step on. As a matter of fact, this reporting of drab, humdrum everyday life produced a vivid response from readers, because it was true to life. Readers turned reporters; they knew where to apply, if they came across something they thought reprehensible. This kind of journalism, combined with careful "nursing" of the news-service started the "Ekstrabladet" on a fantastic career of progress. In 1924, when it was still political and satirical, it had 13,000 readers, but in 1946, with nearly 76,000 copies, it was Denmark's third largest newspaper.

The "Ekstrabladet"s treatment of the news is peculiar in that the editors do not set out to make an all-round newspaper. The feel under no obligation to re-print the news-items of the morning-papers, except in so far as they influence the telegrams and reports received in the forenoon, in which case the earlier news is briefly recapitulated. For the "Ekstrabladet", and other dailies of similar type, are really and truly *extra* newspapers, and nothing more. A reader who based his outlook solely on them would indeed get very queer ideas of World Events.

As we have already heard, Frejlif Olsen had called his young assistants "Madcaps". In doing so, he may have been thinking first of all of that "Revolt of the Types" which they caused, as part of the modern newspaper-technique. After the First World War the typography of many European newspapers was greatly influenced by the American Press, whose "lay-out" was planned on lines derived from psycho-technical experience. The typographical arrangement of an article in such a way as best to catch the readers' eyes had become a science. Headlines were underlined once, or even twice, and might take the saw-, drop-, or pyramid-shapes, or even an artistic combination of all three. This choice was considered all-important. It should be possible to make a headline gentle, but also harsh, nay, brutal. In the columns it was permissible, even useful, to use a variety of types, so as to facilitate reading. The "Ekstrabladet" was the first Danish newspaper to introduce the new lay-out, at first with childish exaggerations, then, gradually, in a more moderate way, which made some impression on other newspapers. The result was a rather more forceful and varied typography in the Danish Press.

The revolt of the types brought with it new ideas of the whole newspaper page, especially the front page. It was now regarded as the newspaper's window-display, which ought to be just as inviting as that of a draper. Some American newspapers, notably the "New York Times", believed in a symmetrical lay-out of the front page, so that, day after day, it kept the same appearance, with, f.inst., 3-column headlines both right and left, over the outer columns, and immediately below the title, irrespective of the varying character and importance of the articles, 2-column headlines at the same height about the middle of the page, etc. It looked very like a building game, arranged—perhaps under the influence of cubism—so as to produce a fine and dignified balance. Other newspapers preferred the so-called circus make-up, which gives a livelier, more varied, but nevertheless planned front page. With this, too, the "Ekstrabladet" experimented after 1924.

The Liberal Press

In the inter-War years the Liberal Press showed little or no change, only the "Kobenhavn" ("Copenhagen") and the "Vestkysten" ("West-Coast") adding new pages to the history of the Press.

When I. A. Hansen took over the "Kobenhavn", he said that his sole task was to make a daily newspaper, without commercial "side-shows" of any kind, and this promise he kept. The "Kobenhavn" became the typical political newspaper, *but* in 1927 Hansen returned to the provincial "Roskilde Dagblad", kr. $1\frac{1}{2}$ million having been sunk in the "Kobenhavn"-experiment.

I. A. Hansen was one of those rare original talents who will not be content to drive in the worn old ruts of the language, but on the contrary, want to blaze new tracks for its use. He turned the language of journalism still further away from academic parlance than Horup and Vilhelm Lassen.

Although, in Ribe County, the Liberals were the largest party, its South-West Jutland Press could not for years hold its own, because it consisted of a number of negligible, small newspapers, all of them privately owned. In the large export centre of Esbjerg, the most widely read daily was the "Vestjyllands Social-Demokrat"; in Ribe the Conservative "Ribe Stiftstidende". During World War I, local Liberals wished to put an end to this state of affairs. A company, ("Den sydvestjyske Venstrepresse") was formed for the purpose of establishing a large up-to-date county-newspaper. It was a democratic company. Each shareholder was only to have one vote, irrespective of the number and value of his shares—issued for amounts as low as kr. 25. Shares were not saleable without the consent of the committee. This clause is important for political enterprises of the kind, and so is found in the regulations of many company or cooperatively owned newspapers. Existing Liberal newspapers, unable to offer much resistance, were bought up, with the exception of the Varde paper (with which an agreement was only reached in 1934, after the Varde district had been conquered), and on July 1st, 1947, the company started business. The title of the new daily was the "Vestkysten", and it began with a nucleus of 2700 subscribers.

The editor chosen for the "Vestkysten" was *Rasmus Benditsen* (1889-1927), who came from the Berg Press, and made himself known as the founder of the "Venstres Ungdom" (Liberal Youth Movement)—When, at the age of only 38, Rasmus Bendtsen died, presumably a victim to overwork and his own fiery temperament, he was succeeded by *Knud Ree* (b. 1895). With Ree in the editorial chair, the paper has stuck to its old line, but often in political issues showed considerable independence, which has met with the approval of its readership. When the present editor took over, the "Vestkysten" had 12,000 subscribers: a great, very skilfully utilized, technical expansion, in 1936, and wide-awake editorship have combined to treble its sales. In 1952, selling 32,000 copies, it was the Liberal Party's largest newspaper, and the third largest Danish provincial daily, having effected the first large-scale amalgamation of small, provincial newspapers.

On November 15th, 1952 the Provincial Liberal Press stated its sales to be 432,000 copies.

The Labour Press in the Inter-War Years

In 1911, after thirty years' service, *Emil Wiinblad* resigned the editorship of the "Social-Demokraten", which he had made the greatest political daily in Copenhagen. He was replaced, as a matter of course, by *F. J. Borgbjerg,* who had for a long time been its most important pen.

F. J. Borgbjerg was a better journalist than editor, and far inferior to Wiinblad as an all-round newspaperman. He was a writer and an orator, for whom the leading article—not infrequently the text of a speech he had recently made—was the most important thing in the newspaper. As chief editor he proved a rather negligent supervisor of the day-to-day editorial routine. In 1924, when Borgbjerg joined the first Labour Government, young *Marinus Kristensen* (1891-1928) became chief editor. He had served through his typographer's apprenticeship, possessed fine natural talents, seemed surrounded by an aura of success, like a favourite of the gods. Already in youth he had attrached public notice by his political insight and rare lyrical eloquence. Marinus Kristensen had joined the staff of the "Social-Demokraten" in 1911, and became, not only a disciple of, but a mouthpiece for Borgbjerg, who soon began to regard this popular young stump-orator as his spiritual son and heir and "Marinus" entered politics like his mentor. More than anything else, he was a controversialist, with a substratum of lyrical humour, but he realized the necessity of making a better newspaper of the "Social-Demokraten". As a result of his efforts such prominent authors as Georg Brandes and Johs. V. Jensen often wrote for the leading Labour daily, while he was its chief. When, at the age of only 37, Marinus Kristensen died, *H.P. Sorensen* (b. 1886), now First Burgomaster of Copenhagen, and at that time Parliamentary Correspondent to the "Social-Demokraten", succeeded him as chief editor. He undertook a technical re-organisation of the "Social- Demokraten" and started a great colour-print Sunday Supplement. As a writer on political subjects, H.P. Sorensen, himself originally a worker, often found adequate expressions for the thoughts and aspirations of the working classes. And at the same time, he had more of the real newspaperman in him than his predecessors. When, in 1941, he was forced out of the editorial chair by the German Occupation, his associate-editor, *P. Tabor* (b. 1891) was appointed chief by the proprietors. Tabor had been imported in 1930 from the provincial Labour Press, and had soon given proof of his prowess as a keen controversialist, a master of verbal imagery.

The official *"History of the Danish Labour Party"* puts the total number of copies printed by the National Organization of the Labour Press at 174,000 in 1921. In 1952, the total circulations were 172,000 of which the Copenhagen "Social-Demokraten" printed 44,000, and the provincial dailies 128,000. Even if these are net figures, they seem, by comparison, to indicate that, in the 1921-46 period, the Labour Press had not got its reasonable share of the increased sales of the total Danish Press, i.e., relatively speaking, it was being left behind. This really seems to have been the case; and causes, or at least probable causes, for it can be adduced. If it is true that, in the course of its history, the Danish Daily Press has passed from the Printer's Era, through its Political Stage, to the Age of Industrialization, (which is true, generally speaking, although several papers have never experienced the first stage, or been "industrialized")—if, then, this is a true outline of Press history, the Labour Press forms a conspicuous exception. It has remained entirely in the political stage. The Socialist dailies were never an end in themselves, always weapons in the struggle for the interests and philosophy of the working classes. Labour Union and political news—controversial and educational matters—held first place in these newspapers—and if a fashionable wedding at Our Lady's or other tit-bits were crowded out, the editors bore it with equanimity. But this attitude, praiseworthy though it might seem, impeded the numerical progress of the Socialist dailies at a time when other newspapers had realized the importance of all-round service. Even loyal party-members would warn their newspaper against becoming too ideological, and especially the women, to whom the choice of a newspaper is often left, missed the "light stuff". It is not possible, from the fact that, at the 1945 Folketing Election, the Labour Party got nearly 672,000 votes (in 1943 over 894,000) to come to any conclusion as to how large the circulation of its Press "ought" to be. In Sweden, where the Labour Party is not far from having the majority, the Labour dailies constitute less than one-sixth of the total Press. In Denmark, too, many are believed to have voted for the Labour Party without, properly speaking, being Socialists. Of these supporters many may have considered the Labour dailies too onesided, a monopolized Labour Union Press. And some might not think it "respectable" to take a Socialist newspaper, even if, in the given situation, the Labour policy seemed to them the right one. But the most remarkable fact is, that not all party members read the party newspaper. In 1952 the Labour Party had 287,288 members, while, as we have seen the Press sold 172,000 copies. However, in this connection it must be borne in mind that fairly large numbers of married women are members of Party organizations along with their husbands. In 1942, the "Sonderjyllands Social-Demokrat" changed its title to "Sonderjyden"; later on the Esbjerg, Aalborg, and Kolding papers became the "Vestjyden", the "Ny Tid", and "Tidens Tegn", and others are expected to follow suit. They seem to have given up the stereotyped old "Socialdemokrat"-titles in the hope of improved sales, outside party-circles, when they do not advertise themselves as a Party Press. At the same time there has been within this wing of the Press a noticeable change from the very lopsided political reporting of former days.

The economic unity of the Danish Labour Press has, in some respects, been advantageous to the Party, and perhaps to this Press as a whole, but it has been a decided disadvantage to certain individual newspapers. The Copenhagen "Social-Demokraten" could not be expected to equal the circulations of the "Berlingske Tidende" or the "Politiken" when, for decades, it had invested millions out of its profits in the provincial Labour Press. By so doing it not only curtailed in its Copenhagen expansion, but also bred a race of rivals in the provinces—where consequently, it could not win the same large following as other Copenhagen newspapers. It was unable to make itself a national daily, because the best of the Copenhagen paper was reproduced in the provincial dailies by means of stereotypography. By and by, when certain provincial dailies became profitable propositions, they, too, had to obey the law of solidarity. Thus, when the Aarhus "Demokraten" began to pay a good dividend, the staff was not allowed free use of the money for replacements of machinery or purchase of telegraphic or pictorial matter. It had to aid in keeping other, less profitable Party newspapers afloat.

The clear political line followed by this wing of the Press commands respect, especially for inspiring educational work among the masses, and fraternal solidarity amongst these newspapers themselves. But, as we have seen, all this did not increase circulations. One reason was that the political newspaper had fallen from favour. Readers no longer want to be told what to think, they want information and to be left to draw their own conclusions. Also, paradoxically enough, the spread of Socialism has impeded the progress of the Labour Press. Power brings with it responsibility. After a Labour majority had been recurred in a number of Town Councils and, in 1917, in the Corporation of the City of Copenhagen, the good old days of Opposition skirmishing were over. If, now, the Labour Press were to stick to its tradition of criticizing the finance policy, administration of justice, poor relief, gas-prices, or even the pavements—it would more often than not hit members of its Party—ministers and burgomasters. The Labour Press had dropped a good hand of cards on the floor, from where it had been picked up by the Opposition, who played it skilfully, and sometimes ruthlessly.

And there were mistakes. The Labour Press was much longer than other sections of the Press in making editorship incompatible with other activities, such as those of a Burgomaster or Member of Parliament. Nor have the proprietors, mostly the Labour Unions, always been willing to pay competitive salaries. Although, throughout the Press, salaries have been going up by leaps and bounds, the Labour Unions are against a journalist earning very much more than a skilled worker, which has led to some emigration from the Labour Press, and a scarcity of new journalistic aspirants.

Generally speaking, then, the Labour Press does not live up to the position of the Party in circulations and economy. It is, nevertheless, a powerful Organization, consisting of 15 fullfledged newspapers with 46 local editions, 2 of which have auxiliary printing houses. It has about 1743 employees, and in 1952 paid salaries and wages amounting to kr. 14,889.000. It owns more than twenty newspaper premises all over the country and uses 12 per cent of the newsprint purchased by the entire Danish Press. Although for years incomes have not been very satisfactory, it has not become necessary to seek an alliance with Capitalism.

The Communist Press

After 1905, when the "Four-Party-System" which has since become traditional had emerged, it looked as if there would be no need for further expansion of the Press. The political struggle went on, of course, but the *Sturm und Drang* period seemed to be over, and with it the incentive to establish new dailies. For the last forty years of the history of the Press the old newspapers have relied more and more on the informed discussion of, f.inst., municipal affairs, which had formerly been treated only in their political or even personal aspects. More and more newspapers are trying to serve their town or district by useful criticism and by encouraging enterprise. They bring to our homes international and home-news, instruction and food for thought, entertainment and advertisements, i.e. commercial and trade news.

For thirty years after 1905 the political balance created in the Danish People, and hence in the Danish Press, was maintained. A few new and small parties or movements, owing their existence to short-lived conjunctures, proved unable to keep going the dailies they started. This is true also of the more durable Danish Henry George Party. This party was founded in 1919 and has started newspapers both in Copenhagen and Aarhus, but is in 1947 without a representative in the Daily Press. Alone the Danish Communist Party, also dating from 1919, has succeeded in keeping alive an addition to the Danish

Four-Newspaper-System. 1910 had seen the first beginnings of Syndicalism, not only in opposition to "bourgeois" parties, but also to the "Prevailing reformism and bourgeois degeneracy" of the Labour Party. During World War I Syndicalist opposition gained a foothold among the youth of the old Labour Party, who thought that the war-time suspension of party rivalries was not in the interest of the working classes. Austerity measures further ruffled popular feelings, and when in 1917 the Russian Revolution broke out there was considerable unrest. About Jan. 1st, 1919, with 70,000 unemployed, there followed sudden strikes and violent demonstrations. The Left-Wingers, who had left the Labour Party, split up into several groups, who would now establish weeklies, now shortlived dailies. Only one weekly, the "Arbejderbladet" managed to keep afloat. At the Folketing Election of 1932 the Communist Party obtained 17,000 votes and won two seats. Then, from new year 1934, the "Arbejderbladet" began publication as a daily. Its format was small, but a subscription among readers and friends enabled them to buy an up-to-date rotary press, and on Dec. 1st, 1937, it changed over to the standard get-up of Danish dailies. In the late thirties the "Arbejderbladet" was gaining ground, but in the winter of 1939-40, the Finno-Russian War roused public animosity against it, and it lost most of its advertisers. It was reduced to four pages on weekdays, and a public subscription became necessary to keep it afloat.

12

Disaccreditation of Journalists

SINCE the system of accreditation of journalists with the Government of India had been done solely with the advice of Central Press Advisory Committee that was nominated by the AINEC. At the time of appointment of the Press Commission in 1952, it was represented to the Commission that, as the representation of working journalist organisations was not in the Committee, the system of accreditation was unsatisfactory. The Commission, therefore, said: "We would recommend the formation of a Central Accreditation Committee in consultation with the different organisations of newspapermen, the committee to consist of six to eight members normally resident in Delhi, of whom 50 per cent may be working editors, elected or nominated by the all-India organisations of editors and 50 per cent correspondents and working journalists selected or nominated by the all-India organisations of working journalists all being of at least five years standing."

This recommendation was accepted by the Government, was placed before the Parliament and endorsed by it and, since then CPAC was reconstituted with representatives of editors and working journalists. Originally, the number was half and half. Later on, representation was extended to representatives of working journalist organisations like the Press Association, News Cameramen Association and the National Union of Journalists. But nobody's share of membership was reduced and this committee functioned well, till the new committee was set up in August 1979, by reducing membership of the AINEC, IFWJ and NUJ and extending its membership to two organisations of newspaper proprietors in the name of small and medium newspapers. This was done contrary to the opinion of the Press Commission and convention, because proprietors have nothing to do with accreditation. It is the business of editors and correspondents and other journalists who become correspondents. And the Committees were so constituted that they would have information and knowledge about the correspondents and journalists whose cases would appear before the committee.

The first act that the Committee did was to do away with the rules and conventions which permitted functioning editors of news media to be accredited since the time accreditation was introduced. After the reconstitution of the Committee, which included Devadas Gandhi, A.E. Charlton, Ranbir, Akshay Kumar Jain, S.A. Sastri, P.K.S. Kutty, D.R. Mankekar and J.P. Chaturvedi, a Sub-Committee was appointed to go into the rules and conventions of the accreditation. This sub-committee was appointed in 1956 and consisted of Shri Charlton, Shri Ranbir, Shri J.P. Chaturvedi and Shri TRV Chari, the Principal Information Officer. On a report of the Committee, the full accreditation committee in its ninth meeting held on 2nd January 1957, adopted the following resolution:

> "Accreditation may be extended as an exceptional measure on application to journalists of long and distinguished service who may be contributing special articles to a number of papers regularly though not attached to any newspaper. It was recognised that such cases would be exceptional."

This convention was followed and later on incorporated in rules of accreditation which were discussed for nearly three months by a sub-committee of the CPAC with Mr. N. K. Trikha as convenor, and, later on, adopted by its meeting held at Hyderabad specially for this purpose, on 17th June, 1978. The rules became effective on that date. According to the resolution of 1957 and the rules, the following distinguished journalists were accredited upto 1978:—

1. Shri E. Narayanana
2. Shri J. N. Sahni
3. Shri B. Shivarao
4. Shri M. Chalapathi Rau
5. Shri D. R. Mankekar
6. Shri E.P.W. Da Costa
7. Shri K. Shankar Pillai
8. Shri S. A. Sastri
9. Shri Mukut Behari Verma (former Editor of *Hindustan*)
10. Shri A. N. Vidyalankar, famous writer and editor of *Nav Bharat Times*.
11. Shri K. Rangachari
12. Shri K. Subbarayan.
13. Shri Pran Chopra
14. Shri P. D. Sharma
15. Shri C. Raghavan
16. Shri Chandulal Chandrakar
17. Shri P. Ramaswami
18. Shri Vishnu Dutt
19. Shri J.S. Indurkar
20. Shri A. N. Das
21. Shri K. R. Sundar Rajan, and
22. Shri B. G. Verghese.

Later on, Shri E. Narayanan and Shri B. Shivarao passed away. Along with the correspondents, Shri Anwar Ahmed was accredited as a cartoonist of long standing and Shri T. S. Nagarajan as a correspondent cameraman of long and distinguished service. Among the photographers, Shri T. Kasi Nath, Capt. D. Arjun, Shri Kundan Lal, Shri B. J. Talreja, Smt. Homai Vyarawala and Shri Abnashi Ram had been accredited in this category. The basic consideration in the case of most of these correspondents was that they had been associated with the reporting of the Government or the Parliament for the last 25 to 30 years and it was deemed necessary to afford them this facility if they wanted to continue in the profession. That this number is very small compared to the total number of accredited correspondents is clear as the list is very extensive and newspaper chains and organisations as well as big news agencies have 20 to 24 correspondents and a sizeable number of photographers on their accreditation list.

That there were strict limitations on accreditation of such correspondents is clear first from the resolution of 1957 as well as from rule 6 passed in 1978 which provided "the CPAC may grant accreditation as an exception to journalists of long and distinguished service to the profession of 25 years who would be contributing special articles to a number of newspapers regularly but not attached to any newspaper which qualifies for accreditation."

It was clearly an institution to help the professional journalists in India without any of them being tied to a newspaper, just as there are columnists in America and Europe whose columns appear in a number of newspapers. Journalists like Chalapathi Rau, Pran Chopra, Chanchal Sarkar, D.R. Mankekar, Da Costa and Rangachari come under this category and are active in a number of papers and this provision was meant to help them through accreditation.

The CPAC in its meeting of 10th and 11th September, 1979 took over the question of review of the rules relating to correspondents on its own without any previous item on the agenda raised by any member, while it referred to, the review of rules relating to TV news and features syndicate to a committee of 7 members. It amended the rules 5 and 6. Rule 5 related to editors of news media. It said that "Editors of news media may in exceptional cases be granted accreditation if CPAC is satisfied that the applicant is genuinely engaged in covering current affairs and news actually for this purpose. Such applicants will be considered by the CPAC. No temporary accreditation will be granted by PIO in such cases." The Committee in a huff changed its rules and without waiting for the confirmation of the rules from the Government also laid down that accreditation cards may not be revalidated for the year 1980 and these categories may be given press release and invitation to Prime Minister's conferences.

There were no valid reasons for the committee to arrive at this decision, specially when bulk of the members of the committee had nothing to do with accreditation as such, because there were only two members who belonged to the older committee. Out of it one was absent and another opposed the proposals. As a result the following editors will be disaccredited. They are Mr. B.P. Agarwal, Chief Editor of Hindustan Samachar, D.V. Gandhi of Samachar Bharti, Editor of India Press Agency, Dewan Birendra Nath Editor, Press Asia International, Shri Inderjit, Editor India News & Features Alliance, Mr. Chandran, Assistant General Manager, PTI, Mr. G.G. Mirchandani, Chief Editor UNI, Mr. K. Rangaswami, Editor, Foreign News & Features, Mr. K.C. Gupta, Editor, National News Service, Mr. Rajindra Sarin, Editor, POTT Analysis and News Service, Mr. Thomas Mullakal, Editor NBI news service, Mr. K.V. Kumar, Editor, Cartographer News Service, Mr. Romesh Chander, Editor Television News Features, Mr. Som Dev, Editor, Publication Syndicate, Mr. Krishan Kumar, Editor Vikrant News Service, Mr. J.K. Jain, Editor, *Doorandesh* Hindi Evening Daily, Mr. Vishwabandhu Gupta, Editor, *Tej* Urdu Evening daily, Mr. C. Ummat of *Eastern Economist*, Mr. G.P. Jain, Editor *Sevagram Weekly* etc. The editors of small newspapers and weeklies were admitted to accreditation by the CPAC in view of their demand that, due to lack of resources, they being residents in Delhi. The Editors of news agencies and features syndicates were admitted because, even while becoming editors, they continue to work as correspondents and were engaged in news gathering for their organisations.

The Committee which is a caricature of the previous accreditation committee has by a stroke of pen removed about 60 journalists from the list of accreditation which is much more severe than what was attempted in emergency, although it was said even at that time that it was based on certain considerations and done on the advice of CPAC. But the Das Committee and the Shah Commission severely criticised it as an encroachment on the freedom of press and all such cases were reviewed and set right by the Janata Government. It is surprising that, while the Press Commission is considering the complaint against the CPAC by the AINEC which has boycotted it because it has been given only one seat, the Government should rush with the formation of the Committee and the Committee should rush with the disaccreditation of such a large number of distinguished and active journalists in the field. It is requested that this decision should be reconsidered, revised and annulled.

Decision of the Press Council of India

In the complaint of Shri. J.P. Chaturvedi, Founder Secretary General and former President, IFWJ and others against the Government of India, rendered on September 25, 1980.

A letter dated October 17, 1979, was addressed to the Chairman of the Press Council signed by Shri J.P. Chaturvedi, Founder Secretary-General and a former President, Indian Federation of Working Journalists and a number of other journalists forwarding a note containing a complaint about the disaccreditation of some 60 editors and distinguished journalists by the Central Press Accreditation Committee. It was urged that as the issue involved was a grave one affecting long established policy and convention relating to the freedom of the press, appropriate action be taken. It was stated in the note that in accordance with the recommendation of the Press Commission in its report submitted in 1954, a Central Press Accreditation Committee (CPAC) was constituted. It consisted of nominees of all-India organisations of editors and working journalists, and later on the representatives from the Press Association, News Cameramen Association and National Union of Journalists.

It was pointed out that in the 9th meeting of the CPAC held on January 2, 1957, a resolution was adopted according to which accreditation could be extended as an exceptional measure to journalists of long and distinguished service who might be contributing special articles to a number of papers regularly though not attached to any newspaper. The resolution was followed as a convention, and was later on incorporated in rules 5 & 6 of accreditation of a meeting held at Hyderabad on June 7, 1978. The names of the distinguished journalists and others from the profession who were given accreditation in accordance with the aforesaid convention and the rules, have been mentioned. The following paragraph from the note may be reproduced:

> "It was clearly an institution to help the professional journalists in India without any of them being tied to a newspaper, just as there are columnists in America and

> Europe whose columns appear in a number of newspapers. Journalists like Chalapathi Rau, Pran Chopra, Chanchal Sarkar, D.R. Mankekar, De Costa and Rangachari come under this category and are active in a number of papers and this provision was meant to help them through accreditation."

It was next stated that CPAC in its meeting held on September 10-11, 1979 took over the question of review of rules 5 and 6 on its own initiative without there being any previous item on the agenda. These two rules were amended. Rule 5 related to editors of news media. According to the changed rules the editors of news media could in exceptional cases be granted accreditation if CPAC was satisfied that the applicant was genuinely engaged in covering current affairs and news. No temporary accreditation cards were to be revalidated for the year 1980 although it was laid down that journalists belonging to these categories could be given press releases and invitation to the Prime Minister's conference.

The main grievance raised in the note was that there was no valid reason for the CPAC to arrive at the above decision especially when bulk of the members of the Committee had nothing to do with accreditation as such. A number of eminent editors (about 60) whose names are mentioned, would lose their accreditation owing to the change of the rules.

The Council Secretariat addressed a letter in November, 1979, to the Secretary to the Government of India, Ministry of Information and Broadcasting forwarding a copy of the representation of Shri J.P. Chaturvedi and others regarding contemplated disaccreditation of editors and distinguished journalists of old standing, and comments were invited. Ultimately after a number of reminders, the Deputy Principal Information Officer, Shri R.K. Kachru, wrote a letter dated May 7, 1980, explaining the circumstances in which the CPAC had taken the impugned action. It was stated that the CPAC had at a meeting held on September 10-11, 1979 decided to review the existing accreditation rules to news media representatives before taking up the question of grant of accreditation to new applicants. The rules regarding grant of accreditation to editors also came up for consideration. It was felt that the editors did not normally require the kind of facilities which were essential for correspondents engaged in day to day news gathering. It was decided that accreditation on exceptional basis to editors of news media was not necessary. Moreover, if accreditation was to be accorded to editors as a rule, it would open flood gates and hundreds of editors might seek accreditation. It was added that the change of rules had affected only ten news editors who were already accredited. The editors of news agencies, news features agencies etc., had already been treated on special footing as they continued to work as correspondents. As regards the category consisting of journalists of long and distinguished standing, they had ceased to do any active work and were not involved in day to day news gathering. They, therefore, did not require accreditation. The CPAC felt that facilities like supply of press material, invitation to press conferences and facility to visit Government offices would serve their purpose. It was decided to do away with their accreditation. In all it affected 27 journalists and cameramen who already stood accredited. It was further stated that the CPAC which met again on March 11-12, 1980, considered the representation of Shri J.P. Chaturvedi to the Press Council. It reconsidered the whole question of grant of accreditation to editors and those who had been accredited would continue to enjoy the accreditation. Similarly, journalists/cameramen accreditated under long and distinguished service rule would also continue to enjoy the accreditation. However, no accreditation would be granted in future to these two categories. But persons belonging to these categories who had retired after 25 years would be provided various functional facilities with CPAC's approval. These would include supply of press material, invitation to press conferences, rail travel concession for professional work and C.G.H.S. facility as also Home Ministry passes. They would not be entitled to housing facility which is given only to accredited correspondents who are engaged in day to day news gathering. It has been pointed out that the CPAC is a body which was first constituted as a result of a recommendation by the Press Commission. With the passage of time, more and more press bodies have been given representation on it with a view to making it more broad-based. The Government by convention, does not interfere with the deliberations of the Committee and its decisions are normally accepted by the Government.

Shri S.L. Kapur, Joint Secretary, Ministry of Information and Broadcasting also addressed a communication dated May 12,

1980, explaining the stand of the Government. Reference was made to the detailed letter of the Press Information Bureau dated May 7, 1980. It was stated that the main grievance voiced by Shri J.P. Chaturvedi had been redressed. It has further been stated that the CPAC is an independent, non-official body and the Government does not normally interfere with its working.

At the sittings of the Inquiry Committee held on August 5-6, 1980, Shri R.K. Kachru and Shri J.P. Chaturvedi were both heard in support of their respective cases. Shri Chaturvedi appeared to be generally satisfied with the decision taken by the CPAC that those journalists who had a distinguished record of service and who had joined him in filing the complaint before this Council would not be disaccredited, and that the decision taken by the CPAC changing the rules would not affect them. But he stressed the necessity of examination of the whole question from the effect the change in rules would have on the freedom of the press as a whole. Mr. Kachru prepared a very elaborate and detailed backgrounder note in a comparatively short time on the CPAC giving the entire history of its establishment and constitution from time to time.

Before the matter is examined further, it is necessary to give extracts of rules 5 and 6 which had been framed by the CPAC and which were changed in September, 1979. These are reproduced below:

> "5. Editors of news media may in exceptional case be granted accreditation if the CPAC is satisfied that the applicant is genuinely engaged in covering current affairs and needs accreditation for this purpose. Such application will only be considered by the CPAC. No temporary accreditation will be granted by PIO in such cases.
>
> 6. The Central Press Accreditation Committee may grant accreditation, as an exceptional measure, to journalists of long and distinguished service of at least 25 years who may be contributing special articles to a number of newspapers regularly but not attached to any newspaper which qualifies to accreditation."

As a result of the decision taken in September 1979 the position as it obtains today is that editors and distinguished journalists/cameramen who had retired after 25 years service would be provided various facilities with CPAC's approval. These have already been mentioned before. The only exception made was as already noticed that those editors and journalists who had been accredited from the category of journalists of long and distinguished service would not lose their accreditation. Mr. Kachru laid a great deal of emphasis on the fact that with the exception of being eligible for provision of housing facilities even those who could take the benefit previously of rules 5 and 6, would get all the other benefits which they were getting on accreditation. The card, however, which would be issued to them would be of a different nature as persons belonging to categories covered by the aforesaid rules would not be regarded as fully accredited. But according to Mr. Kachru in actual practice it would hardly make much difference. It was forcefully urged that very senior journalists who had retired from active work should not be eligible for housing facilities as the queue was very large of those who were doing professional work and who being younger and of less standing in the profession were in greater need of housing and accommodation facility.

From the backgrounder note of accreditation it does appear that in 1971 the CPAC appointed a Sub-Committee to re-examine amongst other things, the accreditation of editors and other deskmen, stringers and correspondents/cameramen of long and distinguished service. The Sub-Committee felt that the accreditation should be given to retired journalists (including editors) if they satisfy the following two criteria:—

- *(a)* They should ordinarily have been active journalists for at least 20 years;
- *(b)* They should not be employed in any other organisation engaged in non-journalistic purpose.

In August 1977, the CPAC appointed a Sub-Committee to make a comprehensive review of rules and conditions governing the accreditation. At the meeting held on February 17, 1978, the CPAC accepted the recommendation of the Sub-Committee in regard to the grant of accreditation to journalists/cameramen under the long and distinguished category. At the meeting held on September 10-11, 1979, rule 5 came in for a detailed discussion. It is stated that most of the members were of the view that the editors did not require normally the kind of facility which was essential for correspondents engaged in news gathering etc. There was, however, a note of dissent contending that a proprietor-editor of a small and medium newspaper was as much a working journalist as any employee-correspondent. The change in rules was made as stated before keeping in view the above considerations.

So far as the denial of accreditation in terms of the erstwhile rule 5 to editors is concerned, the crucial question is whether such a denial would stand in the way of a proper discharge of their duties and functions. The role of an editor hardly needs any elaboration. In regard to the editors of those newspapers which have a fair amount of circulation, there may be a great deal of force in the latest thinking of the CPAC that they do not stand in need of accreditation. They do not have to gather news from day to day or on regular basis and that their work is of such a kind that it would suffice if they got all the facilities which can still be extended to them in terms of the new rule. But there does appear to be some substance in what has been pressed before the Council about those editors who are also proprietors of newspapers. They often manage and run these papers with much more limited resources than bigger newspaper establishments. On several occasions, therefore, they may have to take full advantage of accreditation. It may be observed that the Council has not been given any substantial reason as to why a decision was taken so soon to change the rules in September 1979. Rule 5 had been introduced in February 1978, the interval being comparatively of a short period. When the new rule 5 came into existence in February 1978, it was after the CPAC had appointed a Sub-Committee to make a comprehensive review of the terms and conditions governing the accreditation that a decision was taken to extend the facility of accreditation in exceptional cases to editors. It is equally difficult to understand the argument put forward by Mr. Kachru that by allowing accreditation to editors it would open the floodgate to a very large number of editors seeking accreditation. Even if that be so the discretion would have still rested in terms of rule 5 with the CPAC and it could extend the facility of accreditation only in most deserving and exceptional cases.

Coming to the question of the category covered by the erstwhile Rule 6, journalists of long and distinguished service can have a valid argument in favour of their accreditation in terms of Rule 6. The names of the veterans from the profession illustrates that even though they may have ceased to be very active journalists their contribution as columnists or by way of special articles, can be of immense value to journalistic activity. Although they would be entitled to most of the facilities even now after the change in the rule, regular accreditation possibly carries a certain prestige, and the distinguished journalists would not feel happy about being denied a particular status. The backgrounder note shows that the number of journalists and cameramen belonging to the long and distinguished category is not particularly large, and even in future the number can be kept at a reasonable figure because the discretion rests with the CPAC. If the anxiety is that editors and journalists of long and distinguished standing should not become eligible for housing facility on the basis of accreditation, it is certainly not difficult to say that by convention or otherwise they must give way to younger and more needy people and should not claim housing facilities.

The question, however, still remains whether the denial of accreditation facilities in terms of Rules 5 and 6 to editors and to journalists who have retired from active work but who belong to the categories mentioned in the erstwhile rules 5 and 6, would affect the freedom of the press. It may be open to suggest that depriving such eminent and distinguished members of the profession from getting all the facilities which are available on accreditation or making any distinction between them and other members of the profession would interfere with whatever contribution they can make to free expression of views and comments on matters of great public interest. The Council, however, is strongly of the opinion that it would be in the fitness of things that the CPAC which is the appropriate body to decide all matters relating to accreditation should reconsider the question that have been raised before us in the light of the observations that have been made. The complaint is disposed of accordingly.

Appendix—I

Recommendations of the First Press Commission: An Appraisal

THE report of the Press Commission, made after an exhaustive enquiry, is primarily based upon considerations of public interest. The appointment of the Press Commission was demanded by working journalists and its setting up was welcomed by all persons who believed in the democratic way of life. The Commission has given a unanimous report, excepting on certain aspects of Press laws, where a minority has dissented.

2. Vested interests in the industry have assailed the report, and some of them have described it as amateurish, impractical and unjudicious. In view of this outcry it would be worthwhile to note that the Chairman of the Commission was a judge of the Bombay High Court with wide experience of such enquiries. Another member, Dr. C.P. Ramaswamy Iyer, is a well known jurist, educationist and administrator. Three members of the Commission belong to the industry, Messrs Chalapathi Rau, A.R. Bhat (President of the AINEC and Dr. President of the IENS). Of the remaining, four are Members of Parliament; two of them are well known publicmen and educationists, Acharya

---

This note was circulated to members of Parliament before a discussion on the Press Commission Report in Lok Sabha in 1955.

Narendra Deva and Dr. Zakir Hussain of the remaining two MPs, Mr. T.N. Singh had wide experience of the Newspaper Industry, both on the editorial and managerial sides, while the other Mr. Jaipal Singh had also experience of journalism. Another member, Dr. V.K.R.V. Rao, is an economist of repute. Mr. P.H. Patwardhan, besides his wide experience of public affairs, had also experience of the periodical Press. To characterise the efforts of such a Commission as amateurish or unjudicious is to do violence to the language.

3. No one can dispute the conclusion of the Commission that if Democracy is to survive in this country, and if it is to fulfil its purpose of achieving a Welfare State, there should be a large number of independent papers in the country, particularly at district and state headquarters, presenting differing view-points before the public and thus promoting public discussion. The practitioners of the profession, the journalists, must maintain certain high standards.

4. The Commission found that far from there being a good climate for the growth of a larger number of papers, even existing ones were facing extinction and there was already a high degree of concentration of ownership amongst the about 340 daily papers. Five owners, the Commission found, were controlling 29 papers and 31.2 per cent of the circulation while fifteen owners controlled 54 papers and 50.1 per cent of the circulation (para 818 of the report).

5. The Commission also found that there were certain economic imbalances at work in the Industry, which adversely affected the economy of the smaller or independent papers and tended further to concentrate ownership. It found too that some of the existing methods of ownership and management and control were not conducive to objective presentation of news. The insecurity of service, the deplorable conditions of work, low wages, lack of any leave facilities, and retirement benefits, the Commission reported, were such that journalists could not be expected to discharge adequately their public duty.

6. Considering these various aspects, the Commission has recommended several measures. Some of these, like changes in the form of ownership and management of newspapers are recommendatory to the newspapers. They depend for their implementation on the good sense of the newspaper proprietors,

aided and influenced by pressure of public opinion and awakening of social conscience. A few, like those relating to the reorganisation of the ownership and structure of the news agencies, have also been left for voluntary acceptance by the owners. But Government have been asked to use their good offices to bring about these changes; certain suggested economic aids have been made dependent on such acceptance.

7. The Commission has, however, recommended certain measures such as those relating to government's advertisement policy and tariffs, to be enforced by Government through administrative action, and some other by legislative action. The latter relate mainly to measures aimed at correcting the economic imbalances in the industry arising out of unfair competition and adoption of restrictive practices. Other sets of measures recommended for legislative action seek to provide certain minimum working conditions like fixation of a minimum wage, leave, provident fund, gratuity, notice for termination of service, bonus etc. Items such as salary scales, hours of work, amenities have also been left for mutual negotiations and agreement. The setting up of a Press Council, the appointment of a Press Registrar and the creation of a Press Institute are some of the other items requiring legislative action.

8. It is not the purpose of this note to narrate the various recommendations or give the Federations's view on them. The appended literature deals with these aspects. The present note deals only with certain developments since the submission of the report and answer some of the criticisms levelled against the report.

9. For the purpose of ensuring equality of competition, the Commission recommended the prohibition of certain unfair and restrictive practices like undue sales commission, price cutting, abolition of crossword and other prize competitions or restricting the value of prizes offered to Rs. 500 a month, separation of accounts of chains, combines and multiple units, etc.

10. On the positive side, after carefully considering various measures for improving the economy of smaller and independent papers, the Commission suggested the introduction of a price page schedule. This would mean that the minimum price of a newspaper of standard size would be fixed, depending

on the number of pages. The price would be so fixed that the cost of materials etc. should be met by the sale of the newspaper. The ethics and the intricacies of this particular recommendation is examined in detail in an appended note. It should, however, be mentioned that it is only one of the measures recommended for improving the economy of the papers, though it is an important and positive measure, which if put into effect, would also reduce the concentration of circulations and encourage the growth of a number of district and mofussil papers.

Working Conditions

11. Before dealing with working conditions, certain points should be noted. The inquiry of the Press Commission in this particular field has been preceded by two similar inquiries, on a state level. In 1947-48 the Uttar Pradesh and Madhya Pradesh Governments set up inquiry commissions which recommended special measures to safeguard the wages and working conditions of journalists.

12. The recommendations were never implemented by the newspapers or the governments. However, in U.P., the State Government later referred disputes between the newspapers and their employees over working conditions for adjudication. The reference was however withdrawn soon after the appointment of the Press Commission on the ground that there was to be a comprehensive enquiry which would result in all India legislation.

13. The ILO committee on salaried employees, meeting in Geneva more than three years ago, felt that the conditions of journalists and teachers, among the professional classes, were most deplorable particularly in Asian countries and that their problems required special study and special protection.

14. That is not without significance, in view of the latest cry of the employers who demand why only eight per cent of their editorial employees need special protection. Some of the reasons have been given by the Commission itself, particularly in para 512 of the Report. One fallacy of the employers' argument should however be pointed out here. Industrial labour as such is probably just about 10 per cent of the population of the country but there are any number of laws dealing specially

with Industrial labour conditions, including a number of special laws dealing with special branches of industry and commerce.

15. Whereas other sections of labour in the Newspaper Industry, have had, during the last eight years, the benefits of the States Labour adjudication machinery and have bettered their conditions of work, the privileges of the Industrial Disputes Act have only now been extended to journalists, and that too after a great deal of argument. So till now, only the journalists employees of the Industry have been considered outside the pale of every kind of law or judicial decision.

16. In considering, for example, the question of fixing the minimum wages of journalists, it should not be forgotten that the Minimum Wages Act applies to printing press and newspaper offices and in many states the wages of other sections of labour in this Industry have been fixed under the Act. In Bombay, just now, a tripartite committee is sitting to fix minimum wages of other workers in the printing and newspaper industry. To argue, therefore, that fixation of minimum wages for journalists would mean special patronage by the state to eight per cent of the employees is to forget facts.

17. It has been argued that implementation of these recommendations would cripple the industry and result in closure of several papers. This is a bogey, like others raised by employers to avoid social obligations that might reduce their profits. It should not mislead anyone. But in any event, no Industry has a right to exist on the sweated labour of its employees and working journalists are not going to tolerate such conditions any longer.

18. It is true that the financial condition of some of the smaller papers is bad. But that is due to unfair and unequal competition. Editorial costs in a language paper work out only to ten per cent and even if all the recommendations regarding working conditions are accepted, it would increase this ten per cent by one-third *i.e.* the editorial costs would increase by three or four per cent. The real difficulty of the smaller papers arises, not out of this variation, but the variation in the price of other factors like newsprint, particularly when they are compelled, in the absence of a price page schedule, to indulge in the costly pastime of selling their papers below the cost of production. These smaller papers cannot be saved by refraining from

legislative action for better working conditions or exempting them from such legislation. They can be saved only by adopting economic measures suggested by the Commission, such as the price page schedule. As regards the other papers, it should be understood clearly that the figures of revenue, expenditure and profits given by the Commission were based purely on the accounts submitted by employers. According to these returns, the Commission estimated that the Industry as a whole earned a return of Rs. 6 lakhs on an investment of Rs. 7 crores. But the Commission itself referred to the possibilities of concealment of profits (paras 143, 144). The extent of such concealment was vividly brought to the public eye in a recent dispute between the workers and the management of the Dalmia-owned *Times of India* group of papers. It emerged in the proceedings before the Tribunal, that a sum of Rs. 3 lakhs, shown as expenditure under the head "advertisement commission," really represented payment to a subsidiary of the owners themselves, and the owners were agreeable to treating it as profit rather than disclose details of such payment. This one instance alone thus distorts by 50 per cent the return of the Industry.

19. As has been pointed out earlier, under the Minimum Wages Act, minimum wages of other workers in the Industry have been fixed in many centres and the industry has not suffered. As a result of labour disputes during the last eight years, fair wages have been fixed for other workers; yet the Industry has not been crippled. Fear of closure, if minimum wages, leave, provident fund or gratuity were fixed for editorial employees are therefore nothing more than a scare.

20. It is argued that the Newspaper Industry is now going through a slump, and whatever the merits of the Press Commission's recommendations they should not now be implemented. Facts available do not indicate that there is any basis for this argument. Advertisements placed by advertising agencies with 84 member newspapers of the IENS, for which statistics are available, have been steadily increasing. As against an advertisement revenue of Rs. 1,81,34,876 in 1952, in 1953, it was Rs. 1,93,69,733 and in 1954 Rs. 2,31,47,352. These figures do not include the value of government and institutional advertisements, which have considerably increased, and also direct and classified advertisements.

21. The report of the Press Commission has received wide support among a large section of the Press. Only a small group, which has a vested interest in the continuance of the present state of affairs has opposed the implementation of the recommendations. This small group, however, is today in a dominant position in the Industry, by its control of the PTI, and through proxies and multiple ownership exercises in the IENS an influence out of proportion to its numerical strength. Its voice should not be mistaken to be the voice of the Press. Only those whose non-journalistic, extra-journalistic or monopolistic position in the Industry might be affected are opposing the report and raising bogies.

Resolutions of the IFWJ on Press Commission

(I)

This Indian Federation of Working Journalists' Organisations requests the Government of India to appoint forthwith a Commission to enquire into the conditions of the press in India with a view to improving its place, status and functioning in the new democratic set up.

This Federation holds that the terms of reference of the Commission should be as comprehensive as possible. It suggests the following illustrative list of the lines of inquiry and examination for the Commission.

1. Improvement of the standards of newspaper production;

2. Regulation of the relations of the various interests engaged in the production of newspapers with a view to raising the status of the workers and protecting their rights;

3. Improvement of the conditions of working journalists and other employees in newspaper industry and in particular, security of service, scales of wages and salaries, hours of work, provident fund, gratuity etc., holidays, leave. sickness benefit, and application of general labour welfare laws to this industry;

4. Training of journalists and press industry;

5. Need of cooperative ventures in order to promote the varied public interests through regional papers and for helping the growth of public life;

6. Working of news agencies in the country, both Indian and foreign;

7. Growth of chain newspapers, with their effect on the national well-being; popular education and the workers in the industry, and the need, if any, of legislation to deal with the existing chains in an appropriate manner and to prevent their growth in future;

8. Financial condition of the press during the last two decades, investments, profits and losses, success or otherwise of the enterprises, need of reorganising the basis as well as the functioning of such enterprises;

9. Promotion of a newsprint manufacturing industry in the country in order to satisfy its requirements fully;

10. Possibilities of indigenous manufacture of cheap printing and composing machinery;

11. Effect of publication of newspapers and periodicals by foreign agencies on the people and the operation of foreign influence in the Indian press;

12. The freedom of the Press and repeal or amendment of laws not in consonance with it;

13. Liberal interpretation of the laws relating to contempt of court, etc.;

14. A general council of the press including representatives of all sections of the newspaper, industry and the public and Parliament.

(II)

This session of the IFWJ congratulates the Government of India on having accepted the demand of the Federation, voiced at the last Calcutta Session, for the setting up of a Press Commission to enquire into the state of the Indian Press. The Federation is glad to find that the terms of reference suggested by it has formed the basis of the Government's announcement.

The Federation assures the Commission of its whole-hearted cooperation and hopes that its labours will bring hope and cheer to those engaged in the industry.

The Federation notes from reliable press reports that some newspaper proprietors have not furnished the Press Commission with the information asked for and that such delay is impending its work. The Federation regrets the attitude of such newspaper managements in not extending their cooperation to the Commission. It apprehends that some of the proprietors are attempting to sabotage the efforts of the Commission and its possible recommendations in advance. The Federation desires the Commission to take a serious view of the failure of such proprietors to cooperate in its work.

(III)

The Indian Federation of Working Journalists places on record its appreciation of the work of the Press Commission particularly the speed and thoroughness with which the Commission has gone into the various aspects of the newspaper industry and produced a report which is unanimous in all matters of vital concern to working journalists and the industry as a whole. The Federation is specially gratified that the Commission had laid bare the gravest weaknesses of the industry and analysed the causes preventing the healthy and democratic development of the press.

The Federation is happy that the Commission has accepted the stand that the newspaper industry should be treated on a footing different from other industries because of its special relations with and influence on the public and of the special position of the employees. In view of this vital difference the Federation agrees that the profit motive should not have free play in this industry.

The Federation notes the various suggestions made by the Press Commission to promote the growth of a healthy, vigorous and independent press and in particular welcomes:

1. The proposal to appoint a press registrar. The Federation feels that his functions should be different from and larger than those exercised by the registrar of joint stock companies;

2. The proposal to set up a Press Council. The Federation is convinced that the professional members of the Council should be chosen exclusively from a panel submitted by the Indian Federation of Working Journalists and that the constitution of the Press Council is an integral part of a larger scheme of reorganisation of the industry and its constitution

would be futile unless effect is given to the other recommendations of the Commission;

3. The proposal to extend to working journalists the benefit of the machinery for settlement of disputes. This could be achieved by including working journalists in the definition of "employee" or "workman" in the proposed Industrial Relations Bill or by specific provision in the proposed Newspapers and Periodicals Bill or by an appropriate ordinance whichever can be secured earliest;

4. The proposal to recognise unions of journalists as industry's bargaining agents. The Federation reiterates that the right of collective bargaining is the exclusive right of a trade union and the suggestion made in certain quarters that such a right should be conferred on mixed organisations of employees and employers or on "professional organisations" not registered as trade unions is inconsistent with the basic principles of trade unionism and collective bargaining and should on no account be countenanced;

5. The recommendations of the Commission on the crossword and other prize competitions. The Federation calls for immediate legislative action to make the conducting of such competitions a penal offence.

The Federation is glad to note the care with which the Commission has examined the working conditions in the industry and its proposals for strengthening the position of the working journalists and the editors. The Federation acknowledges the reasonableness of the scheme suggested by the Commission under which the "clear profit" is to be divided into three parts—one to be ploughed back into industry, the second to be distributed amongst employees in the form of bonus, and the third as dividend among the shareholders.

The Federation, however, considers that recommendations to improve the present working conditions of employees in the newspaper industry do not go far enough. The Federation is particularly disappointed at:

I. The absence of specific recommendations to prevent the appointment of "nominal editors" who may delay or defeat the proposals for the reorganisation of the industry;

II. The failure to give full effect to the Federation's modest and reasonable demands with regard to minimum wages, scales of pay and classification of areas;

III. The distinction between one category of working journalists and another in the matter of notice for termination of service and the inadequacy of the provisions for notice period for all categories. The minimum notice period for termination of service should be six months;

IV. The absence of adequate protection of the interest of reporters and correspondents with regard to hours of work, emoluments, etc.;

V. The meagre provision for sick leave;

VI. The inadequacy of the provisions for retirement benefits which are hardly distinguishable from the retrenchment benefits under the Industrial Disputes Act; and

VII. The exclusion of proofreaders working exclusively on the editorial side of a newspaper from the category of working journalists.

Despite the shortcomings pointed out above, the Federation calls upon the Government to proceed with the implementation of the Press Commission's recommendations specially by enacting the following legislative measures:

(a) The Newspapers and Periodicals Act;

(b) The Act to establish a Press Council;

(c) The Act to bring into existence a state trading corporation for dealing in newsprint and the levy of a cess to finance the working of the Press Council and the Press Institute;

(d) The reorganisation of the ownership, management and structure of the newspaper industry and the news agencies providing in addition to matters specially recommended by the Press Commission for:

(i) The inclusion of the proofreaders within the definition of working journalists, *(ii)* the appointment of the editor from the journalistic profession and making any case of appointment liable to be challenged before the appropriate authority and *(iii)* the formation of a staff council in every newspaper establishment with the members of the editorial staff for advising the editor in the exercise of his disciplinary jurisdiction.

II. Proposals on Industry's Reorganisation

The Indian Federation of Working Journalists welcomes the Press Commission's recommendations for the reorganisation of the ownership, structure, management and finance of the newspaper industry. The Federation is satisfied that these recommendations are designed to curb the growth of monopolies and to democratise the press.

Toward this end the Federation supports:

(I) The principle of a price-page schedule;

(II) Provisions designed to end price-cutting and other unfair and restrictive practices;

(III) The insistence on the maintenance of separate accounts as between the units of a chain or multiple unit and on separate revenue and cost accounts for each paper of a group;

(IV) The principle that government advertisements should be distributed on an equitable basis among newspapers:

(a) Taking into consideration such factors as circulation, standing, class of readership, area of coverage and multiplicity of readership;

(b) Treating newspapers as separate units and

(c) In accordance with the principles of telescopic maximum rate.

(V) The principle that a reasonable return on capital should not be confused with a quest for large-scale profits leading to commercialisation, vulgarisation and sensationalism. The Federation agrees that the initial return on capital should be limited to half per cent above the bank rate or four per cent, whichever is higher.

The Federation demands that the Government should take immediate steps to give effect to these recommendations by legislative or other action.

III. Reorganisation of News Agencies

The Indian Federation of Working Journalists endorses the recommendations of the Press Commission in regard to the reorganisation of the news agencies.

The Federation is of the opinion that for the proper development of small and regional papers and to ensure to the readers a comprehensive and objective news service it is essential immediately to convert the Press Trust of India into a public corporation with adequate representation for employees on the board of trustees. The Federation is convinced that this is the only way to secure the wholehearted cooperation of the employees and urges that immediate steps should be taken towards this end. The present management of the PTI by its rejection of the reasonable and moderate proposals of the Press Commission has forfeited the confidence of the smaller newspapers, the employees and the public. The Federation endorses the view of the Commission that the recommendations with regard to the reorganisation of the PTI should be implemented in full and that no financial assistance should be given to it till such reorganisation is effected.

The Federation also endorses the recommendations of the Press Commission that the United Press of India should be converted into a public trust with representation for its employees and for subscribing newspapers on its board of trustees. The Federation urges the UPI management to take immediate steps in this direction and expresses the hope that in that event the Government of India will give the UPI financial assistance on easy terms to enable it to get over its present difficulties and expand and improve its service.

IV. Objectionable Press Laws

The IFWJ is in complete agreement with the note of dissent on the press laws added by four members of the Press Commission.

The Federation urges:

I. That article 19(2) of the Constitution be amended on the lines suggested in the note;

II. That the Press (Objectionable Matters) Act should be allowed to lapse;

III. That the scheme of the Criminal Procedure Code in regard to defamation should not be disturbed, and defamation should continue to be an offence against an individual and there should be no discrimination in procedure as between a public servant and a private citizen.

The Federation also urges that the unanimous recommendations of the Commission for amending, modifying and repealing various press laws should be implemented forthwith.

(IV)

1. The Indian Federation of Working Journalists places on record its deep sense of sorrow at the passing away of Mr. Justice G.S. Rajadhyaksha, Chairman of the Press Commission, whose report is destined to mark the beginning of a new era in Indian journalism. Mr. Rajadhyaksha was a distinguished judge whose objectivity, judicial poise and earnest capacity for probing the truth, have given to the report and authority that cannot be shaken. The Federation mourns him even more as a true friend of the journalist.

The Federation is of the view that the best and most appropriate monument to his memory is an early implementation of the recommendations of the Commission.

2. The Indian Federation of Working Journalists welcomes the enactment of the Working Journalists (Industrial Disputes) Act and congratulates Parliament for its commendable speed and unanimity is placing this law on the statute book.

While welcoming this initial step towards the implementation of the recommendations of the Press Commission, the Federation regrets that the Government has so far made no move either to bring forward the comprehensive Industrial Relations Bill, or to amend the Industrial Disputes Act to remove defects that have been revealed in the course of its administration. It draws particular attention of the Government to the discontent and disquiet in all sections of Labour at the Working of the Labour Appeallate Tribunal, the failure of the Government to administer the Industrial Disputes Act and other labour and urges that early steps be taken to redress the grievances.

Bad administration will defeat the objectives of Labour laws as an instrument for the promotion of social progress, and will result in labour losing faith in the capacity of the present State machinery to bring about social changes necessary for the establishment of a Welfare State.

The Federation however urges working journalists in general and the units of the Federation in particular to make the utmost use of the machinery provided by the Act to remove grievances.

3. The Indian Federation of Working Journalists notes with regret that little progress has been made on the implementation of the recommendations of the Press Commission, as demanded by the Federation at Bombay in October last, despite the promises made in Parliament. This has led to a feeling of disquiet among working journalists and there is a growing suspicion that this inaction is due to sustained pressure from proprietorial interests. The Federation also regrets to note that the recommendations of the Press Commission in regard to minimum wages and other working conditions are sought to be whittled down by proprietorial interests, who are also carrying on a subtle and persistent campaign to discredit and sabotage the report of the Commission. In view of the attempts being made by some proprietors to prejudice government steps to implement the recommendations of the Press Commission by premature retirements and indiscriminate dismissals, the Federation urges Government to take steps to see that the conditions of working journalists are not changed for the worse in the interim period.

The Federation reiterates its demand for the immediate implementation of the Commission's recommendations, particularly in regard to (1) proposals for the reorganisation of ownership, structure, management and finance of the newspaper industry and the news agencies, (2) the introduction of a price-page schedule, (3) measures to end price-cutting and other unfair and restrictive practices, (4) proposals to change the system of advertisement tariffs and restraint on the proportion of advertisements, (5) proposal to ban crossword puzzles and other competitions, (6) the proposal to appoint a Press Registrar, (7) the proposal to set up a Press Council and (8) proposals for the improvement of working conditions of journalists.

4. The Indian Federation of Working Journalists records its appreciation of the action of the Government of India in reconstituting the Central Accreditation Committee on the lines suggested by the Press Commission.

It requests the Government of India to advise the State Governments of the action taken and demands that State Governments should take similar action.

5. The Indian Federation of Working Journalists regrets that many newspaper owners are trying to destroy the trade union movement among working journalists by forcing out of service active trade union workers under various pretexts, by discouraging, dissuading, and threatening employees to prevent them from joining the unions, and by inspiring or supporting the formation of unrepresentative and quasi-journalistic organisations.

The Federation feels that the employers ought to realise the spirit of the times and appreciate that the stand taken by the Press Commission and the Federation is guided by the desire for the promotion of public interest. The proprietors will be furthering the cause of healthy journalism and a sound industry only by discarding their attitude of distrust and hostility.

The Federation calls upon all working journalists in the country to discard fear, avoid the confusion of divided loyalties and rally under the leadership of the Federation.

6. This session of the Indian Federation of Working Journalists calls upon the Working Committee to launch and direct a sustained programme to activise the rank and file of working journalists and to mobilise public opinion in support of the implementation of the Press Commission's recommendations.

The programme should include:

(a) a drive for increased membership of existing affiliated units and the starting of units where there are none and the formation of journalists clubs for the promotion of cultural activities and social relations among the members;

(b) drafting and presentation of a petition to the Lok Sabha in terms of the resolutions passed at the present and last session of the Federation during the ensuing session of Parliament;

(c) a nation-wide signature campaign among journalists and informed members of the public in support of this petition;

(d) the taking of steps to start a journal, entitled "The Working Journalist" to promote the interests of journalists and to serve as the mouthpiece of the Federation;

(e) taking of steps to start negotiations with proprietors or their organisations for regulating working conditions and guide units in similar efforts;

(f) setting up of legal aid machinery at the centre and by the units;

(g) a collection drive for campaign funds, part of which must be constituted into a special fund for aiding victimised workers; and

(h) fixing of a day to be observed all over the country to focus public attention on the delay in the implementation of the recommendations of the Press Commission.

7. The Indian Federation of Working Journalists regrets the failure of the government to undertake the reorganisation of the Press Trust of India and the United Press of India in terms of the recommendations of the Press Commission. The Federation feels that the transfer of the administration of the UPI to a businessman highlights the urgency of transforming the two news agencies into a public corporation and a public trust respectively and urges the government to take steps forthwith towards this end.

The agreement recently arrived at between the employees and the employers of the PTI should not distract attention from the major recommendations of the Press Commission about the form of organisation of the PTI. The Federation also reiterates its support to the stand of the Commission that all its recommendations in regard to the PTI should be implemented together.

FEDERATION COMMITTEE FOR PRESS COMMISSION

Summary of proceedings and conclusions reached at meeting on 22.9.1952.

Messrs K. Rama Rao, T. Fernandez, S.A. Shastri, S.P. Thiagarajan, K. Ishwara Dutt, Tarachand Gupta, J.P. Chaturvedi and C. Raghavan were present. Messrs Chalapathi Rao, Jwala Singh and Sudhanshu Basu were also present.

Administrative:

1. Mr. Ishwara Dutt will be deputy chairman.
2. The Delhi members will act as a sub-committee.

3. Mr. Chaturvedi should collect all the literature on the press laws committee report, British Royal Commission report, Miss Margaret Barne's book, UP and MP Committee reports etc. He will also try and obtain earliest the evidence of the official witnesses.

4. A circular letter to branches asking them to set up similar committees. Central members will become automatically members. On a number of points (circular letter copy separately) they should also send in their views (preliminary) immediately on how work should be done etc.

5. In formulating any proposals, the subcommittee should see that methods of giving effect to such proposals should also be mentioned.

The Central memorandum will be drawn up in consultation with the units and will be sent to them when finalised. The state memoranda should be broadly within the fundamental principles enunciated in the central one but with local variations and colour.

The state units must concentrate on and immediately begin gathering data for state memoranda covering subjects like salaries and wages, conditions of service, freedom of the editors and financial control of newspapers, study of balance-sheets etc. A special study into the history of each paper, the vicissitudes through which they have gone through, change of control and so on.

Eight study groups were set up to concentrate on study of various subjects and prepare notes. These groups consist mainly of persons in Delhi. But those outside might please indicate to central office subjects on which they will prepare notes and submit.

Group A: Messrs Ishwara Dutt, Rama Rao, Shastri and Chaturvedi will study improvement of standards of newspapers, training of journalists, press laws, Press Council and code of ethics.

Group B: Messrs Fernandez, Tarachand Gupta and J.P. Chaturvedi will study regulation of relations of various interests engaged in the industry, improvement of conditions of working journalists, security of service etc. Mr. Jayadev Gupta will be submitting notes on some of the points in above.

Group C: Messrs Jwala Singh and Ishwara Dutt will go into questions relating to cooperative ownership of newspapers; and so on.

Group D: Messrs Fernandez, Shastri, Rana Jung Bahadur Singh, Jwala Singh and Raghavan will go into question of working of news agencies, both Indian and foreign, effect publication of periodicals and newspapers with foreign assistance and operation of foreign influence on Indian press.

Group E: Messrs Jung Bahadur Singh, Rama Rao and M.K. Bose will go into questions about growth of chain newspapers, fiancial conditions in the press during the last two decades, investments, profits, losses etc.

Group F: Mr. Chaturvedi and Mr. Jayadev Gupta and Mr. R.K. Sharma (Cawnpore) will go into application of labour laws, trade unions etc.

Group G: Press advising and Accreditation: Messrs S.A. Shastri, Fernandez, J.P. Chaturvedi and Raghavan.

Group H: Mr. Sane: Indian language papers and their problems.

Report on Working of the Federation

The Indian Federation of Working Journalists was established in 1950 at an All-India convention of Working Journalists held at New Delhi, under the presidentship of Mr. M. Chalapathi Rau. The conference was attended by delegates of 23 organisations of journalists in the country. The Convention, besides adopting a number of resolutions on the problems connected with the press and pressmen in general, appointed a Drafting Committee to draft the constitution and adopted a code of conduct for journalists. This Committee had representatives of all the leading journalist organisations in the provinces like the Indian Journalists' Association of Calcutta, Bombay Union of Journalists, U.P. Working Journalists and the South Indian Journalists' Federation. The Committee's draft constitution which provided for the organisation of journalists on a trade union basis, was adopted at a special session of the Federation held at Bombay on April 14, 1951. The special session was attended by delegates of all the organisations that had participated in the first convention except representatives of the

S.I.J.F. The S.I.J.F. representative on the Drafting Committee had also disagreed with the report, which was otherwise unanimous on the principle of trade unionism. After the adoption of the constitution, the Federation had two sessions, one at Calcutta on April 12 and 13, 1952, and the other at Trivandrum on May 29 and 30, 1953.

After the formation of the Federation, new organisations of journalists were formed in Rajasthan, Madhya Bharat, Madhya Pradesh, Gujarat, Maharashtra, Hyderabad, Travancore-Cochin, Punjab, Vindhya Pradesh and Bhopal. The journalist organisations in West Bengal, Bihar, Pepsu, Orissa and Mysore have converted themselves into trade unions. The bodies in U.P., Bombay and Delhi had already converted themselves into trade unions long before the Federation came into being. The Federation has been during this period, devoting its attention to the individual as well as collective grievances and difficulties of its members. It has also taken active interest in maintaining and raising the standard of journalism and safeguarding freedom of the press. The Federation opposed the Press Objectional Matters Act when it was introduced in Parliament and waged a sustained fight against it. A memorandum was submitted to the Select Committee of Parliament in this respect, and as a result, a number of harsh provisions of the Bill were deleted. Its title was changed and its term limited to two years. When the matter came again before Parliament, the Federation again objected to it. In its evidence before the Press Commission, it put forth all available evidence against such an Act. Similarly the Federation was the first and the only organisation that opposed the proposed amendment in the Criminal Procedure Code making defamation of public servants a cognizable offence. In its evidence before the Commission it argued against its inclusion and submitted a petition to Parliament and a memorandum before the Joint Select Committee. The Federation representatives were the only body asked to give oral evidence before the Joint Select Committee and after hearing them for four days, the Committee agreed that defamation of public servants should not be made a cognizable offence.

The Federation and its various branches appeared before the Press Commission and presented memoranda on various problems affecting the press. As it was the Working Journalists'

Federation that demanded the appointment of a Press Commission at its Calcutta session, it had a particular responsibility in seeing that the Press Commission got full cooperation from working journalists. Actually the Federation had demanded at its first convention an enquiry into the conditions of journalists and later on when the Press (Objectionable Matters) Bill was introduced in Parliament, the Working Committee of the Federation made a demand for the appointment of a Press Commission which was subsequently put forth in the form of the Calcutta resolution. As a result of the evidence tendered by the Central Committee and various units of the Federation, much light has been thrown on the newspaper world in the Press Commission report.

The Federation also took note of the growing tendencies of legislatures in restricting freedom of newspapermen and resolutions were passed at the Calcutta session as well as at the Trivandrum session on the subject. The Federation and its units also took up cases of restrictions on the freedom of correspondents by State Governments in places like West Bengal, U.P., Delhi and Pepsu. In U.P., Pepsu and Delhi prohibitory orders were withdrawn or amended as a result of this protest. In Calcutta the Indian Journalists Association had to wage a full-fledged fight with the police administration of West Bengal in what is known as the Maidan Incident. That I.J.A. produced evidence, and later on rebutted the findings of the Mukherjee Commission.

The Federation presented two memoranda to the Company Law Reform Committee, and later on when the Companies Amendment Bill was presented and referred to the Select Committee, presented a memorandum before the Committee. It also tendered oral evidence to support the cases of employees for protecting them in case of liquidation of newspaper companies and improve the financial administration of newspaper companies.

The Federation had also to take up cases of working journalists. While local and provincial units took up the cases in various labour tribunals and courts, the Legal Adviser's Bureau established at the Centre fought two cases in the Supreme Court. In one case, the employees of *Vishwamitra* were not only reinstated, but also paid arrears of pay for the period the litigation went on. In another case of Mr. V.N. Sinha of Bihar, special leave application could not be accepted by the Supreme Court on technical and legal reasons.

The Federation, in view of the conflicting opinions of the Industrial Tribunals, had demanded that journalists should be declared workmen. This demand was supported by all the trade unions in the country and was accepted by the Standing Labour Committee which consisted of representatives of Labour, Industry and Government. A resolution was moved in the House of People which was supported by all sections of the House and now the Press Commission has also expressed the same opinion. Cases relating to journalists were raised in civil or labour courts of Hyderabad, Bombay, Madhya Bharat, U.P., Bihar and West Bengal. Some of them are pending even now. The Bennett Coleman and Company having decided to close the *Times of India* Calcutta edition and its allied publications, namely. *Nav Bharat Times* and *Satyug*, the Working Committee immediately appealed to the Government of India to intervene in the matter and the matter was also raised before both the Houses of Parliament. As a result of the intervention by the Central Government, the matter was referred to an industrial tribunal which held the closure unjustifiable and awarded unemployment and retrenchment relief to the employees. The Federation had to fight an order of the editor of the *Searchlight* of Bihar prohibiting membership of the Bihar Working Journalists' Association, that had to be withdrawn by the management later. Similarly the Federation was called upon this year to protest against the order of the management of the Prajatantra Prachar Samiti prohibiting its members from joining the Utkal Journalists' Association and dismissing two employees for their trade union activities. The management has been forced to withdraw the order, but the question of the dismissed employees is before the labour authorities of Orissa. Owing to successful intervention by the Federation and the Bombay Union of Journalists, a contract prejudicial to journalists was withdrawn by the Bennett Coleman & Co.

The Federation has addressed the Labour Ministry of the Central Government and other State Governments over the extension of benefits of labour laws to journalists. Deputations of the Federation met the Labour Ministers of the Central

Government, Mr. Jagjivan Ram and Mr. V.V. Giri in this respect. The demands of the Federation have now been held reasonable and essential by the Press Commission.

The Federation was invited by the U.N.O. to send its views regarding holding of an International Conference for evolving an International Code of Ethics. The Federation was one of the principal journalists organisations to accept such an invitation. It has been asked by the U.N. to express its views on the steps to protect the sources of information of journalists. The Federation has also been invited to participate in a International Conference of Newspaper Entities to be hel Sao Paulo in the middle of November, 1954. The Federation was requested to participate in goodwill delegations to Holland, China and Argentina. Nominees of the Federation were sent to Holland, China and a nominee is going to be sent on the trip to Argentina and Brazil. The I.F. Journalists which met in Brussels on May 4, 1952 invited the Federation to affiliate with it. An observer on behalf of the Federation attended the Second Congress of this organization held at Bordeaux this year. A similar invitation was also received from the I.O.J. which has its headquarters at Prague. The Federation has as yet not decided to affiliate with either of these bodies. An invitation was received from the Syracuse University of U.S.A. to send a team of 24 journalists for training in journalism every year but the Federation refused the scheme after going through the conditions and the programme. Later on, the Government of India also rejected the scheme although it was accepted by the A.I.N.E.C. The Federation has close fraternal relationship with the Pakistan Union of Journalists, All China Journalists Association, National Union of Journalists, London, American Newspaper Guild and the Australian Journalists' Association.

Appendix—II

General Usage, Abbreviations, and Symbols

Abbreviations and Symbols

Abbreviations given below are all acceptable; those marked with an asterisk must be defined at first mention in the text or in a table, preferably also in a 'list of abbreviations used' early in the paper. This list is compatible in most respects with abbreviations given by *Biological Abstracts* (1974); *Quantities, Units and Symbols* (Royal Society, Symbols Committee, 1971); and *Units, Symbols and Abbreviations* (Ellis [Royal Society of Medicine] 1972).

absorbance; absorbancy: *A*
acceleration due to gravity: *g* (9.81 m/s^2)
acidic dissociation constant: K_a
ad libitum: ad lib.
alternating current: a.c. or AC
and others: *et al.* (*with* the stop)
anno Domini (with dates): A.D.
ante meridiem (before noon): a.m. *Prefer* 24-hour clock: 0930 or 11:45 etc.
atomic weight: at. wt.; atomic mass preferred
bacille Calmette-Guerin: BCG
basal metabolic rate: BMR*
before present (with ages): B.P.*
blood pressure: BP*
boiling point: b.p.
centrifugation, speed and duration: *g*-min
cerebrospinal fluid: CSF
change per 10 K rise: Q_{10}

circa (about): ca.
compare: cf.
concentrated: concd
concentration: concn
constant, equilibrium: *K*
correlation coefficient: *r* (of observed sample). ρ (of hypothetical population)
date: prefer from 15 February 1974, abbreviated if necessary to 15 Feb 74 or 1974-02-15
degrees of freedom (statistics): df
density: ρ (mass); *d* (relative)
dextro: D
dextrorotatory: (+)-
direct current: d.c. or DC
effective dose, median: ED_{50}
electrocardiogram: ECG*
electrocencephalogram: EEG*
electron paramagnetic resonance: EPR or epr
electron spin resonance: ESR or esr
enzymes: In general, do not abbreviate; give Enzyme Commission number at first mention
equation: Eq.
equivalents: eq or equiv (use moles if possible)
erythrocyte sedimentation rate: ESR*
et alii: *et al*. (*with* the stop)
et cetera: etc. Use rarely and only when you have specific things in mind
experiment: expt
experimental: exptl
exponential: exp
extinction [$\log_{10}(I_o/I)$] : *E*
extinction coefficient, molar: Ξ
female: F; ♀
figure, figures: Fig., Figs.
first filial generation: F1
focus-forming units: FFU*
for example: e.g. (exempli gratia)
freezing point: f.p.
gas-liquid chromatography: GLC*
gravity, unit of acceleration of: *g* (9.81 m/s^2)
greater than: >
half-life: $T_{\frac{1}{2}}$
hydrogen ion concentration, negative log of: pH
infective dose, median: ID_{50}*
infrared: i.r. or IR
inner diameter: i.d. or ID
inside diameter: i.d. or ID
intelligence quotient: IQ
international unit: i.u. or IU
intra-arterial(ly): i.a.*
intracutaneous(ly): i.c.*
intradermal(ly): i.d.*
intramuscular(ly): i.m.*
intraperitoneal(ly): i.p.*
intravenous(ly): i.v.*
isoelectric point: pI
laevo (configuration): L
laevorotatory: (-)-
less than: <
lethal dose, median: LD_{50}
logarithm: log (base 10 understood): In (base *e*); $\log_n$ (any base specified by *n*)
longitude: long.
male: M: ♂
maximum, maximal: max
median effective dose: ED_{50}*
median infective dose: ID_{50}*
median lethal dose: LD_{50}*
melting point: m.p.

meta-: *m-*
metabolic quotient: Q
minimum, minimal: min
molar extinction coefficient: Ξ
molecular optical rotation: $[M]^{20}{}_D$
molecular weight: mol. wt.; M
normal temperature and pressure: Use standard temperature and pressure
not determined: ND*
not significant: NS*
nuclear magnetic resonance: NMR or nmr
number: no.
observed, observation: obs.
opere citato (in the work cited): op. cit.
optical rotation, molecular: $[M]^{20}{}_D$
optical rotation, specific: $[\alpha]^{20}{}_D$
optical rotatory dispersion: ORD*
ortho-: *o-*
osmotic pressure: Π
outside diameter: o.d. or OD
para-: *p-*
partial specific volume: $\bar{v}$
parts per million: parts/10^6
per cent (Brit), percent (US): %
per thousand: /10^3. Avoid %o
phenylketonuria: PKU*
plaque-forming units: PFU*
plus or minus: ±
post meridiem (after noon): p.m. *Prefer* 24-hour clock: 1530 or 21:40, etc.
potential difference: p.d.
precipitate: ppt.
probability: P or *P*
proton magnetic resonance: PMR or pmr
radioisotopes: ^{14}C, ^{3}H, etc.; carbon-14 permissible
rapid eye movement: REM*
red blood corpuscle: *prefer* erythrocyte
refractive index: n; $n^{20}{}_D$
respiratory quotient: RQ*
retardation factor (chromatography): R_f
reticuloendothelial system: RES*
rhesus (blood factor): Rh
sedimentation coefficient: *s*
simian virus: SV*
specific activity: sp. act
specific gravity: sp. gr.
standard deviation: SD
standard error (of sampling): SE
standard error of the mean : SEM
standard temperature and pressure: s.t.p.
Student's t: *t* (with number of degrees of freedom)
subcutaneous(ly): s.c.*
temperature: temp; *T* (absolute, in equations); *t* (empirical)
temperature-sensitive: ts*
that is: i.e. (id est)
thin-layer chromatography: TLC*
ultraviolet: u.v. or UV
uniformly labelled: U-
unit: U or u
vapour density: v.d.*
vapour pressure: v.p.*
variance ratio: *F* (statistics)
versus: vs.

volume: vol

volume ratio: v/v (two components only; otherwise 'by vol.')

wavelength: λ

weight per volume: wt/vol; *Prefer* mass/vol

weight ratio: wt/wt

white blood corpuscle: *Prefer* leucocyte

Science Writer's Abbreviations

Abbreviations in biochemistry and taxonomy are given here because these two disciplines have applications in much of biology and because abbreviations tend to proliferate in both of them. More advanced guidance is given in Sober (1968) and *Biological Abstracts* (1974) respectively.

Abbreviations given below are all acceptable; those marked with an asterisk must be defined at first mention in the text or in a table, preferably also in a 'list of abbreviations used' early in the paper.

acetate: OAc

acetyl: Ac

n-acetyl: NAc

acetyl coenzyme A: CoASAc; acetyl-CoA

N-acetylglucosamine: GalNAc

adenosine: Ado; A (in sequences)

adenosine 5′-phosphates: AMP, ADP, ATP

adenosine-ribosylthymine: A-T

adrenocorticotropin: CTH

alanine residue: Ala

amino acids: use 3-letter symbols only for aminoacyl residues in sequences, not for free aminoacids. See under each amino acid for its symbol

arginine residue: Arg

asparagine residue: Asn

asparagine or aspartic acid residue: Asx

aspartic acid residue: Asp

complement and its components: C, C1, C2, etc*

cultivar: cv.

cysteine residue : Cys

cystine residue: Cys; Cys

cytidine: Cyd; C (in sequences)

cytidine 5′-phosphates: CMP, CDP, CTP

deoxy: d (in nucleotides)

deoxyribonuclease: DNase

deoxyribonucleic acid: DNA
deoxyribosylthymine: dThd; dT (in sequences)
dextro: D
dextrorotatory: (—)-
O-(diethylaminoethyl) cellulose: DEAE-cellulose*
3,4, dihydroxyphenylethylamine: dopamine
3,4-dihydroxyphenylalanine: dopa
dimethylaminonaphthalene-*S*-sulphonyl: dansyl, Dns*
2,4-dinitrophenyl: DNP* (with trivial names); Dnp (with amino acid symbols)
diphosphopyridine nucleotide, oxidized form: NAD*
diphosphopyridine nucleotide, reduced form: NADH
doubtful name: nom. dub.
emendation, emended: emend.
enzymes: in general, do not abbreviate; give Enzyme Commission number at first mention
ethylenediaminetetraacetic acid or acetate: EDTA
familia nova: fam. nov.
flavin-adenine dinucleotide: FAD
flavin-adenine dinucleotide, reduced form: $FADH_2$
flavin mononucleotide: FMN
follicle-stimulating hormone: FSH*
forma: f.
forma specialis: f.sp.
formylmethionyl: fMet
fructose residue: Fru
fucose resdue: Fuc
furanose: *f* (as suffix)
galactosamine: GalN
galactose residue: Gal
genus novum: gen. nov.
gluconic acid: GlcA
glucosamine: GlcN
glucose: Glc (residue); G (in some combinations)
glucose 6-phosphate: Gle-6-P; G-6-P
glucuronic acid: GlcUA
glutamic acid residue: Glu
glutamic acid or glutamine residue: Glx
glutamine residue: Gln
glutathione, oxidized: GSSG
glutathione, reduced: GSH
growth harmone: GH*
guanosine: Guo; G (in sequences)
guanosine 5′-phosphates: GMP, GDP, GTP
haemoglobin: Hb
histidine residue: His
hydroxylysine residue: Hyl
hydroxyproline residue: Hyp
immunoglobulins: IgA, IgD, IgE, IgG, IgM
incertae sedis (uncertain position): inc. sed.
inorganic phosphate: P_i
inosine: Ino; I (in sequences)
inosine 5′-phosphates: IMP, IDP, ITP
invalid name: nom. nud.
isoleucine residue: Ile
lactose residue: Lac
laevo (configuration): L
laevoratatory: (—)-
leucine residue: Leu
luteinizing hormone: LH*
lysergic acid diethylamide: LSD*
lysine residue: Lys

maltose residue: Mal
mannose residue: Man
melanocyte-stimulating hormone: MSH*
messenger ribonucleic acid: mRNA*
meta-: *m-*
methionine residue: Met
methyl: Me
Michaelis constant: K_m or K_m
minimum, minimal: min
molar extinction coefficient: Ξ
morpha (form): m.
myoglobin: Mb
myoglobin, carboxy: MbCO
myoglobin, oxy: MbO_2
N-acetylgalactosamine: GalNAc
N-acetylglucosamine: GlcNAc
new combination: comb. nov.
new family: fam. nov.
new genus: gen. nov.
new name: nom. nov.
new species: sp. nov.
new subspecies; ssp. nov.
new variety: var. nov.
nicotinamide-adeninedinucleotide: NAD
nicotinamide-adenine dinucleotide, oxidized form: NAD*
nicotinamide-adenine dinucleotide, reduced form: NADH
nicotinamide-adenine dinucleotide phosphate, oxidized form: NADP*
nicotinamide-adenine dinucleotide phosphate, reduced form: NADPH
nicotinamide mononucleotide: NMN
nomen conservandum: nom. cons.
nomen dubium: nom. dub.
nomen nudum: nom. nud.
nomen rejiciendum: nom. rej.
nuclear RNA: nRNA*
nucleoside, unspecified: N (*not* X)
optical density: OD (for suspensions); substitute absorbance *(A)* for solutions
ornithine residue: Orn
ortho-: *o-*
orthophosphate: P_i
oxyhaemoglobin: HbO_2
oxymyoglobin: MbO_2
para-: *p-*
parts per million: ppm
perchloric acid: $HClO_4$ *not* PCA
phenyl: Ph*
phenylalanine residue: Phe
phosphate, inorganic: P_i
phosphate other than inorganic: *P* (sometimes *p*)
phosphocreatine: *P*-creatine
phosphoenolpyruvate: *P*-enolpyruvate
preoccupied: preocc.
proline residue: Pro
pseudouridine: Ψrd; Ψ (in sequences)
pseudouridine 5′-phosphates: ΨMP, ΨDP, ΨTP
purine nucleoside, unspecified: Puo; R (in sequences)
pyranose: p (as suffix)
pyrophosphate, inorganic: PP_i
rejected name: nom rej.
retained name: nom. cons.

riboflavin 5′-phosphate: FMN
ribonuclease: RNase
ribonucleic acid: RNA
ribose residue: Rib
ribosomal RNA: rRNA*
ribosyl (where needed before nucleotide symbol): r
ribosylnicotinamide residue: Nir
ribosylthymine: Thd: T (in sequences)
ribosyluracil: Ψrd; Ψ (in sequences)
sensu lato: s.l.
sensu stricto: s.s.
serine residue: Ser
soluble RNA: Substitute tRNA
sorbose residue: Sor
species: sp., spp.
species nova: sp. nov.
subspecies: ssp., sspp. (plural)
subspecies nova: ssp. nov.
sucrose residue: Suc
sulphydryl: SH
thiol: SH
threonine residue: Thr
thymidine: dThd; dT (in sequences)
thymidine 5′-phosphates: dTMP, dTDP, dTTP
thyroid-stimulating hormone: TSH*
tobacco mosaic virus: TMV*
transfer RNA: tRNA
trichloroacetic acid: TCA*; Prefer CCl_3COOH
1, 1, 1-trichloro-2, 2-bis (*p*-chlorophenylethane): DDT*
O-(triethylaminoethyl)cellulose: TEAE-cellulose*
triphosphopyridine nucleotide, oxidized form: NADP*
triphosphopyridine nucleotide, reduced form: NADPH
tris(hydroxymethyl) aminomethane: Tris*
tryptophan residue: Trp (*not* Try)
tyrosine residue: Tyr
uridine: Urd; U (in sequences)
uridine 5′-phosphates: UMP, UDP, UTP
valine residue: Val
variety: var.
variety, new: var, nov.
xanthosine: Xao X (in sequences)
xanthosine 5′-phosphates: XMP, XDP, XTP
xylose residue: Xyl

Expressions to avoid

Readers are advised to work through the whole list to get the flavour of the suggestions rather than use it as a reference tool, since alphabetization is so arbitrary. Do *not* regard the list as a dictionary: the word or phrase in the second column is not by any means always an exact equivalent of that in the first.

Avoid	*Usually prefer*
aliquot	portion, sample {an aliquot is an integral subdivision of the whole: 2 ml can be described as an aliquot of 10 ml, but 3 ml cannot]
alternate (adjective)	[see pp. 43-44; you probably need ' alternative']
anticipate	expect
approximately	about
are of the same opinion	agree
area	*see* 'woolly words' below
as already stated	[omit]
as can be seen from Fig. 1, growth is more rapid	growth is more rapid (Fig.1), *or* Fig. 1 shows that growth is more rapid
as far as our own observations are concerned, they show	our/my observations show
as far as this species is cornerned, it as follows:—	this species is [omit 'as follows' and the dash; the colon is sufficient]
as for these experiments, they are	these experiments are
as of now	now, from now on
as shown in Fig. 11	Fig. 11 shows that
as regards this species, it	this species is
assist(-ance)	help, aid
at some future time	later
at the present moment, at the present moment in time, at this time	now
author(s), the	I / we
bright red in colour	bright red
case	patient
[colourless past participles: accomplished, achieved, attained, carried out, conducted, done, effected, experienced, facilitated, given, implemented, indicated, involved, made, obtained, occurred,	[avoid; use a meaningful verb instead]

performed, proceeded, produced, required]	
commence	begin, start
comparatively	[avoid, unless you are making a real comparison of one item with another]
concerning this effect, it may be borne in mind that	[omit]
conducted inoculation experiments on	inoculated
considerable amount of	much
considerable number/proportion of	many, most
contemporaneous in age	contemporaneous; the same age
created the possibility	made possible; enabled (a person); allowed (an action)
data	facts, results, observations
decreased number of	fewer, less
decreased relative to	less than, lower than
demonstrate	show
due to the fact that	because
during the time that	while
elevated	raised, higher, more
employ	use
encountered	met
encountered frequently (e.g. 'this effect was encountered frequently')	common ('this effect was common')
equally as well	equally well
exhibit; X exhibits good stretch properties	show; X stretches well
fairly	[omit]
fewer in number	fewer
following (the operation)	after (the operation)
for the reason that	because, since
from the standpoint of	according to
goes under the name of	is called
greater/higher number of	more
hospitalize	admit to hospital

hydroxylation reaction	hydroxylation [-tion ending denotes a reaction]
if and when	[use one of these prepositions alone]
if conditions are such that	if
in a considerable number of cases	often
in all cases	always
in connection with	about, for
increased relative to	more than
in few cases	sometimes, rarely
in excess of	more than, above
in order to	to
in regard to	[use the appropriate preposition, e.g. in, for, about with]
in relation to	
in respect of	
in terms of	
in the case of	
in the context of	
in the event that	if
in the present communication	here; in this paper
in this connection the statement may be made that	[omit]
in view of the fact that	since, because
it has long been known that	[omit]
it is apparent, therefore, that	hence, therefore
it is of interest to note that	[omit]
it is often the case that	often
it is possible (probable) that	possibly (probably)
it is this that	this
it may, however, be noted that	nevertheless, but
it may be said that	possibly
it seems to the present writer	I think
it will be seen upon examination of Table 5 that	Table 5 shows that
it would thus appear that	apparently
large number(s) of	many
large proportion of	much, most
lazy in character	lazy
lesser extent, degree	less
level	concentration, content

literature, e.g. it is reported in the literature that	others have reported that
made a count	counted
majority of	most
mental patients	patients with mental disorders
moment in time	time
much	[omit]
multiple	several, different
number of	several, some
of large size	large
of such strength that	so strong that
on the basis of	from, by, because
owing to the fact that	because
parameter	index, criterion, factor, characteristic, measure, value, variable
pertaining to	on, about
prior to; prior to that time	before; before that
proportion of	some
quite	[omit]
rather	[omit]
regime	regimen
relatively	[avoid, unless you are calculating a real quotient]
relative to ('This letter is relative to')	about
respectively	[avoid, unless you are sure you are using the word correctly, as in 'Absorption measurements for cadmium vapour at 50,70, and 100 nm give cross-sections of 0.7, 0.9, and 1.2 fm^2, respectively.']
reveal	show
sacrifice (experimental animals)	kill
serves the function of being	is
significantly	much, appreciably, definitely [but correct and desirable if statistical tests of significance have been made]
similar in every detail	the same
small numbers of	few
sophisticated	advanced, new, expensive
species in shape, square-shaped	square

sufficient number of	enough
subsequent to	after
terminate	end
the test in question	this test
the tests have not as yet	the tests have not
the treatment having been performed,	after treatment
there can be little doubt that this is	this is probably
there is, there are	[often unnecessary: e.g. change 'There is much work being done on . . .', to 'Much work is being done on . . .']
there will always be a miscellany of quality in terms of illustrations	the quality of illustrations will always vary
they are both alike (similar)	they are alike (similar)
throughout the entire area	throughout the area
throughout the whole of the experiment	throughout the experiment
two equal halves	halves
upon	on
using	[test whether it is an unattached participle; if so, try 'by', 'with', 'by means of']
utilize, utilization	use
very	[omit]
while	although
with reference to	about
with regard to	in, to
[woolly words: area, character, conditions, field, level, nature, problem, process, situation, structure, system]	[avoid: change to more precise words]

Index